Scotland for Kids

Anne Shade

MAINSTREAM
PUBLISHING

EDINBURGH AND LONDON

First published in Great Britain in 1993 by
MAINSTREAM PUBLISHING COMPANY (EDINBURGH) LTD
7 Albany Street
Edinburgh EH1 3UG

ISBN 1 85158 533 8

A catalogue record for this book is available from the British Library

Illustrations by Bob Dewar
Map Credits
Glasgow, Edinburgh
and Aberdeen:
Natalie Hunter
Scotland: Wendy Price

Typeset in Monophoto Optima by Lasertext Ltd., Stretford, Manchester

Printed in Great Britain by BPCC Wheatons, Exeter

CONTENTS

ACKNOWLEDGMENTS

I would like to thank all the tourist information centres, district and regional councils for the help they have given me in putting this book together.

Thanks too, to parents and children all over Scotland who provided me with help and information, especially: Elizabeth Newton, Joan Shade, Maggie and Steve Wright, Katie Wood, Meg and Jim Kendall, Gail and Bill Savage, Maggie Alpine, Sandra and James Brownhill, Sue Band, Fiona Celli, Mary Dower, Bedoch Eliasieh, Portia File, Margot and Phil Gribbon, Mary Gillies, Sarah and Charles Hirom, Anne and Neil Horne, Katalin Illes, Dave and Donella Kirkland, Alison Lowe, Maeve McDowell, Sarah McIntyre, Lesley McDonald, Rea Powlesland, Chris Tauber, Fiona McLauren, Jennie Jacob, Sheila Hansom, John Wigzell, Hilary Russell, May Tweedie, Maureen McLennan, Anne Booth, Anne-Marie Mackin, Mrs Reville, Julie Baxter, Val Harling, Mrs Bremner, Gillian Lake, Gail Montague, Carolyn Thompson, Gill Wardell, Pam Alari, Isobel Triay, Stella Douglas, Christine Mitchell, Ann Campbell, Kate Cromb, Marion McLeod, Margaret Murray, Mary McNicol, Irene Motion, Diana Douglas, Doreen Riddell, Fiona McLennan, Helen Docherty, Doreen Routledge, Elma Matheson, Fiona Page, Linda Davidson, Joan Burnett, Penny Thomson, Lesley Sinclair, Maureen Drummond, Julie Radcliff, Sue Digby, Irene Morris, Janet Gibson, Linda Livingstone, Margot McKenzie, Lesley Johnston, John Anderson, Lynette Provan, Anne Robertson, Diane Battrick, Jane Collantine, Marjorie Coull, Gillian Stewart, Liz Somerville, David Fryer, Margaret Houlihan, Jenny Stook, Frances Shaw, Margaret Ferguson, Pam Meiklejohn, Fiona Renton, Susan Murray, Vivienne O'Duffy, Karen Robertson, Liz Alexander, Jinny Gribble, Judith Harkin, Moira Watson, Eleanore Glennie and John MacDonald.

And, last but definitely not least, my special thanks to John, Robbie and Katie Shade for their great patience, encouragement and constructive criticism.

PREFACE

Are your children ever bored, hungry or tired? Are you ever at your wits' end trying to think of something to do with them during the holidays or on long wet weekends?

As your answer is bound to be 'yes' this is just the book for you.

The idea for it was born almost four years ago. We were on a self-catering holiday with a four-year-old and a toddler, there was sleet in the air, the local tourist information centre was closed for the season, and we had little more than books, felt pens and stickle bricks to keep the children amused if the weather didn't improve. What was there to do in the area? The answers, I realised, would be found in a comprehensive guide to Scotland for families and children. The only problem, of course, was that we didn't have a copy of it (and as I later discovered such a book didn't even exist). In the event, the weather got crisper, the sleet turned to powdery snow and we had a very pleasant time tracking rabbits through the snow, swimming in the local pool, and walking.

When we returned home, I tried to find a book that might provide the kind of information we needed. In my search I came across a number of guides for families with children but, in general, they concentrated on English attractions. Looking at the entries for those parts of Scotland that I knew well, it was clear that the coverage was woefully inadequate.

The book I wanted didn't exist and there seemed no alternative but to do something about it myself. I started to gather material and, as the information flooded in, I was pleasantly surprised to discover just how much there is to do in Scotland. What resulted is a compilation of the very best that Scotland has to offer families with children. Whether toddlers or teenagers or somewhere in between, there is sure to be something to interest or amuse them. And hopefully you will no longer have to listen to cries of 'I'm bored' two days into the summer holidays.

INTRODUCTION

Scotland has come a long way in the last 20 years and now has a great deal to offer families with children of all ages. From cold Victorian swimming pools to state-of-the-art leisure centres; from museums with unchanging displays in glass cabinets to visitor centres with hands-on exhibits and costumed guides; from play areas with hard surfaces and dangerous equipment to challenging adventure playgrounds: it is heartening to see how much things have changed for the better.

This is a book to dip into for fresh ideas for outings in your neighbourhood. The places that amused and interested your children last year may be old hat a second time round. But don't worry—there are so many ideas in the following pages that some at least should be new.

If you are planning a holiday it is worth browsing through it to get a clear picture of what is available. Some areas like the south-west and the Borders are ideal for quiet, relaxing holidays, walking, building sandcastles, pony-trekking and off-the-road cycling. For older and more energetic children, it is worth considering skiing in the Highlands or watersports on the west coast or the big inland lochs. On the other hand, older children may well prefer the excitement of the big cities with their wealth of modern leisure complexes, sophisticated visitor centres and top quality museums.

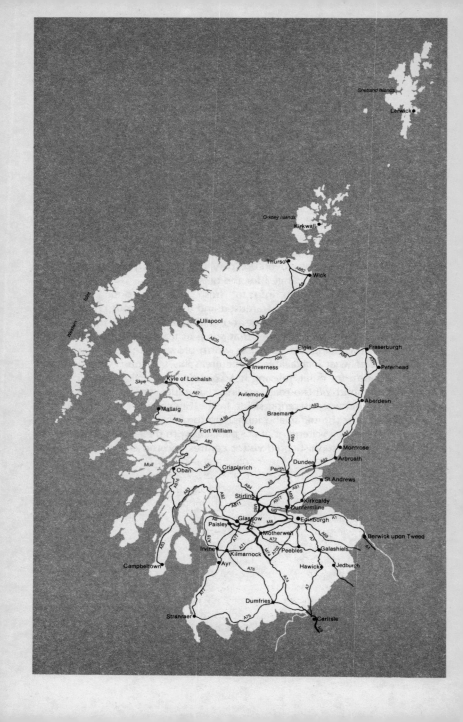

ABOUT THE BOOK

The country splits naturally into areas accessible from the main road and rail networks, and entries for each area are arranged, town by town, under various activity headings. You will find descriptions of hundreds of things to see and do in all weathers and all seasons, including museums, country parks, swimming pools, caves, ghost walks, theatrical groups, sport and leisure centres, zoos, open farms and much more. These are the best of what is on offer in Scotland, but outstanding attractions are marked with asterisks (**).

Each entry comes complete with details of the address, telephone number, opening hours and, where necessary, directions to help you find the place. Information on parking arrangements is also given.

The existence of public toilets in parks and so on is noted as this is essential information for families, particularly those with tiny tots in tow. Some enlightened establishments provide baby changing facilities while others have risen to the dizzy heights of a mother and baby room, and this is mentioned where appropriate.

Disabled access and facilities are also noted wherever they are known to exist. Developments and changes are taking place all the time and it would always be worth checking with other places to see whether they have improved the facilities since going to press.

Entry charges are graded, £, ££ and £££, and are explained in more detail at the end of this section. Suffice to say that if you are keeping to a tight budget you should look out for those places marked £ or, better still, **Free**. Parks, playgrounds, country parks, walks and so on are all free unless otherwise indicated, and **free attractions** are noted in the index at the end of the book. Places owned by the National Trust for Scotland (NTS), Historic Scotland (HS), Scottish Wildlife Trust (SWT) and Royal Society for the Protection of Birds (RSPB) are marked, as members may get free entry.

There is also a brief note on catering facilities. Knowing whether there are picnic or barbecue areas is important when you are planning an outing. And if you forget to pack the sandwiches and apples it is useful to know whether you can get a drink or a light lunch. Please note though, that the mention of a café or restaurant on the premises does not guarantee that the food will be great — only that it is available.

ENTRY CHARGES FOR PLACES TO VISIT
£   — up to £1 for children; up to £2 for adults
££   — up to £2 for children; up to £3 for adults
£££ — up to £3 for children; up to £5 for adults

MINIMUM COST OF THINGS TO DO — RIDING, WATERSPORTS AND
WINTER SPORTS
£   — under £6
££   — up to £8
£££ — over £8

Please note that these prices are approximate and may change (usually upwards).

EATING OUT

All parents know that a regular intake of food and drink helps to keep children cheerful. Sometimes a snack is all that is required, but for birthdays and treats it is nice to go somewhere a little bit special. I asked parents the length and breadth of the country to recommend places to eat but, of the dozens I questioned, most said they took snacks and picnics with them on outings. Many families confessed that when they did eat out, they only patronised the fast food chains as they could be sure the food would appeal to their children. The general feeling was that very few places really welcome families with small children and that meals are often overpriced or of poor quality. Compared to many parts of Europe where families eat out regularly, it is little wonder that parents are not prepared to spend money on poor food and indifferent service.

In spite of this, I am pleased to say that there are some recommendations to pass on. Prices vary but many of the hotels, restaurants and cafés would be no more expensive than eating in one of the fast food chains. The choice is wide ranging: hotels serving lunches and traditional high teas; French, Italian, Indian, Chinese and American-style restaurants; tea and coffee shops; fish and chips; baked potatoes with fillings; sandwich bars; pub lunches and ice-cream parlours. The chains have also been included because they are conveniently situated in town centres and by main roads and because so many people rely on them.

At the very least you should expect reasonable food and a warm welcome even with children in tow. High-chairs, booster seats, feeder beakers, bottle-warming, and mother and baby rooms may also be available. Many places have children's menus but these generally offer the standard repertoire of burgers, fish fingers or chicken nuggets, chips and ice-cream.

It is worth encouraging children to be more adventurous in their eating habits, so check out those places that serve small portions off the adult menu, or that let parents have a sideplate so they can share their own meal at no extra charge. Some places have toys to keep children amused while others provide crayons and placemats that can be coloured in.

Families with older children are not necessarily looking for these facilities. They are more interested in the quality of the food and the fun factor. Amongst the recommendations are places with interesting decor, or where children can help to make their own pizza, or where birthday meals can be celebrated in style.

Tea-rooms, ice-cream parlours and take-away sandwich bars are good for boosting flagging spirits mid-afternoon, while fish and chips and filled jacket potatoes make a great high speed supper.

McDonald's and Burger King offer burgers, French fries, soft drinks and milkshakes, and both are good bets if you want a quick but not very substantial meal in clean surroundings. High-chairs are available for babies, and there are bright play-eating areas set aside for children's parties where members of staff help to entertain the guests.

The branches of the Pancake Place have a bias towards pancakes with sweet or savoury fillings, but it is also possible to order baked potatoes, club sandwiches and so on. There is a children's menu or you can choose small portions off the main menu. High-chairs and clip-on chairs are available.

Olivers Coffee Shops offer quick snacks and light, reasonably whole-some lunches including more adventurous things like garlic bread. There are placemats to colour in at mealtimes and high-chairs for toddlers and babies. Some branches will open outside normal hours for children's parties.

It is not hard to guess what Pizza Gallery, Pizza Hut and Pizza House specialise in! Pizzas come in various sizes to suit all appetites. They have high-chairs and children's menus, and often have promotional offers on meals.

Little Chef restaurants are generally situated close by major roads and motorways. The restaurants have high-chairs and free baby food, and in some instances they have baby changing facilities.

PLACES TO STAY

Each chapter ends with information on places to stay, with recommen-dations for caravan and campsites, youth hostels with family accommod-ation, and top-quality hotels with lots of leisure facilities. It would have been nice to include child-friendly guest houses and self-catering places too but there were very few recommended. Guest houses providing bed and breakfast fall between the two stools of budget and luxury accommodation and, as such, probably appeal more to families touring Scotland from abroad. Only Edinburgh Tourist Board would give me information on child-friendly guest houses; the other area tourist boards were not prepared to make any recommendations because, they say, they are obliged to give all members equal prominence. I do hope that personal callers get a more helpful response.

Camping and caravanning holidays are very popular with families at least in part because of the cost. Apart from the initial expense of buying the equipment (which can be a bargain second-hand), it can cost as little as 35p per night to stay on a very basic site. This is exceptional, however, and generally the prices are more likely to be between £5 and £10 per night per family. The most basic sites have only a cold tap and toilets, but most have hot showers, flushing toilets, dish and clothes-washing facilities, a play area, and electrical hookups for caravans, while the most luxurious have TV and games rooms, sports facilities, a swimming pool, shops, restaurant and bar. Once children, even toddlers, are used to spending the night in a sleeping bag, camping is the next best thing to home – perhaps even better. Some sites also have static caravans which may be rented by the week.

If you prefer a roof over your head, mod cons, and a bit more privacy than you get on a campsite, it is worth looking at self-catering holidays. You still have the housework and cooking to do but you benefit from not having to disrupt your normal routine which can be very important to young children.

Hostels are useful if you want to have a budget holiday without the hassle of real camping. They are a good bet in early spring and late autumn when the weather can suddenly turn seriously nasty – especially in the Highlands. Anyone over the age of five may join the Scottish Youth Hostel Association (SYHA) for a small annual fee. Families whose children are five or over can share family rooms at certain hostels, while those with younger children may stay at hostels with special family units. Two adults and two children can stay at a youth hostel for around £20 or less per night. For more information contact SYHA at 7 Glebe Crescent, Stirling, FK8 2JA (tel: (0786) 51181).

Travelodges, part of the Little Chef chain, provide bargain accommodation for travellers on their way to somewhere more interesting. A family room costs £30 per night and can sleep up to five. Tea, coffee and an alarm clock in the room are all part of the service.

Bed and breakfast accommodation in guest houses, especially farmhouse B&Bs, where you usually get good home cooking, can be a real treat. Some have family rooms which are ideal for young children who would be afraid if they awoke alone in a strange room. There may even be toys and other children to play with.

At the top end of the scale are hotels and hydros with every facility you could hope for. This luxury comes at a price, of course, though it may be possible to get special deals at off-peak times. Most places in this category have swimming pools, sports facilities, play areas inside and outside, kids' clubs, and a baby listening service or babysitting.

SCALE OF CHARGES FOR CARAVAN AND CAMPING SITES
£   – up to £5 per pitch per night
££   – up to £8 per pitch per night
£££ – £8 or more per pitch per night

HOTELS AND GUEST HOUSES (COST OF BED & BREAKFAST PER ADULT)
£   – under £20
££   – £20–£25
£££ – £25 or more
Please note that these prices are approximate and may change (usually upwards).

SHOPPERS' CRECHES

One thing that came to light during the compilation of this book is the general lack of shoppers' creches. It is one thing to have information on places to go for family outings, but what about the more mundane times when Mum or Dad has to go shopping, pay bills or simply needs a break? Creches are fun – indeed most children would consider it a treat to spend an hour or two playing in a ball pond, building models, doing messy paintings and watching videos. The charge is not prohibitive and the benefits are great. Imagine the pleasure of shopping without whining and tantrums or those heart-stopping moments when you think that your child has got lost in the crowds. The more you can enjoy a shopping trip, the more likely you are to spend your money, so surely the logical approach would be for shopkeepers and local councils to set up creches all year round (not just at Christmas) for our mutual benefit.

YOUR COMMENTS

I would be pleased to hear from anyone with comments on any of the places mentioned in this book, or details of any new ventures that you or your children have come across. Please write to me c/o Mainstream Publishing, 7 Albany Street, Edinburgh EH1 3UG.

AYRSHIRE AND THE SOUTH-WEST

The south-west corner of Scotland, from Dumfries over to Stranraer, is off the main tourist route which makes it an excellent place for a quiet holiday with young children. There are enough clean, sheltered and unspoilt beaches along the Solway coast to keep the bucket and spade brigade happy for weeks. Youngsters will also enjoy the open farms, the fish pond at Port Logan and the aquarium at Gatehouse of Fleet. Further inland, the Galloway Forest Park is a good place for walking — perhaps to the summit of one of the 2000ft peaks, and there's off-road cycling and pony-trekking too.

This is also notable as Robert Burns country. Dumfries has a good museum covering the Bard's life and works. (And another famous Robert — Robert the Bruce may have been born in Turnberry though there are rival claims for this honour.) You could spend a whole day in the village of New Lanark finding out about the cotton industry, and there are other fascinating examples of Scotland's industrial past at Dalmellington and Wanlockhead. There are also a number of small leisure centres, but the main attractions are outdoors — for instance, the country parks at Culzean Castle, Drumlanrig and Kelburn could well occupy a whole day each. The island of Arran has good beaches, quiet roads for cycling, open farms, a fine country park and a number of riding and trekking centres.

City kids who like video games, high-tech swing parks and that sort of thing might be better off going to the Ayrshire coast. The closer you get to Glasgow, the more sophisticated the attractions become — Butlin's Wonderwest has a huge range of fun activities, while the Magnum and Galleon centres have impressive skating rinks and modern leisure pools.

The main road, the A74, runs roughly along the eastern edge of this area, while the railway travels from Glasgow down the coast to Stranraer.

A shoppers' creche is provided by the local authority in the centre of Dumfries, while Stranraer has a small, privately operated creche in the Ryan Centre. Ayr has two creches: children between 5 and 10 can be left at 'Jump for Joy' in the town centre, while a shoppers' creche in Burns Statue Square caters for children from aged one-and-a-half to 12.

PLACES TO VISIT

Aeroplanes

DUMFRIES AND GALLOWAY AVIATION MUSEUM
Former Control Tower, Heathall Ind. Est.
Dumfries
Tel: (0387) 65957/710491
Open: Easter – Oct, Sat/Sun 1000 – 1700
£
P: Available
There are aircraft with strange names like Mystere IV, Vampire T11, Super Sabre and Meteor T7 at this former RAF airfield as well as relics and flying clothes dating back to 1914. Climb aboard a helicopter or an aeroplane and pretend to fly them.

PRESTWICK AIRPORT
Tel: (0292) 79822
Free

An outing to the airport to watch planes landing and taking off is always popular with 5 to 8-year-olds.

Ancient Monuments

SWEETHEART ABBEY (HS)
nr Dumfries
Tel: (031) 244 3101 (HS, Edinburgh)
Open: Daily
£
A ruined abbey with a wall made of enormous boulders. Don't miss the afternoon teas at ABBEY COTTAGE –
see **PLACES TO EAT.**

WHITHORN DIG
Priory Visitor Centre and Museum,
George Street, Whithorn
Tel: (09885) 508

18

Open: Daily Easter – Oct, 1030 – 1700
£
Picnic area

See archaeologists at work uncovering 1500 years of history at the site of Scotland's first recorded Christian settlement. There are raised viewing platforms from which the friendly guides can point out interesting finds. Learn about St Ninian, pilgrimages and Vikings in the visitor centre which has exhibitions and a 'picture show'. There are re-enactments of medieval activities and demonstrations of traditional craft skills, a herb garden, and a play area. A good day out for all the family.

Animals and Birds

GREENHILL COVENANTER'S HOUSE
Burn Braes, Biggar
Open: Easter – Oct, daily 1400 – 1700
£

See rare breeds of sheep, pigs and poultry. The farmhouse has been moved and rebuilt 10 miles from its original site. Inside there is a display of costume dolls.

LANARK MARKET – *see* SCOTLAND AT WORK

KIRKCUDBRIGHT WILDLIFE PARK
Lochfergus Plantation, Kirkcudbright
1 mile from town centre, on B727
Tel: (0557) 31645
Open: Easter – Oct, 1000 – 1800
££
Tea-room, picnic areas

Try to distinguish the various owls which include eagle owls, snowy owls and barn owls. There are some unusual animals and birds to be seen – porcupines, coaties and wallabies – as well as more common creatures like buzzards, pheasants, fallow deer, pigs, feral goats, pygmy goats, ducks and geese. School bookings welcome.

CLATTERINGSHAWS WILDLIFE CENTRE
nr New Galloway
6 miles W of New Galloway on A712
Tel: (06442) 285
Open: Apr – mid Oct, daily 1000 – 1700
Free
P: Small charge
Light refreshments

This is part of Galloway Forest Park. The Forestry Commission display shows local wildlife, ecology and forest management and a reconstruction of a Romano-British homestead.

THE WILDFOWL AND WETLANDS CENTRE
Eastpark Farm, Caerlaverock nr Dumfries DG1 4RS
8 miles S of Dumfries, signposted or follow B724 and B725 from Annan
Tel: (038777) 200
Open: Daily, mid Sep – Apr, 0930 – 1700 (except 24/25 Dec)
££
Limited disabled access

Every winter the entire population of 12,000 barnacle geese return here from Spitsbergen. With them are thousands of swans, ducks, waders and other water birds which you can see from the viewing towers or one of the 20 hides. The reserve is also the home of the most northerly colony of natterjack toads. Take care of the tides and areas of quicksands if you are out walking. An educational service is available.

T&C BREWSTER
Bandirran, Kirtlebridge by Lockerbie
Tel: (04615) 459
£
Disabled facilities and access
Spend an hour meeting all the Clydesdale horses including mares and foals.

KIRROUGHTREE VISITOR CENTRE
Palnure nr Newton Stewart
3 miles E of Newton Stewart
Open: Daily, Easter – Sep 1000 – 1700
Free
P: Available
Tea-room
Part of the Galloway Forest Park. Watch an audio-visual display, look in the wildlife pond, or go on the bird trail or one of the forest trails which start from here.

Beaches

It is unfortunate that only a few of the beaches on the Ayrshire coast have been monitored for sewage pollution. Going 'doon the watter' and spending a day at the beach could leave you with an upset stomach. Following recommendations in the 1992 Good Beach Guide you should avoid IRVINE (BEACH PARK), PRESTWICK, AYR and TURNBERRY as they all failed to meet the required standard. Only SALTCOATS, TROON (SOUTH) and GIRVAN were listed as having reasonably clean water and of these, only TROON (SOUTH) has consistently met the grade. There is not enough information on other beaches along the Clyde coast to know how they compare.

The coastline in the far south-west tends to be cleaner and there are many delightful beaches. However, the water can be quite chilly on the exposed westerly beaches. Don't go to STRANRAER MARINE LAKE, STRANRAER COCKLE SHORE, SANDHEAD, ROCKCLIFFE or ANNAN WATERFOOT though, as these have not reached EC standards.

Some of the beaches on the eastern shores of the Solway Firth are swept by very fast tides. Bathing at SANDYHILLS and POWFOOT is safe at high tide but it is dangerous to cross long stretches of sand to meet incoming tides.

POWILLIMOUNT
Between Dumfries and Dalbeattie
A710 and unclassified road passing Arbigland
P: Pay to park
Sand and rock.

SOUTHERNESS
Between Dumfries and Dalbeattie on A710 and unclassified road to Southerness
P: Available
Large sandy beach suitable for children and less mobile visitors. Swim at high tide only.

CASTLEPOINT
nr Dalbeattie
A710 and unclassified road to Rockcliffe
P: Free at Rockcliffe
Follow footpath for 1 mile to Castlepoint beach, which is a mixture of sand and rocks.

KIPPFORD
nr Dalbeattie
A710 and unclassified road to Kippford
P: Free in village
Disabled facilities
Toilets

Half-mile walk to a beach made up sand, shingle and rocks—a good place for little ones to search for shells and peer into rock pools.

BRIGHOUSE BAY
Between Kirkcudbright and Gatehouse—
B727, then unclassified road to beach
P: Pay to park
Safe, flat beach.

CARRICK SHORE
Between Kirkcudbright and Gatehouse
B727 then unclassified road
P: Free
Sandy beach with surrounding rocks.

SANDGREEN (AIRDS BAY)
nr Gatehouse of Fleet
A75 then unclassified road
P: Pay to park
Sandy beach with some rocks between two low rocky headlands. Portaloos in carpark.

CARDONESS
Between Gatehouse and Newton
Stewart
Off A75
P: Pay to park
Very attractive beaches with rocky surroundings and rocky outcrops. Portaloo.

SANDYHILLS
nr Dalbeattie
A710 S of Dalbeattie
P: Pay to park
Disabled facilities
Toilets
Large sandy beach with rocky outcrops, intersected by a river. (See introduction to BEACHES.)

POWFOOT
Between Annan and Dumfries
B724 and unclassified road to village of
Powfoot

P: Available
Sandy. Suitable for picnics or paddling. (See introduction to BEACHES.)

MONREITH
nr Wigtown
A747 to Monrieth, beside St Medan's
Golf Course
S of village
P: Free in village
Two beaches by the golf course, and others at the foot of cliff paths at Monreith village. Portaloos and small carpark at N beach. Look out for the otter memorial to Gavin Maxwell who wrote *Ring of Bright Water.*

PORT LOGAN
B7065 S of Stranraer
P: Free
Picnic area
Pleasant beach though the sea on this exposed coastline is noticeably colder than along the Solway coast. Portaloos.

Bike Hire and Cycle Routes

Cycling with, or without, children can be a nightmare on busy roads. But you can relax and enjoy a bike ride if you are away from traffic. Stretches of disused railway track have been turned into long-distance cycle routes at Saltcoats and Irvine. Contact the District Council or Tourist Information Centre for leaflets describing the routes in detail. There are also waymarked routes at DRUMLANRIG (*see* COUNTRY PARKS), MABIE FOREST and GLENTROOL — *see* WALKS.

MINI GOLF CYCLE HIRE
Brodick, Isle of Arran
Tel: (0770) 2272
From £ per day
Adults' and children's bikes for hire

including tourers, mountain bikes and BMX bikes.

WHITING BAY HIRES
The Jetty, Whiting Bay, Isle of Arran
Tel: (077 07) 382
From £ per day
Adults' and children's bikes for hire on 2-hourly, daily or weekly basis.

THE SPINNING WHEEL
The Trossachs, Corrie, Isle of Arran
Tel: (077 081) 640
From £ per day
Adults' and children's bikes for hire. Also half-day and weekly rates.

BRODICK CYCLES
Brodick, Isle of Arran
Opposite village hall
Tel: (0770) 2460
From £ per day
Adults' bikes, junior mountain bikes, children's single-speed bikes, and carrier cycles with a seat for a small child are all available for hire from 2 hours up to a fortnight.

KLR CYCLES
15 High Street, Gatehouse of Fleet
Tel: (0557) 814392
From £ per day
Cycles for hire include children's bikes. A child's seat is also available.

NITHSDALE CYCLE CENTRE
Rosefield Mills, Dumfries
Tel: (0387) 54870
£ per day
Adults' and children's bikes for hire on a daily or weekly basis. Family rates. Bikes can be delivered to your holiday base if required.

MERRICK CARAVAN PARK
Bargrennan nr Newton Stewart
A714 NW of Newton Stewart
Tel: (067184) 280

From ££ per day
Mountain bikes are suitable for touring and off-road use in Glentrool Forest Park. There are lots of trails to explore as well as touring routes on quiet roads. Route guides available. Adults' and children's bikes, also child seats.

Boats and Boat Trips

MV THE SECOND SNARK
Princes Pier, Greenock
Tel: (0475) 21281
Open: May – Sep
From ££ for a return trip
P: Available
Light refreshments
Pack a picnic and take a boat trip to Ailsa Craig. It is known locally as 'the fairy rock' or 'Paddy's milestone' because of its position on the sea route between Ireland and the Clyde, and is actually the core of an extinct volcano. Its towering cliffs are a sanctuary for huge colonies of seabirds. Trips go from Greenock to Helensburgh, Kilcreggan, Dunoon and Loch Goil, Rothesay and Tighnabruaich, Kyles, Loch Riddon, Loch Striven, Millport, Largs and round the Cumbraes.

Camera Obscura

THE OBSERVATORY
Dumfries Museum, Dumfries
Tel: (0387) 53374
Open: Apr – Sep, Mon – Sat 1000 – 1300,
1400 – 1700, Sun 1400 – 1700
£
Disabled facilities and limited access
The Camera Obscura was installed in 1836 when the windmill tower was

being converted into an observatory. On the table-top screen you can see a moving panoramic view of Dumfries and the surrounding countryside – weather permitting. It's fun for children to try 'catching' cars and people as they move across the screen. *See* DUMFRIES MUSEUM – **MUSEUMS**.

Castles

NEWARK CASTLE (HS)
Port Glasgow
Tel: (0475) 41858
Open: Apr – Oct
£
P: Available
Picnic area
A 15th-century castle on the edge of the Clyde which was the home of Patrick Maxwell. He was infamous for murdering 2 neighbours and beating his wife – who still managed to have 16 children. Nearby is Kelburn park with a play area and a slipway for small boats. The jetty is popular with sea anglers of all ages.

LOCH DOON CASTLE (HS)
nr Dalmellington
From A713 S of Dalmellington, take road to Loch Doon
Tel: (031) 244 3101 (HS, Edinburgh)
Open: All reasonable times
Free
P: Available
Picnic areas
Early 14th-century castle devised to fit the island on which it was originally built. It was dismantled and rebuilt on the shores of the loch when the water level was raised due to a hydro-electric scheme. The walls vary from 7 to 9ft thick and stand 26ft high.

CRAIGNETHAN CASTLE (HS)
nr Lanark
5.5 miles WNW of Lanark off the A72
Tel: (055 568) 364
£
The castle is protected on 3 sides by steep gorges. There is a caponier or stone vaulted artillery chamber. Some people say that the ghost of Mary Queen of Scots appears there occasionally.

CAERLAVEROCK CASTLE (HS)
nr Dumfries
Off B725, 8 miles SE of Dumfries
Open: End Mar – Sep, Mon – Sat 0930 – 1900, Sun 1400 – 1900;
Oct – Mar close at 1600
£
P: Available
An unusual triangular castle with a water-filled moat. Substantial ruins have survived in spite of its battle-torn past. There is a full-sized reconstruction of a medieval mangonel, or catapult, as would have been used when the castle was besieged by Edward I of England in 1300. It was beseiged again for 13 weeks by the Covenanters in 1638.

THREAVE CASTLE (HS)
nr Castle Douglas
N of A75, 3 miles W of Castle Douglas
Tel: (031) 244 3101 (HS, Edinburgh)
Open: Mon – Sat 0930 – 1900, Sun 1400 – 1900 (1600 Oct – Mar)
Free but £ for ferry
P: Available
No disabled access
Early stronghold of the Black Douglases, on an island in the Dee. The 4-storeyed tower was built in the 17th century.

Caves

KINGS CAVE
Blackwaterfoot, Isle of Arran
Free
No disabled access
Legend has it that Robert the Bruce watched the spider try, try and try again while hiding in this cave. It takes about 1.5 hours to walk along the shore path from the golf course to Drumadoon Point and Kings Cave. There is also a signposted path across a field from the third tee.

ST NINIAN'S CAVE
Isle of Whithorn nr Whithorn
On shore, 2 miles W of Isle of Whithorn
Open: All times
Free
No disabled access
A short attractive walk leads to the cave which is reputed to have been used as a retreat by St Ninian. There are carvings of crosses on the cave walls which date from the 8th century.

Country Parks

KELBURN COUNTRY CENTRE
nr Largs KA29 OBE
On A78 Fairlie/Largs, free minibus from Largs Station in Jul/Aug
Tel: (0475) 568685
Open: All year; centre: Easter – mid Oct, daily 1000 – 1800
££: free to Blue Peter Badge wearers
P: Free
Tea-room, picnic area
Disabled facilities
Explore the natural woodland via pathways linked by wooden bridges across the waterfalls and gorges of the Kel Burn. If that is not enough, have a go on the Commando course which was built by the Marines.

Younger children can play in the wooden stockade with its battlements, towers and slides. Join in the fun events, nature activities and guided walks. Find out about the Earls of Glasgow at the cartoon exhibition. There are 10-minute paddock rides for very young children (pricey at ££).

EGLINTON COUNTRY PARK
nr Irvine
2 miles N of Irvine
Tel: (0294) 51776
Open: Centre 1000 – 1630 (Apr – Sep 1900 – 1700)
Come along to a Fun Day or go on a ranger-led walk in this beautiful country park. The visitor centre has displays on natural history.

CORNALEES BRIDGE
Clyde-Muirsheil Regional Park, Inverkip nr Greenock
Follow signs for Loch Thom from A78 W of Greenock after IBM complex
Tel: (0475) 521458
Open: All year
P: Available
Picnic areas
Toilets
The beach at Lunderston Bay is a mixture of sand and pebbles and is very popular for picnics on sunny days. There are scenic coastal paths and guided walks in summer. Sea angling. Further inland there are walks (*see* GREENOCK CUT – **WALKS**), nature trail (unsuitable for pushchairs), visitor centre and a ranger service with special activity days and guided walks.

DEAN CASTLE COUNTRY PARK
Dean Road, Kilmarnock
Off Glasgow Road

Tel: (0563) 27702/26401
Open: Grounds daily dawn – dusk; castle 1200 – 1700
Grounds free; Castle £
Tea-room, picnic areas
Garden for the disabled

Walks and nature trails through 200 acres of countryside. The field centre has worksheets and games on wildlife themes, and is the meeting point for the Young Naturalist Club. Small children like the aviary and farm. There is an adventure playground and a riding school which welcomes beginners. Try on some armour in the medieval castle, and look for the ghost – which might be lurking in the dungeon.

LANARK MOOR COUNTRY PARK
Hyndford Road, Lanark
Tel: (0555) 661331
Open: Park all year; amenities Apr – Sep
Picnic areas
Toilets

Fishing and boating on Lanark Loch with putting, pitch and putt and play areas in the surrounding wooded park.

CLYDE VALLEY COUNTRY ESTATE
Crossford, Carluke ML8 5NJ
A72 to Crossford, then B7056 to Roadmeetings
Tel: (055 586) 691
Open: Daily
£ – ££ for trips on the railway
P: Available
Restaurant, coffee shop and picnic areas

A restored Victorian country estate with a narrow gauge railway which runs for 1 mile along the banks of the Clyde. At Christmas there is a special trip to visit Santa in his grotto. Adventure playground, woodland and riverside walks.

BRODICK CASTLE, GARDEN AND COUNTRY PARK (NTS)
Brodick, Isle of Arran
1.5 miles N of Brodick Pier
Tel: (0770) 2202
Open: Goatfell, park and gardens, daily 0930 – sunset
££ – castle and gardens; £ – gardens only
P: Available
Restaurant and tea-room
Disabled access to specially designed nature trail

The country park has nature trails and an adventure playground. Guided walks start from the ranger centre. There is a formal garden dating from 1710 and a woodland garden with some of the finest rhododendrons in Britain. Goatfell (2866 feet) may be climbed by the energetic.

CULZEAN CASTLE AND COUNTRY PARK (NTS)
Maybole nr Ayr KA19 8LE
Off A719 Maybole/Girvan
Tel: (06556) 269/274
Open: Park all year 0900 – 2230; castle end Mar – Oct 1030 – 1730
Castle – ££s; Grounds – pedestrians free; car and passengers £££
P: Available
Self-service and picnic areas
Disabled facilities

Scotland's first country park won a Scottish Tourism Oscar in 1990. The 593-acre grounds include woodland walks, 3 miles of coastline with rocky and sandy beaches, grass play areas and a treetop walkway and adventure playground for 3 to 8-year-olds.

Go on a ranger-led walk or discover the secrets marked on the mystery map. Find out about local otters and other wildlife at the film nights or by joining the Young Naturalists' Club (over-6s). Wear old clothes and take a torch if you are planning to explore the caves which were once linked by a passage to the castle. The walled garden, camellia house and orangery, aviary and swan pond are all worth visiting too.

At the last count 475 schools and 20,000 pupils have learned about the castle's history on one of the award-winning educational tours led by guides in period costume. Find out about WWI and do some rifle duty; try on an 18th-century hairpiece and use a fan to hide your rotten teeth and dispel your bad breath. There is even a Dolphin Tour for toddlers who try to find all the animals incorporated in the Robert Adam plasterwork. With all that is on offer, it is not surprising that Culzean is one of the most popular attractions in Scotland.

DRUMLANRIG CASTLE
nr Thornhill
Off A76, 3 miles N of Thornhill
Tel: (0848) 31555
*Open: End Apr – Sep, Mon – Sat 1100 –
1800, Sun 1200 – 1800*
££ for castle; £ for grounds
Tea-room
Wheelchair path round loch
Woodlands with adventure play area including aerial ropeways, high-level walkways, giant slides and wild west fort. Also signposted walks and nature trails, ranger-led walks and cycle hire. The visitor centre has videos and a countryside exhibition, and you can see craftsmen and women making toys, leatherwork and jewellery in the craft workshop (*see* DRUMLANRIG CASTLE – SCOTLAND AT WORK). There are adventure days in the summer with mountain biking and other activities.

Fairgrounds

BEACH PARK – see PARKS AND PLAYGROUNDS

Farms

BLACKSHAW FARM PARK
nr West Kilbride
*On B781 between West Kilbride and
Dalry*
Tel: (0563) 34257
*Open: Easter – Sep 1030 – 1700, Sat, Sun
and Mon only in Sep*
£
P: Available
Coffee shop, picnic and barbecue areas
Disabled facilities and limited access
Toilets
A working farm with 300 sheep and a herd of beef cattle. Watch the daily routine of dipping and shearing sheep, milking cows and feeding calves. There is a herd of red deer and a pets' corner with peacocks, geese, rabbits, kittens and a Clydesdale horse. Walk round the nature trail, ride the ponies and donkeys, or take a tour on the tractor and trailer. Older children can drive 4-wheeler motorbikes round a track or try grass sledging. There are indoor and outdoor play areas and picnic sites to cater for changeable weather. Old clothes and wellies are recommended as no child could stay clean here and enjoy themselves.

Birthday parties can be arranged. Park rangers take school groups on educational tours.

INVERCLYDE ENVIRONMENTAL PROJECT
Hole Farm Glen, Greenock
Behind Overton housing scheme
Open: Mon–Fri 0900–1700, Sat–Sun 1200–1400
Free
Snacks available
The farm is in the process of expanding and now includes a nature trail with bird boxes. There are rare breeds of sheep, poultry, pigs and rabbits, as well as peacocks and pheasants. A small wildlife centre will be available for school groups. Contact Inverclyde District Council for further information.

SOUTH BANK FARM PARK
East Bennan, Isle of Arran
At S end of Arran, on A841 between Kildonan and Kilmory
Tel: (077082) 221
Open: Easter–Oct, Mon–Sun 1100–1800
£
Picnic area, tea-room
A working farm with sheep and cattle. Besides the more usual farm animals there are various less common breeds of sheep, cattle, poultry, goats and smaller pets such as rabbits and guinea pigs which you can feed. A good outing for pre-schoolers.

NORTH SANNOX FARM PARK
North Sannox, Arran
Tel: (077 081) 222
£
Picnic area
Walk around the paddocks and see farm animals, llamas and chipmunks.

A pets' corner, play area and free pony rides make this fun for under-5s.

BLOWPLAIN OPEN FARM
Balmaclellan, New Galloway DG7 3PY
2 miles from Balmaclellan off A712, 12 miles from Castle Douglas via A713
Tel: (06442) 206
Open: Easter–end Oct daily. Tour at 2pm daily (Sat by appointment only)
£
P: Free
Go on a 2-hour guided tour to see day-to-day life on a small hill farm. There are cattle and calves, sheep, peacocks, pheasants, poultry and ducks, as well as a pets' corner. Winner of the best Scottish Farm Tour Award in 1987.

BRIGHOUSE BAY HOLIDAY PARK – *see* SPORT AND LEISURE CENTRES

MOSSBURN FARM ANIMAL CENTRE
Hightae, Lockerbie
Off B7020 SW of Lockerbie
Tel: (0387) 811 288
Open: Daily 1030–1600
Free (donation)
Picnic areas, snack bar
A good range of weird and wonderful animals including Vietnamese pigs and Ardwell Belties, rabbits and geese. Children can hold some of the animals. Signposted countryside walks, educational projects, pony rides and treasure hunts.

PALGOWAN OPEN FARM
Bargrennan, Newton Stewart
4 miles N of Glentrool on Straiton Road
Tel: (0671) 84 231
Open: Easter, mid-May, Jun, Sep, Oct; Tue–Thu; Jul–Aug, Mon–Fri at 1400
£

Picnic areas
Disabled access
A hill farm with Highland and Galloway cattle, sheep and working sheep-dogs. Go on a 2-hour conducted tour and watch dry-stone dykes being built, walking sticks being made and animal skins being cured. School visits may be booked in advance.

LOWER KNOCK OPEN FARM

Monreith nr Port William
4 miles from Port William, 7 miles from Whithorn on A747
Tel: (09887) 217
Open: All year 1000 – 1700
£
This farm specialises in breeding exotic ducks and also has tiny African pygmy goats, Shetland ponies and other animals. There is also an adventure play area.

Fish

FENCEBAY FISHERIES

Fairlie nr Largs
Tel: (0475) 568918
Open: Daily
Free
Feed the trout in the fish ponds. See live crabs and lobsters.

MARINE STATION

nr Millport, Isle of Cumbrae
Tel: (0475) 530581/2
Open: Mon – Fri 0915 – 1215, 1400 – 1630; also Saturdays from Jun – Sep
£
This marine station has been open for more than 100 years and has an excellent aquarium and museum.

McCRIRICK & SONS

38 John Finnie Street, Kilmarnock
Tel: (0563) 25577
From £
Great value day tickets for children with easy access to lochside from car park.

NEWMILL TROUT AND DEER FARM

nr Lanark
On A706, 3 miles from Lanark
Tel: (0555) 870730
Free but you can pay for fish you catch
Café
Loch and river fishing with a children's fishery where they are guaranteed to catch a fish. Deer, wild boar, Clydesdale horses, calves and pets' corner.

HB WILLIAMS

10 The Crofts, Kirkcudbright
Tel: (0557) 30367
Open: Phone after 1800 for bookings and sailing times
Sea angling on a large modern boat with safety equipment. Rods for hire, families welcome, tuition if required.

SKYREBURN AQUARIUM

Skyreburn, Gatehouse of Fleet
Beside A75, 2 miles W of Gatehouse of Fleet
Tel: (067182) 204
Open: Apr – Oct, Sun – Fri 1000 – 1700 (also Sats in July/Aug)
£
P: Available
Disabled facilities
See creatures that are normally hidden away in the burns and rivers or the sea in this underwater wildlife centre. There are over 50 species of local saltwater and freshwater fish and animals including sticklebacks, pike, starfish, lobsters, rays and dogfish.

THE MOFFAT FISHERY AND FISH FARM

Selkirk Road, Moffat
Entrance 300yds out of Moffat on A708
Tel: (0683) 21068
Open: Daily, 0800 – dusk
£££ for a parent and child day ticket
Refreshments, or barbecue your catch on the banks of the loch
Disabled access
Toilets

A trout farm where youngsters can feed the fish or try angling. Rods for hire. Beginners and families welcome.

LOGAN FISH POND

nr Stranraer
Off B7065, 14 miles S of Stranraer
Tel: (0292) 268181
Open: Easter – Sep, daily 1200 – 2000
£
No disabled access

This tidal pool in the rocks, 30ft deep and 53ft round, was completed in 1800 as a fresh-fish larder for Logan House. It was damaged by a mine in 1942 but re-opened in 1955. It holds about 30 fish, mainly cod, which are so tame that you can feed them by hand.

BEACH PARK – *see* PARKS AND PLAYGROUNDS

Forest Parks

GALLOWAY FOREST PARK

nr Newton Stewart
Off A714, 10 miles NW of Newton Stewart
Tel: (0671) 2420
P: Available
Café
Disabled facilities

It is said that while Robert the Bruce was hiding in a cave here, he was inspired by a spider 'to try, try and try again' to defeat the English. There are waymarked trails suitable for walking or cycling in the 250 square miles of magnificent countryside which includes Merrick (2765 feet), the highest hill in southern Scotland. Look for salmon, deer, golden eagles and peregrines, otters and pine martens. If you don't see them in the wild, have a look round the deer museum instead. Some of the riverside trails are suitable for wheelchairs.

Gardens

BELLEISLE ESTATE

nr Ayr
Cafeteria

Grounds and gardens, pets' corner, deer park, aviary.

ROZELLE ESTATE

Alloway nr Ayr
1.5 miles S of town centre
Tea-room

Well-kept gardens, shrubbery, walks and sculpture park.

BARGANY ESTATE GARDENS

nr Girvan
4 miles E of Girvan on B734
Picnic areas

Woodland walks.

THREAVE GARDEN (NTS)

Castle Douglas
Tel: (0556) 2575
Open: Daily 0900 – sunset
££
Restaurant
Disabled access and facilities

29

The gardens are at their best in the spring when almost 200 varieties of daffodils are in flower. Children also like the unusual giant tree ferns, palm trees, eucalyptus and spiky rhubarb.

ARBIGLAND GARDENS
Kirkbean, Dumfries
Tel: (038788) 283
Open: May – Sep, Sun/Tue/Thu 1400 – 1600
£
Tea-room
Admiral John Paul Jones, the founder of the US Navy, was born in a cottage in the grounds and worked here as a boy. The formal woodland and water gardens lead down to a sandy beach which children enjoy. There is also a small play area.

ARDWELL GARDENS
Ardwell nr Stranraer
10 miles from Stranraer on A716 to Drummore
Tel: (0776) 86 227
Open: Mar – Oct, daily 1000 – 1800 (1700 Mar/Apr/Oct)
£
Picnic site on shore
Beautiful spring flowers especially the daffodils and rhododendrons. Walk round the ponds, walled garden and greenhouses, or pick-your-own fruit in season.

CASTLE KENNEDY GARDENS
Castle Kennedy, Stranraer
Tel: (0776) 2024
Open: Easter – Sep, daily 1000 – 1700
£
Tea-room
The attractive gardens include a sunken garden, the 'Giant's Grave'. There's a long avenue of monkey puzzle trees, too – how do monkeys climb back up the downward-pointing spikes of the branches?

LOGAN BOTANIC GARDEN
Port Logan nr Stranraer
On B7065, 14 miles S of Stranraer
Tel: (077686) 231
Open: Mid Mar – Oct, 1000 – 1800
£
Salad bar
A specialist garden of the Royal Botanic Garden, Edinburgh, where many exotic plants grow in the mild west coast climate. The famous walled garden has palm trees, tree ferns and cabbage palms from the southern hemisphere as well as woodland and water gardens.

GALLOWAY HOUSE GARDENS
Garlieston nr Wigtown
8 miles S of Wigtown
Tel: (098 86) 225
Open: All year, all reasonable times
Free (donation)
Teas in village
Disabled access
The gardens, which cover about 30 acres, go down to the sea and a sandy beach. Among the fine old trees there is a handkerchief tree which is at its best in May – June. There are lots of seasonal flowers, a walled garden with greenhouses and a camellia house.

MEADOWSWEET HERB GARDEN
Soulseat Loch, Castle Kennedy
Open: May – early Sep, Tue – Thu 1200 – 1800
£
Learn about medieval, culinary, pot-pourri and medicinal herbs and their history.

Heritage Centres

ROBERT BURNS CENTRE
Mill Road, Dumfries
Tel: (0387) 64808
Open: Apr—Sep, Mon—Sat 1000—2000,
Sun 1400—1700; Oct—Mar,
Tue—Sat 1000—1300, 1400—1700
Free
Café, picnic area
Older children would enjoy a visit
to this 18th-century converted mill,
especially if they were doing a project on the Bard. There is lots of
information about his life and work
including a life-size model of Burns
as an exciseman. Younger children
like the scale model of 18th-century
Dumfries, the diorama, the deer
enclosure, the riverside walk and the
play area.

Indoor Fun

COLVEND FAMILY POP-IN
Colvend Hall nr Dalbeattie
On A712
Open: Mornings Mon—Fri, mid Jul—end
Aug
Light refreshments
Quizzes, games, prizes, suggestions
for walks and visits. Maps, reference
books etc. Wildlife information.

LUCE BAY SHORE CENTRE
nr Port William
The displays are based on seashore
life. Go on one of the nature trails
or guided walks, watch videos, or
try driftwood doodling, puzzles and
games.

Museums

SCOTTISH MARITIME MUSEUM

Laird Forge Building, Gottries Road, Irvine
KA12 8QE
A736, A71 Kilmarnock/Irvine
Tel: (0294) 78283
Open: Apr—Oct, daily 1000—1700
£
P: Free
Partial disabled access
Climb aboard the puffers, tugs, traw-
lers and lifeboat in the harbour. See
an Edwardian shipworker's flat.

HM CUSTOMS AND EXCISE
Greenock Custom House, Customhouse
Quay, Greenock
Tel: (0475) 26331
Open: Mon—Fri 0900—1200, 1300—
1630
Free
An exhibition of the work of the
Customs and Excise including a display on Robbie Burns who was an
exciseman at one time. Children can
handle objects which have been
used, without success, for smuggling
and then they can test their knowledge by playing a computer game
in which they have to search a ship
for smuggled goods.

McLEAN MUSEUM AND ART GALLERY
Kelly Street, Gourock
Tel: (0475) 23741
Open: Mon—Sat 1000—1200, 1300—
1700
Free (£ for organised activities)
Who needs to go to the zoo when
you can see tiger and bongo (a
large striped African antelope) in the
natural history section? Model ships
and engines. Worksheets for the
under-10s makes learning fun, as do
the special activities on Saturdays
and during the holidays (booking
advised).

DICK INSTITUTE

Elmbank Avenue, Kilmarnock
Off London Road
Tel: (0563) 24601
Open: Mon/Tue/Thu/Fri 0900 – 2000,
Wed/Sat 0900 – 1700
Free

Find out the names of different types of rock in the geological section. Imagine fighting battles with the broadswords and firearms on display. The children's library (in the same building) organises quizzes and other activities during summer months.

GLADSTONE COURT STREET MUSEUM

North Back Road, Biggar
Tel: (0899) 21050
Open: Easter – Oct, daily 1000 – 1230,
1400 – 1700, Sun 1400 – 1700
£
P: Available
Partial disabled access

An indoor reproduction of a Victorian street with grocer, library, dressmaker, bank, school, photographer, ironmonger, chemist, china merchant, telephone exchange etc.

NEW LANARK CONSERVATION VILLAGE AND VISITOR CENTRE

New Lanark Mills, Lanark ML11 9DB
Signposted off A70
Tel: (0555) 661345
Open: Centre daily 1100 – 1700; village at all times
£
Picnic areas, café
Disabled access to centre

Spend a day in New Lanark and go back in time to a cotton-milling village in the early 19th century. The Falls of Clyde used to power the mills but now they are the home of 'ghosts' which disappear behind the spray. The visitor centre has a magical history tour of life in the 1820s complete with the sound of voices and the smell of soup. Your guide is a little girl called Annie McLeod (a hologram). Run your fingers through raw cotton in the exhibition area and find out what life was like for children in those days. You can even join in the games they played. There are walks by the Falls of Clyde and through the nature reserve. And, if anyone has time to get bored, there is a small adventure playground. Winner of a Scottish Tourism Oscar in 1991 and nominated for a 'World Heritage Site' award.

MOAT PARK HERITAGE CENTRE

Lanark
Tel: (0899) 21050
Open: Mon – Sat 1000 – 1700, Sun 1400 – 1700

A local history museum with displays covering 6000 years – from volcanoes and glaciers to yesterday's newspapers. There are splendid models portraying life in different eras of the Clyde Valley's history.

ISLE OF ARRAN HERITAGE MUSEUM

Rosaburn, Brodick, Isle of Arran
Tel: (0770) 2636
Open: May – Sep, Mon – Sat 1000 – 1300 and 1400 – 1700
£
Picnic area and tea-room
Disabled facilities

A group of old buildings which were originally an 18th-century croft farm on the edge of the village. Smithy, cottage furnished in the late 19th-century style, stable block with displays of local history, archaeology and geology. Occasional demonstrations of spinning and other handcrafts. The inexpensive tea-room serves light lunches, snacks and home-baking.

DUMFRIES MUSEUM
Tel: (0387) 53374
Open: Apr—Sep, Mon—Sat 1000—1300, 1400—1700, Sun 1400—1700 (closed Sun/ Mon from Oct—Mar)
Free
As well as the CAMERA OBSCURA, you can see stones that glow in the dark and the first-ever bicycle.

GALLOWAY FARM MUSEUM—
see SCOTLAND AT WORK

MOONSTONE MINIATURES
4 Victoria Street, Kirkpatrick Durham
Tel: (055665) 313
Open: Mid May—mid Sep, 1000—1700, closed Thu/Sat
£
Unique collection of 1:12 scale miniatures, lavishly furnished houses, stately homes and shops.

HENRY DUNCAN SAVINGS BANK
Ruthwell
6.5 miles W of Annan
Tel: (038 787) 640
Open: Easter—Sep, daily 1000—1300, 1400—1700 (closed Sun/Mon in Oct—Mar)
Free
This is where the first savings bank was founded in 1810. Interesting exhibits for those aged 8+.

GLENLUCE MOTOR MUSEUM
Glenluce
Half a mile N of centre of Glenluce
Tel: (05813) 534

Open: Mar—Oct 1000—1900; Nov—Feb 1100—1600; closed Mon and Tue
£
P: Available
Tea-room
Disabled facilities
Toilets
The farm buildings contain a collection of vintage and classic motorcars and bikes. Restoration work is also on display along with authentic period costumes, a replica of a garage workshop, and miniature cars. Winners of the children's competitions get a ride in a vintage car, while anyone can climb aboard the fire engine.

CREETOWN GEM ROCK MUSEUM AND CRYSTAL CAVE
Chain Road, Creetown
A75, S of Newton Stewart
Tel: (067182) 357/554
Open: Daily 0930—1800
(sunset in winter)
P: Available
£
Tea-room
Disabled access
Toilets
An award-winning museum filled with examples of almost every known gemstone and mineral. The crystal cave has fluorescent lighting which gives a magical air to the exhibits. Watch jewellers at work in the lapidary workshop.

Novelties

ELECTRIC BRAE
Also known as Croy Brae nr Ayr
A719 9 miles S of Ayr
Motorists are completely confused by an optical illusion which makes

it seem as if the car is going downhill when it is in fact going up. It was once thought to be caused by a powerful magnetic effect, hence the name.

Parks and Playgrounds

GOUROCK PARK
Broomberry Drive, Gourock
Gourock used to be a major holiday resort when Glaswegians went 'doon the watter', but nowadays it is much quieter. The park has a lovely walled flower garden, pets' corner with rabbits and guinea pigs, toddlers' playground, 4 tennis courts, bowling, 18-hole pitch and putt course and a heated outdoor swimming pool.

BEACH PARK
Irvine
Adjacent to the MAGNUM LEISURE CENTRE — see **SPORT AND LEISURE CENTRES**
Tel: (0294) 214100
Picnic areas
Various charges for facilities
Disabled access and facilities
A large park with boating, pitch and putt, maze, fairground (Tel: 0294 311967), trim track with facilities for the disabled, BMX track, Seaworld Marine exhibition (Tel: 0294 311414). These attractions will all help you avoid the beach which suffers from pollution and has failed EC water quality tests for the past 6 years.

KAY PARK
Kilmarnock
Tel: (0563) 21140
Open: Park dawn — dusk; facilities open during summer months
P: Available
Toilets

Children love to ride their bikes round the cycle proficiency track. Other amusements include crazy golf, pitch and putt, trampolines, a boating pond, an adventure playground and assault course, and a museum.

BIGGAR PARK AND LANARK LOCH
Off Hyndford Road, Lanark
Tel: (0555) 61331
Picnic areas
Toilets
Good play areas for under-5s, and lots of open space as well as woodlands. Boating pond, tennis, putting, pitch and putt, and fishing. Caravan site.

BIGGAR BURN BRAES
Biggar
Picnic areas
A large play area for toddlers, lots of open space, paddling pools and a wobbly bridge over the burn — bring spare socks! There are two heritage museums close by.

CASTLEBANK PARK
Lanark
Picnic areas
Playground suitable for disabled children
Large Victorian-style park with play area, woodland walks, formal gardens. Ideal day out with under-5s.

HAZELBANK PARK
Hazelbank nr Lanark
On the A72
Picnic areas
Play area on the banks of the Clyde suitable for under-5s.

BOATING LAKE
The Promenade, Girvan
Pedal boats, bouncy castle, trampo-

lines, crazy golf, play area and fun fair.

LOCHSIDE PARK
Castle Douglas
Open: From Easter weekend
Picnic tables
Rowing boats and canoes for hire, putting, play area, tennis.

COLLISTON PARK
Dalbeattie
Open: From Easter weekend
Paddle boats, putting, trampolines, tennis and multi-purpose play area.

BRIGHOUSE BAY — *see* SPORT AND LEISURE CENTRES

CASTLEDYKES PARK
Dumfries
Open: Daily, dawn – dusk
Picnic tables
Attractive play area at site of former castle.

DOCK PARK
Dumfries
Open: Facilities open Apr – mid Aug, Mon – Sat 1300 – 2100,
Sun 1300 – 1900
Tennis, putting, crazy golf, trampolines, children's play area, paddling pool, swingball, mini-golf, croquet, draughts, chess, table-tennis, cycle track, skateboarding.

McJERROW PARK
Lockerbie
Open: Evenings and weekends May/Jun, afternoons and evenings Jul/Aug
Children's play area, putting, table-tennis, swingball, tennis, paddling pool.

STATION PARK
Moffat
Open: May – Aug, Mon – Sat 1000 –

2000, Sun 1300 – 1900; weekends in Sep
Picnic area
Boating, putting, paddling pool and adventure play area all in beautifully laid-out grounds.

AGNEW PARK
Stranraer
Boating, putting, crazy golf and mini cars, and canoeing and windsurfing on Marine Lake.

Playschemes and Creches

JUMP FOR JOY
Nile Court, Ayr
Opposite Littlewoods
Open: Mon – Sat 1000 – 1700,
Sun 1230 – 1700
£
Refreshments
A creche with a ball swamp and soft play area for under-10s. Under-5s must be accompanied but older children may be left at parents' discretion. Parties can be arranged.

SHOPPERS' CRECHE
Ground Floor, Burns House, Burns Statue Square, Ayr KA7 1UT
Tel: (0292) 284968
Open: Mon – Sat 1000 – 1730
(closes 1300 on Wed)
£
Leave your children for up to 2 hours with qualified staff. The spacious creche is for under-12s (minimum age 18 months).

RUMBLE TUMBLES
26 Castle Street, Dumfries
£
The soft play centre can be used as a shoppers' creche for up to 3 hours. Suitable for children aged 2 to 8.

THE PIED PIPER PLAYROOM
THE RYAN CENTRE – *see* SPORT
AND LEISURE CENTRES

A small, privately run creche where children aged 3 to 5 may be left for up to 2 hours.

Railways

DOON VALLEY HERITAGE – *see*
SCOTLAND AT WORK
CLYDE VALLEY COUNTRY
ESTATE – *see* COUNTRY PARKS

LITTLE WHEELS
6 Hill Street, Portpatrick DG9 8JX
S of Stranraer on A77
Tel: (077 681) 536
Open: Easter – Oct, 1100 – 1600, closed Fri; extended hours during Jul/Aug
£
P: Free
Hot and cold drinks available
Disabled access and facilities

Children can marvel while parents reminisce over 60 working model locomotives, 1000 model cars and other forms of transport, and a variety of dolls. The model railway has over 100yds of track set out in three tiers. Of the 16 complete trains there are usually 4 or 5 working at a time and children can sometimes get a turn operating the controls. More energetic children can climb aboard various vintage machines and pretend to drive them. And to help them remember what they've seen, there is a children's quiz.

Riding

KELBURN COUNTRY CENTRE –
see COUNTRY PARKS

WEMYSS BAY RIDING CENTRE
Wemyss Bay
Between Denny's and Wemyss Bay Holiday Park
Tel: (0475) 521415
££ per hour
Disabled riders welcome

Horse and pony rides in the hills behind Wemyss Bay. Safe treks through woodland, glens and along farmland tracks. Beginners and school parties welcome. Birthday party treks. Escorted pony walks for children. Hats for hire.

GLEDDOCH RIDING SCHOOL
Gleddoch, Langbank
Tel: (047554) 350
£££

Riding lessons and escorted pony walks for children. Treks for more experienced riders.

LANARKSHIRE RIDING CENTRE
The Race Course, Lanark
Tel: (0555) 661853/665498
££

Lessons for children of 4 and upwards.

AYRSHIRE EQUITATION CENTRE
Castlehill Stables, Hillfoot Road, Ayr KA7 3LF
Tel: (0292) 266267
££ per hour

BHS, RDA, POB, ABRS, STRA approved. Unaccompanied children over 7 welcome. There are 30-minute lessons for 3 to 4-year-olds. Beach riding, cross-country.

NORTH SANNOX POINT
TREKKING CENTRE
Laimrig, Sannox, Isle of Arran
Tel: (077 081) 222
From £ per hour

Children can go on 1 and 2-hour treks accompanied by an experienced leader. Beginners very welcome. Half-day and day treks by arrangement. Hard hats available. There is also a farm park with a wide range of unusual animals – see **FARMS**.

CAIRNHOUSE TREKKING CENTRE
Blackwaterfoot, Isle of Arran KA27 8EU
Tel: (077 086) 256
Open: Easter – Oct
From £ per hour
Riding and trekking accompanied by an experienced rider. Hourly rides in the mornings, afternoon hacks for experienced riders. Qualified instruction available. Novice riders welcome. Hard hats provided. STRA approved.

CLOYBURN TREKKING CENTRE
Brodick, Isle of Arran
Tel: (0770) 2108
Open: Summer months only
From £ per hour
Horses and ponies to suit all ages. Short treks of 1 or 2 hours, and rides for small children.

HIGH MAINS FARM
Wallacetown, Maybole
Between Kirkoswald and Dailly on Wallacetown road
Tel: (046 581) 504
£ per hour
Fully supervised riding. Hats provided.

BAREND RIDING CENTRE
Sandyhills, Dalbeattie DG5 4NU
Tel: (038 778) 663
Open: All year
££
Restaurant

Introductory courses, lessons in the outdoor riding school, cross country course, seasonal trekking, barbecue and picnic rides. BHS, STRA approved. Cool off in the indoor swimming pool afterwards.

BRIGHOUSE BAY – *see* SPORT AND LEISURE CENTRES

WEST DRUMRAE FARM
Ravenstone nr Whithorn
Tel: (09887) 518
£ per hour
A small riding and driving centre where young children are welcome. Accompanied rides and lessons.

Science and Technology

HUNTERSTON POWER STATION
nr West Kilbride
Off A78 just N of the town
Tel: (0800) 838557
Open: Daily throughout the summer
Free
Guided tours of the nuclear power station.

TONGLAND POWER STATION
Tongland nr Kirkcudbright
On A762
Tel: (0557) 30114
Open: Summer, Mon – Sat; tours at 1000, 1130, 1400, 1530 by appointment only
£
Watch a video on the production of hydro electricity, visit the turbine hall and the dam where you can see salmon going up the fish ladder on their journey back up river.

Scotland at Work – Past and Present

DALGARVEN MILL
Dalry Road, Kilwinning KL13 6PN
29 miles from Glasgow on A737 between Dalry and Kilwinning
Tel: (0294) 52448
Open: Mon – Sat 1000 – 1700,
Sun 1230 – 1730
£
Coffee room, bakery

Working flour mill with a 20ft diameter water wheel. The museum of country life has objects of industrial and archaeological interest as well as children's toys – bowls, quoits, draught boards, chess sets and sledges. Displays of local costumes include clothes that were worn in 1780. Imagine the womenfolk washing clothes, milking cows and thinning turnips all day, then working by candle-light to produce intricate Ayrshire embroidery, crochet and lace work. Have real 'plooman's lunch', or sample the home-baked bread, oatcakes and scones from the bakery.

DOON VALLEY HERITAGE
Dalmellington KA6 7JF
Tel: (0292) 531144/5
Open: Official opening due in summer 1993
£
P: Free
Tea-room
Disabled facilities

Discover what life was like for the Ayrshire weaving communities during the 18th century and have a look round the reconstructed weavers' room and audio-visual show. There is also an exhibition telling the story of the Dalmellington Iron Company.

Some of the iron workers' houses have already been reconstructed but an open-air museum is still being developed. You can watch the work progress or join in as a volunteer.

The Scottish Industrial Railway Centre at Minnivey Colliery has 8 steam locomotives on display, 12 diesels and a large collection of rolling stock. Children can have a ride in a brake van pulled by a steam loco over a short distance of restored track. There are plans to run a regular passenger service between the ironworks and the colliery, and perhaps occasional services from Ayr.

BIGGAR GASWORKS MUSEUM
Gasworks Road, Biggar
Tel: (031) 225 7534
Open: End May – Sep, Mon – Thu 1400 – 1700, Sat – Sun 1200 – 1700
Free
Disabled access

Britain's oldest surviving rural gasworks, built in 1839. See machinery in action and life-size figures 'at work'. Video show. Phone for details of live steam and working exhibits.

LANARK MARKET
Lanark
Tel: (0555) 2281
Open: Mondays only
Free
Restaurant

There is plenty of hustle, bustle and noise at this large livestock auction market.

GALLOWAY FARM MUSEUM
nr New Galloway
From New Galloway take A712 W for 1 mile

Tel: (06443) 317
Open: Easter – Jun, Sun only;
Jul – Sep, Sun – Fri
£
P: Available
Disabled access

Farming was hard work in the early 19th century as you will find out when you see farm horses at work and hear the talks on crop production. Children (and adults) can have rides on horse-drawn carts and sleighs.

THE WEATHER CENTRE
Lauriston nr Castle Douglas
7 miles from Castle Douglas
Tel: (06445) 264
Open: Tours on Tue – Fri, Sun at 1030 and 1430
£

See a range of weather recording instruments and satellite pictures of moving cloud sequences. Try the computerised weather quiz and speak to a real weather forecaster.

GALLOWAY FOOTWEAR CO-OPERATIVE
Balmaclellan, nr Castle Douglas DG7 3QE
By church in Dalry, on A712
Tel: (06442) 465
P: Available

Do you know how shoes are made? Here is a chance to watch the various processes involved in making clogs, shoes and other footwear. Please phone in advance.

NEW ABBEY CORN MILL (HS)
New Abbey nr Dumfries
8 miles S Dumfries on A710
Tel: (0387) 85260
Open: Mon – Sat 0930 – 1900, Sun 1400 – 1900 (reduced hours Oct – Mar)
£

No disabled access

A most attractive 19th-century water-powered mill which has been restored to working order, complete with millpond and water wheel. It is worth walking round the conservation village of New Abbey too.

COMLOGON CASTLE
Clarencefield, Dumfries DG1 4NA
On B724
Tel: (038 787) 283
Open: Mar – Dec, daily 1000 – 1700
£

Watch a skilled blacksmith at work making arms – claymores, broadswords, targes, dirks and sgian dubhs – and armour. Go on a tour of the castle as well.

DRUMLANRIG CASTLE CRAFT WORKSHOPS
Drumlanrig Castle, Thornhill DG3 4AG
18 miles N of Dumfries on A76
Tel: (0848) 31555
Open: May – Sep, Fri – Wed 1100 – 1800
P: Available
£ (admission to workshops and country park)
Tea-room

There should be something to interest everyone here – leatherworker, potter, jeweller, silversmith, weaver, woodturner and painter.

MUSEUM OF SCOTTISH LEAD MINING
Wanlockhead nr Sanquhar
On B797, 8 miles ENE of Sanquhar
Tel: (0659) 74387
Open: Easter – Oct, daily 1100 – 1600
£
P: Available
Disabled facilities

The area around Wanlockhead and Leadhills was once known as 'God's treasurehouse in Scotland' because of the gold, silver and lead which was found there. Go underground in the lead mine, which was worked till 1860, and see life-size models of miners working in very cramped conditions, then follow the visitor walkway and explore the miners' cottages, beam engines, smelt mill, and miners' library at your own pace. Prospectors used to wash gold from the banks of local streams.

Sport and Leisure Centres

MAGNUM LEISURE CENTRE
Harbourside, Irvine KA12 8PP
A71, 900yds Irvine Station
Tel: (0294) 78381
Open: All year, daily 0900 – 2230
£ for swimming or skating
P: Free
Full catering
Disabled access and facilities
Two leisure pools with exciting giant water slides. The ice-rink can be used for skating, curling, hockey and discos. Young children like the soft playroom and superbounce area with its giant inflatable elephant and a mountain slide. Sports available include squash, badminton, table-tennis, soccer, basketball, volleyball and golf practice. Right beside the centre is BEACH PARK with boating, pitch and putt, trim tracks, a maze, a fairground and picnic areas. There is a SEA WORLD centre (Tel: 0294 311414) where you can see conger eels, lobsters, anemones and starfish in underwater caverns. All in all, this is one of Scotland's most popular attractions (and it keeps the children away from the sea and the sand – *see* BEACHES).

HARVIE'S LEISURE CENTRE
Stevenston
Tel: (0294) 605126
£
Cafeteria
Learn to swim in the pool or skate on the ice-rink. Ice discos, figure skating club and ice dancing.

PAVILION BOWL
Winton Circus, Saltcoats KA21 5DA
Tel: (0294) 62457
Open: Daily, 1000 – late evening
P: Free
From ££
Snack bar
Ten-pin bowling is suitable for kids over 5. There are 6, 7 or 8lb balls for children as well as bump 'n' bowl, where 2 enormous airtubes fill the gutters to keep the ball on course for the pins, and scores are automatically recorded on a computer. Parties can be arranged complete with invitation cards, a cake and a photograph (good for 7+).

GALLEON CENTRE
99 Titchfield Street, Kilmarnock KA1 1QY
Tel: (0563) 23156
Open: Daily, 0900 – 2300
From £
Vending machine
Swimming, fun sessions, lessons. Skating, ice disco, ice hockey, curling, squash, badminton, table-tennis, basketball, indoor hockey, 5-a-side football, trampolining, netball, volleyball, gymnastics, martial arts. Shipmates club during holidays, soft play area. Creche.

BRIDGEHOUSE BAY HOLIDAY PARK
13 Borgue Road, Kirkcudbright DG6 4TS
Tel: (05577) 267
Various charges

Day visitors welcome for windsurfing, sailing, canoeing, water skiing, jet skiing—beginners' classes. There is a 2-hour guided tour by tractor and trailer around an award-winning farm trail on a beef breeding and dairy farm where you can see cows being milked (open most afternoons in July—Aug). Other activities include riding at the STRA and BHS approved trekking centre, ornithological walks, boating pond and mini-golf.

SOUTH OF SCOTLAND ICE-RINK
Glasgow Road, Lockerbie
Tel: (05762) 2197
Open: Mid Sep—early Apr
£
Children-only sessions: Sat 1400—1630, 1900—2130. Skates for hire.

EVERHOLM SPORTS COMPLEX
Battery Street, Annan
Tel: (0461) 205874
Open: Apr—Sep, Mon—Fri 1000—2100, Sat—Sun 0930—2000; reduced hours Oct—Mar
£
Picnic areas, snack bar
Putting, swingball, table-tennis, canoeing, trim track. Summer sport bus providing sporting entertainment and coaching at various venues (8 to 15-year-olds).

BEECHGROVE SPORTS CENTRE
Moffat
Tel: (0683) 20697
Open: Mon—Fri 1300—2200, Sat—Sun from 1000
£
Badminton, football, karate, basketball, indoor tennis, babybounce sessions, Moffat Minor's Club, Supersport sessions and summer sports activities including competitions and a bouncy castle.

RYAN LEISURE CENTRE
Stranraer
Tel: (0776) 3535
Open: Daily 1000—2300
£
Cafeteria
Badminton, football, children's parties. There is a youth theatre for kids over 11 where they can try acting and working backstage as well as going to shows. Shoppers' creche— *see* PLAYSCHEMES AND CRECHES.

Swimming

LARGS SWIMMING POOL
24 Greenock Road, Largs
Tel: (0475) 674872
Open: Mon—Sat from 0900, Sun 0930—1630
£
Disabled access and facilities including diving
Children's pool with fun equipment, children's and parent and baby lessons. Baby changing facilities including playpens.

HECTOR McNEIL BATHS
Inverkip Road, Greenock
Tel: (0475) 22909
£
Cafeteria
The main pool has diving boards which are quite a novelty in this era of leisure pools. There are lessons to increase pre-schoolers' confidence as well as beginners' and improvers' classes and a disabled swimming club.

NEW CUMNOCK SWIMMING POOL
The Castle, New Cumnock
Tel: (0290) 38501
Open: End Apr – Sep, Mon – Fri 1000 –
1800, At 1000 – 1630, Sun 1200 – 1630
£
Outdoor swimming pool

AUCHRANNIE HOTEL
Brodick, Isle of Arran
1 mile from ferry terminal in Brodick
Tel: (0770) 2234
£
Restaurant
A new swimming pool which is open to non-residents.

KINLOCH HOTEL
Blackwaterfoot, Isle of Arran
Tel: (0770 86) 444
£
Dive in for a swim even if you are not staying at the hotel.

GREENSANDS
Dumfries
Tel: (0387) 52908
Open: Daily
£
Light refreshments
Mother and toddler sessions, family sessions, fun sessions with a giant chute and an obstacle course along an inflatable aqua run. Birthday parties can be arranged.

ANNAN SWIMMING POOL
St John's Road, Annan
Tel: (0461) 204773/203311
Open: Evenings and weekends in term-time, daily during holidays
£
Vending machines
Disabled facilities and access
Children's splash sessions with infla-tables and rafts. Baby changing tables. Lessons.

GOUROCK PARK – *see* **PARKS AND PLAY-GROUNDS**,

BAREND RIDING CENTRE – *see* **RIDING**,

MAGNUM LEISURE CENTRE, HARVIE'S LEISURE CENTRE, THE GALLEON CENTRE – *see* **SPORT AND LEISURE CENTRES**,

BUTLIN'S WONDERWEST – *see* **THEME PARKS**.

Theatres and Cinemas

BIGGAR PUPPET THEATRE
Broughton Road, Biggar ML12 6HA
On the B7016 E of Biggar
Tel: (0899) 20631
Open: Mar – mid Jan, Mon – Sat 1000 –
1700, Sun 1300 – 1700, closed Wed
£££; free to Blue Peter Badge wearers
P: Free
Tea-room and picnic area
Prior notice required by disabled visitors
Complete Victorian theatre in minia-ture, seating 100. Puppet plays, guided tours, exhibition, outdoor Victorian games.

RYAN LEISURE CENTRE – *see*
SPORT AND LEISURE CENTRES

Theme Parks

BUTLIN'S WONDERWEST WORLD
Dunure Road, Ayr KA7 4LB
4 miles S of Ayr on A719
Tel: (0292) 265141 x211
Open: May – Sep, 1000 – 1900
££££
P: Free
Full catering
Limited disabled facilities

Scotland's largest theme park has a sub-tropical water-world where you can spiral down the gigantic slides or ride the rushing flumes. The fun-world has an adventure play area for younger children complete with bouncy castles, climbing nets and rope ladders. But the big attraction for older children is the breathtaking roller-coaster and other funfair rides. There is a roller-skating rink, crazy golf and a children's afternoon show as well. The entry charge covers almost all the amusements but there is a small additional charge for the mini-motorbikes, go-karts, BMX track and bumper boats.

Walks

THE GREENOCK CUT
nr Greenock
The nature trail goes through Shielhill Glen (a Site of Special Scientific Interest) and along part of the Greenock Cut. It takes less than an hour but there is a circular walk of about 7 miles for the more energetic along the Cut, an old aquaduct built in the 1820s to supply Greenock with water and power. It is easy walking since the Cut only drops 27ft along the length.

STARR FOREST
Galloway Forest Park
Off A713 S of Dalmellington
Tel: (0387) 68171
Walk from Balloch Lodge or Loch Doon Castle.

LOUDOUN HILL
by Darvel
Off A71, E of Kilmarnock

A hill formed by a volcanic plug. Site of a battle in 1307 where Robert the Bruce put the English to flight.

ENTERKINE NATURE TRAIL
nr Tarbolton
B744
Natural woodland with badgers' setts, pond and varied birdlife.

RIVER AYR GORGE
Failford, nr Ayr
On A758
Nature trail along the gorge.

DALBEATTIE FOREST
nr Dalbeattie
On A710
Tel: (0556) 3626
P: Available
Picnic area
Waymarked walks in the forest and along the hillside.

FLEET FOREST
nr Gatehouse
1.5 miles W of Lauriston
P: Available
Picnic area
Fleet Oakwoods Interpretive Trail is a 2-mile all-weather trail through broadleaved wood. Some trees are name-tagged to help with identification.

RAIDERS ROAD FOREST DRIVE
nr New Galloway
Connecting A712 at Clatteringshaws and A762 at Mossdale
P: Available
Picnic area
Forest walk suitable for wheelchairs
Toilets
10.5 miles of forest drive with 4 forest walks.

MABIE FOREST
nr Dumfries
4 miles SW of Dumfries, off A710
Tel: (0387) 86247
P: Available (50p)
Picnic site
2 trails for the disabled
Several waymarked walks and cycle trails between 1 and 4 miles long through mixed woodland. Children especially enjoy the 'adventure trail'. The picnic site is good.

DEVIL'S BEEF TUB
nr Moffat
On east side of A701, 5 miles N of Moffat
Swirling mists were welcomed by the Border reivers (thieves) when they hid stolen cattle in this huge, natural depression in the hills. It can be seen from the road but if you walk there take care at the edge.

WOOD OF CREE
nr Newton Stewart
Through Minnigaff, 4 miles N of Newton Stewart
RSPB Nature Reserve in deciduous woodland, with marked walks and impressive waterfalls. This is one of the finest areas of native birch and oak woodland in Scotland.

GLEN TROOL
Off A714 at Bargrennan, entrance at Stroan Bridge
Open: Daily, all year
Waymarked forest trails through spruce and larch trees.

Watersports

SUB AQUA
Kip Marina, Inverkip
Tel: (0475) 521281
From ££

Windsurfing equipment for hire. Instruction given.

KINGS CROSS, WHITING BAY
Isle of Arran
Tel: (077 07) 442
From £ per hour
Dinghy sailing for kids over 9. Tuition available. Hourly and half-day rates.

KILBIRNIE LOCH
Kilbirnie, Ayr
Tel: (0475) 673765
P: Available
From £
Picnic areas
Water-skiing and canoeing.

BRODICK BOAT HIRE
The Beach, Brodick, Isle of Arran
Tel: (0770) 2388
From £
Fishing dinghies with engines, rowing boats, canoes, windsurfers and wet suits, pedaloes and fishing rods for hire.

LEISURE MARINE HIRE
Machrie, Isle of Arran
Tel: (077 084) 231
£
Fishing boats, rowing boats and canoes for hire.

GALLOWAY SAILING CENTRE
Shirmers Bridge, Loch Ken nr Parton DG7 3NQ
10 miles N of Castle Douglas on A713
Tel: (06442) 626
Meals available
From ££ per half day
Dinghy sailing and windsurfing tuition. Ideal for families and beginners. Canoes, rowing boats, sailing dinghies and surf boards for hire.

Waterfalls

GREY MARE'S TAIL (NTS)
nr Moffat
Off A708, 10 miles NE of Moffat
Tel: (041) 552 8391
No disabled access
A spectacular 200ft waterfall formed by the Tail Burn dropping from Loch Skene. The area is rich in wild flowers and there is a herd of wild goats. NB: It is extremely dangerous to leave the paths – this is not a walk for very young children. There are regular guided walks in the summer.

Winter Sports

KILMARNOCK DRY SKI SLOPE
Newmilns nr Kilmarnock
Tel: (0560) 22320
££
Ski hire.

PLACES TO EAT

Hotels and Restaurants

ARDSTINCHAR INN
70 Main Street, Ballantrae
Tel: (046 583) 254
High teas from 1730.

AUCHEN CASTLE HOTEL AND RESTAURANT
Beattock, Moffat DG10 9SH
On A74, 1 mile N of village
Tel: (06833) 407
Children welcome. A little French spoken. Bar lunches 1200–1400 are recommended in the Taste of Scotland guide.

BEECHWOOD COUNTRY HOUSE HOTEL
Moffat DG10 9RS
On road between church and school at N end of High Street
Tel: (0683) 20210
Open: Daily 1200–1400
Disabled access
Snacks are available Mon–Sat from £2. Children's portions available. Recommended in the Good Food Guide.

THE BOW WINDOW
38 Main Street, Ballantrae
Tel: (046 583) 308
High teas.

BRAMBLES BISTRO
Auchrannie Country House Hotel, Brodick, Isle of Arran
Meals from 1200–2130.

CLONYARD HOUSE HOTEL
Colvend, Dalbeattie DG5 4QW
4.5 miles S of Dalbeattie on A710
Tel: (055 663) 372
Disabled facilities
Six acres of woodland for children to explore. French and some German spoken. Bar lunches served 1200–1400. Recommended in the Taste of Scotland guide.

CROWN HOTEL
95 High Street, Portpatrick
Tel: (077681) 261
Bar lunches and suppers.

KINGS ARMS HOTEL
36 Main Street, Ballantrae
Tel: (046 583) 308
Pub lunches – children welcome.

LITTLEJOHNS
231 High Street, Ayr
Tel: (0292) 288666
Lots of fun for all the family, and good food as well! The walls and ceiling are decorated with 1960s' memorabilia guaranteed to keep youngsters amused while they wait to be served.

THE STABLES RESTAURANT AND COFFEE SHOP
Queen's Court, Sandgate, Ayr KA7 1BD
Behind Tourist Information Centre
Tel: (0292) 283704
Open: Mon–Fri 1000–1700, Sat 1000–2200 and Sun 1300–1700
Part of a small Georgian courtyard dating from the 1760s. Children are welcome. Recommended in the Taste of Scotland guide.

WHEELBARROWS RESTAURANT
39 Charlotte Square, Ayr KA7 1EA
Tel: (0292) 263814
Lunches, suppers, traditional Scottish high teas. Children's menu.

Quick Meals and Snacks

ABBEY COTTAGE COFFEES AND CRAFTS
26 Main Street, New Abbey, nr Dumfries
Tel: (038785) 377
Open: Easter – Oct, daily 1000 – 1700
Light lunches, home-baking, Egon Ronay recommended.

THE HUNNY POT
37 Beresford Terrace, Ayr KA7 2EU
Tel: (0292) 263239
Open: Mon – Sat 1000 – 2200,
Sun 1400 – 1730
A small coffee shop and health food restaurant. Plenty to interest children as the decor is based on teddy bears. Recommended in the Taste of Scotland guide.

BLACKWATERFOOT GOLF TEA-ROOM
Isle of Arran
Play a round on the putting green (child-size 'putters' available) and then boost your energy with tea and delicious baking.

LOCHRANZA GOLF COURSE TEA-ROOM
Isle of Arran
Delicious (but expensive) home-made bread and jam.

MAUCHRIE VILLAGE HALL
Isle of Arran
The café provides good simple food like toasties, hamburgers, baked potatoes, filled rolls, home-made soup, apple pie and fresh baking. A favourite lunch or snack stop with families as there is a play area outside.

STATION BAR
Annan
Tables and seats are arranged like old railway carriages. Inexpensive, children's menu.

Pubs

JOLLY SHEPHERD
1 Glenginnet Road, Barr
Tel: (046 586) 233
Children welcome for bar lunches (half portions available).

PARAFFIN LAMP
Lugton, Ayrshire
Tel: (050 585) 288
Food served from 1130 – 2200. Children's menu.

RIVERSIDE INN
Canonbie, DG14 0UX
Tel: (038 73) 71512
Children welcome for bar lunches. Children's menu and half portions available.

Fish and Chips

MARINE FISH BAR
Girvan
Great fish and chips.

Ice-Creams

DRUMMUIR FARM ICE-CREAM
Clarencefield Road, Collin, nr Dumfries
Tel: (038775) 599
Open: Apr – Oct, Tue – Sun 1100 – 1800;
Nov – Mar, Fri afternoons and weekends
1000 – 1700
A variety of flavours of luxury dairy ice-cream with no artificial ingredients.

NARDINI'S

The Esplanade, Largs KA30 8NF
Tel: (0475) 674555
Superlatives abound for Nardini's ice-cream.

ROYAL CAFÉ

11 New Road, Ayr KA8 9JQ
Tel: (0292) 263058
Open: 0930–2230
Ayr's oldest Italian café serves meals all day as well as award-winning ice-cream.

Bakeries

TAYLOR THE BAKER

Waterside Bakery
10 and 11 Waterside Street
Strathaven
Tel: (0357) 21260
The emphasis is on Austrian baking. Take home some mouthwatering delicacies from the bakery or have coffee and cake at the continental café just across the street. Children might like the gingerbread men baked according to a German recipe.

Fast Food Chains

BURGER KING

158–160 High Street, Ayr
Tel: (0292) 610348

LITTLE CHEF

Gretna Green
On A74, 8 miles N of Carlisle (N bound)
Tel: (0461) 37567
and
Johnstone Bridge (N and S bound carriageways)
On A74, 6 miles N of Lockerbie
Tel: (05764) 432
Disabled facilities (N bound)
and
North Shore, Ardrossan
On A78
Tel: (0294) 63841
Open: Daily 0700–2200
and
Collin, nr Dumfries
On A75 1 mile E of Dumfries
Tel: (038 775) 379
Children's menu, high-chairs and free baby food.

OLIVER'S COFFEE SHOP AND BAKERY

135–139 High Street, Dumfries
Tel: (0387) 61381
and
174 High Street, Ayr KA7 1PZ
Tel: (0292) 285605

THE PANCAKE PLACE

20 English Street, Dumfries

PLACES TO STAY

Hostels

SYHA – AYR
Craigweil Road, Ayr KA7 2XJ
Tel: (0292) 262322
Book in advance to be sure of a family room.

SYHA – LOCHRANZA
Isle of Arran KA27 8HL
Tel: (077083) 631
Book in advance to be sure of a family room.

SYHA – WHITING BAY
Brodick, Isle of Arran KA27 8QW
Tel: (07707) 339
Family rooms are available. There is also a chalet bungalow for family use with a sitting/dining-room, kitchenette, toilet and shower and 2 bedrooms with bunks for 6.

Caravan and Camping Sites

CALDONS CAMPING AND CARAVAN SITE
Glentrool
Turn R at Bargrennan on the A714
Tel: (0671) 2420
Open: End May – Aug
£
A top-grade Forestry Commission site with a play area, table-tennis and pool room. There is a stream running through the site. Bring your bikes and follow the waymarked cycle routes which start from here.

GLEN ROSA FARM
nr Brodick, Isle of Arran
Tel: (0770) 2380
£

A very basic campsite with cold water and toilets (no caravans). It is possible to leave your car on the mainland, cross to Arran on the ferry and then walk 1.5 miles to the campsite, which nestles in the shelter of the hills – a great adventure for hardy children.

HORSESHOE HOLIDAYS
Fairgirth Smiddy, Ruthwell DG1 4NN
Tel: (0387) 87648
Hire fully equipped 2 and 5-berth gipsy caravans with 24-hour backup. Overnight camping at well-appointed sites.

TALNOLTRY CARAVAN AND CAMPING SITE
On A712 7 miles E of Newton Stewart
Tel: (0671) 2420
Attractive forest walks start from this Forestry Commission site.

Hotels

AUCHRANNIE COUNTRY HOUSE HOTEL
Brodick, Isle of Arran KA27 8BZ
Tel: (0770) 2234
£££
A top-quality hotel with a leisure centre and 20m indoor swimming pool (open to non-residents too). Choose from family suites with a baby listening service or the lodges which sleep 6. Recommended in the Taste of Scotland guide – try BRAMBLES BISTRO for a light meal – *see* **PLACES TO EAT**.

CALLY PALACE
Gatehouse of Fleet
Tel: (0557) 814341
£££
A hundred acres of gardens with putting, croquet and tennis. The indoor leisure centre has a swimming pool.

KINLOCH HOTEL
Blackwaterfoot, Shiskine, Isle of Arran
Tel: (077086) 444
£££
Plenty of activities to choose from as the hotel has a swimming pool and leisure centre with snooker, watersports, fishing, pony-trekking, cycling, climbing and tennis.

PORTPATRICK HOTEL
Portpatrick, Wigtown
Tel: (077681) 333
Open: Mar – Nov
£££

Play area and children's pool in the gardens. Indoor playroom.

SEAMILL HYDRO
Tel: (0294) 822217
West Kilbride, Ayrshire
£££
Family rooms with reductions for children and babysitting service if required. Toys are provided for younger children and older children are in their element as there are tennis courts and a swimming pool at the hotel, and the beach is on the doorstep.

TRAVELODGE
Gretna Green
See LITTLE CHEF – **PLACES TO EAT**
£
Cheap and cheerful family accommodation for people on their way to somewhere more interesting.

THE BORDERS

Although the people of the Borders still have a fierce national pride, the days of Border skirmishes and set battles between the Scots and English are long gone. Nowadays, you'll find this a tranquil and attractive area where families can have a low-key, relaxing holiday away from the hustle and bustle of the big cities. There is plenty of scope for outdoor activities ranging from pony-trekking, cycling on waymarked trails, and gentle walking, to sailing on St Mary's Loch.

Many of Scotland's greatest rugby players hail from this area and there may even be a chance to see the Grand Slam heroes on their native turf.

Dull days can be brightened by a visit to a number of interesting museums where you can see teddy bears, old schools and jails, or even try typesetting or some ornamental plastering. The modern leisure pools are small and generally uncrowded so they are great for younger children. And all the attractions of the Edinburgh area are only an hour or two away by car.

Avoid Eyemouth beach if you are heading for the coast as it is badly polluted, but other beaches in the area and north-east of Edinburgh are much cleaner and more attractive.

Trains from Carlisle to Glasgow stop at Carstairs to the west, while the nearest station on the east coast line is at Berwick-upon-Tweed. There is a good network of quiet roads linking the small country towns. There are no shoppers' creches but the traditional shops are quite interesting in themselves, especially if you usually only go to supermarkets.

PLACES TO VISIT

Adventure Playgrounds

PAXTON HOUSE
Berwick-upon-Tweed TD15 1SZ
3 miles off Berwick-on-Tweed bypass on
B6461
Tel: (0289) 86291
Open: Grounds open all day; House
1000 – 1700
£
Tea-room
Toilets
A new adventure playground right on the Scottish/English border with a variety of equipment. Best for 8 to 14-year-olds but younger children enjoy some of the features. The house is too staid for a visit with children.

BOWHILL – *see* COUNTRY PARKS

Ancient Monuments

JEDBURGH ABBEY (HS)
Jedburgh
Tel: (0835) 63925
Open: Apr – Sep, Mon – Sat 0930 – 1900;
reduced hours on Sunday and in winter
£
There are four famous abbeys in the Borders but Jedburgh is particularly suitable for children because of its good interpretation centre. There are displays on life in a medieval monastery plus a collection of important finds which were uncovered during excavations.

Animals and Birds

BORDERS WOOL CENTRE
North Wheatlands Mill, Wheatlands
Road, Galashiels
Off A72 NW of Galashiels town centre
Tel: (0896) 4293/4774
Open: Apr – Oct, Mon – Fri 0900 – 1700
(Sat 1600); Nov – Mar, Mon – Fri 1000 –
1600
Free
P: Available
Coffee shop
Hand spinning, wool sorting, and weaving demonstrations are brought to life by seeing real sheep in the enclosure. Try to spot the different breeds – e.g. Jacob and Soay – and find out how well you have done by checking the display panels of British sheep breeds.

JEDFOREST DEER AND FARM PARK
Mervinslaw Estate, Camptown, Jedburgh
Off A68, 3 miles S of Jedburgh
Tel: (0835) 4364
Open: End May – Oct, daily 1000 – 1730
££
P: Available
Coffee shop, picnic area
A working farm where you can see red deer and farm animals including rare breeds of sheep, pigs, cattle, chickens and ducks. Children can stroke and feed tame animals. There are marked farm paths, a nature trail and an adventure playground.

ST ABB'S HEAD (NTS)
Coldingham nr Eyemouth
Off A1107
Tel: (08907) 71443

Open: All year, sunrise – sunset
Free
P: Small charge for parking
Tea-room

A spectacular headland with 300ft-high cliffs, home to colonies of guillemots, kittiwakes, razorbills, shags, puffins, fulmars and herring gulls. Lighthouse, loch, remains of a medieval monastery and a visitor centre.

TWEEDHOPE SHEEP DOGS
Tweedhopefoot, Tweedsmuir ML12 6QS
On A701, 6 miles from Tweedsmuir
Tel: (08997) 267
Open: Mon – Fri, demonstrations at 1100, 1400, 1500, closed Sat
£
P: Available
Light refreshments

Sheepdog demonstrations with award-winning Border Collies. Small children can ride on a tame Cheviot ram and play with the collie puppies. There are dry-stane dyking demonstrations and a craft shop. A photographic exhibition of shepherds and their dogs is displayed in what used to be the smallest school in Scotland.

Beaches

So many of our beaches are polluted with raw sewage these days, it is wise to take heed of the most recent Good Beach Guide which gives details of those beaches which have achieved minimum EC standards. According to the 1992 guide, EYEMOUTH should be avoided, though COLDINGHAM BAY and PEASE SANDS are fine.

PEASE SANDS
Cockburnspath

Follow a steep road from A1107 just S of jnct with A1
P: Available
Toilets at carpark

Almost a mile of sand backed by red cliffs. Safe bathing. There is a small shop close by as well as a large caravan and campsite. If you tire of building sand-castles there are good walks nearby.

Bike Hire and Cycle Routes

COLDSTREAM CYCLES
The Lees Stables, Coldstream TD12 4NN
Off A697 near The Hirsel
Tel: (0890) 3456/3349
Duet Wheelchair Tandem bikes available

A wide range of bikes are available including children's bikes, tricycles, child seats, trailers and trailer bikes. Panniers, maps, helmets and drinking bottles are also available. Locks and puncture kits are provided. French, German and Spanish-speaking guides can be arranged.

GLENTRESS MOUNTAIN BIKE CENTRE
Enquiries to Drummore, Venlaw High Road, Peebles EH45 8RL
Forestry Commission carpark 2 miles from Peebles on A72
Tel: (0721) 20336
Open: Easter – Oct, closed Wednesday
P: Available
Picnic area at carpark

Morning and afternoon rides on adult and child-size mountain bikes along waymarked routes. Maps are provided.

BOWHILL – see COUNTRY PARKS

Castles and Stately Homes

THIRLESTANE CASTLE
Lauder
Signposted off A68 and A697
Tel: (05782) 430
Open: Afternoons only; May/Jun/Sep,
Wed/Thu/Sun; July/Aug, Sun—Fri
££
Picnic area, tea-room
One of Scotland's oldest castles, with exhibitions of country life. The children's nursery has several thou-sand early toys. There is a woodland walk in the grounds.

TRAQUHAIR
Innerleithen EH44 6PW
A703 to Peebles then follow signs
Tel: (0896) 830323
Open: End May—Sep, Easter, weekends in May
££
Tea-room
Disabled access (except to upper floors)
Toilets

The Traquair Fair takes place on the first weekend in August, with lots of family entertainment including children's theatre, face-painting and swingboats. Even at other times, there is still plenty to do. The house has a spooky cellar and a secret staircase, as well as a children's questionnaire to make your visit interesting. Look out for the sound sculpture area and its unusual musical instruments and maze and the small play area in the extensive grounds. There are also walks through the woodland and by the river. If the weather is poor you can look round the craft workshops and a working brewery.

Country Parks

BOWHILL
nr Selkirk TD7 5ET
3 miles W of Selkirk on A708
Tel: (0750) 20732
Open: End Apr – Aug, Sat – Thu 1200 – 1700 (Sun 1400 – 1800)
£ for grounds
Picnic area, tea-room at weekend only (daily in July)

Children aged four and upwards will enjoy the outstanding adventure playground with aerial ropeways, giant slides and a wild west fort all set in beautiful woodlands. The visitor centre has displays and information on local wildlife. Wander along the many miles of paths and nature trails either on your own or on a ranger-led walk (phone 0750 22326 for details of walks and educational visits). Don't forget to visit the Victorian kitchen filled with strange cooking utensils, or the fire-fighting

display complete with a 19th-century horse-drawn fire engine.

BOWHILL RIDING CENTRE – *see*
RIDING
Open Easter – Oct.
Tel: (0750) 20192/21432
Mountain bicycle hire during summer. Tel: (0750) 22515

THE HIRSEL
Coldstream TD12 4LP
Tel: (0890) 2834
Open: Ground all year
P: Available
£1 per car
Refreshments available, picnic areas
Disabled access and facilities

The Homestead Museum contains displays of stuffed birds and animals, old tools, a dovecot and finds from an archaeological site dating back 1000 years. A room can be used for educational visits. There are nature walks around the lake and grounds which, in spring, are filled with snowdrops, daffodils and rhododendrons. Watch leatherworkers, potters, weavers, woodworkers and jewellers plying their trades in the craft centre or come to a craft fair.

Farms

CRUMSTANE FARM PARK
Crumstane Farm, Duns
On A6105 near Duns
Tel: (0361) 83268
Open: May – Sep, 1000 – 1800; closed Tue
£
P: Available
Picnic area

See unusual breeds of cattle, sheep, goats, pigs, horses, ducks and geese on a working farm which uses traditional methods. Children can stroke small animals such as rabbits, and lambs or calves in spring.

LEGERWOOD FARM TRAIL

Legerwood, Earlston nr Lauder
2 miles N of Earlston off A68, 3 miles E of Lauder off A697
Open: Jun – Sep, 1000 – 1900
P: Available

The waymarked trail is about 2.5 miles long and starts at the carpark. Remember there will be farm animals about so leave your dog at home. And wear wellie boots as the ground may be muddy – or worse!

Fish

ABBEY ST BATHANS TROUT FARM

Duns
Open: Afternoons in summer, weekend afternoons at other times
£
Picnic area, tea-room

The water in the trout ponds looks like it is boiling when the fish start jostling for food pellets. There are very pleasant short walks from the farm (*see* WALKS). A potter can sometimes be seen at work in the tea-room/craft centre.

Gardens

MERTOUN GARDENS

St Boswells nr Galashiels
Tel: (0835) 23236
Open: Apr – Sep, Sat, Sun and Mon public holidays 1400 – 1800
£
P: Available
Partial disabled access

Delightful walks round the walled garden and 20 acres of beautiful grounds filled with fine trees, herbaceous borders and flowering shrubs.

PRIORWOOD EVERLASTING FLOWER GARDEN

Melrose
Tel: (089 682) 2965
Open: Mar – Dec, Mon – Sat 1000 – 1730 (Sun 1330 – 1730 May – Oct)
Free
Picnic area

See about 100 varieties of 'everlasting' flowers being grown and dried. Leaflets explain how to 'do-it-yourself' if you are inspired by the displays. Near the walled flower garden there is a wild garden with more flowers and trees. If you like apples, take a stroll along the Apple Walk which demonstrates the development of apples from Roman times to today.

HARESTANES VISITOR CENTRE

Monteviot nr Jedburgh
3 miles N of Jedburgh at jct A68 and B6400
Tel: (08353) 306
Open: Easter – Oct 1030 – 1730
Free
P: Available
Tea-room
Disabled facilities including a woodland trail

Do you know how to play Nine Men's Morris or Pharoah's Pyramids? Can you complete the Joiner's Cross or the Pyramid Puzzle? Try these and other giant board games in the visitor centre set in an old farm in a large country estate. The exhibits relate mainly to the use of woodlands and timber with carvings and woodwork, profiles of famous plant explorers and a slide show. Have a picnic in the woods, play in the adventure playground or go on a ranger-led walk through the woodland.

KAILZIE GARDENS
Kailzie, Peebles EH45 9HT
2.5 miles from town centre on B7062
Tel: (0721) 22807
Open: End Mar – Oct
£
Tea-room and restaurant
Disabled facilities
Walled gardens with a large greenhouse, 15 acres of wild garden with woodland and burnside walks, ornamental ducks on the pond and a small adventure play area.

DAWYCK BOTANIC GARDEN
nr Stobo EH45 9JU
On B712 8 miles SW of Peebles
Tel: (07216) 254
Open: Mid Mar – Oct, 1000 – 1800
P: Available
Limited disabled access
A lovely place to walk, especially in the spring when the woods are full of daffodils and flowering rhododendrons. The arboretum is a good place to teach children how to identify trees.

Graveyards and Gruesome Places

JEDBURGH CASTLE JAIL
Castlegate, Jedburgh
Tel: (0835) 63254
Open: Easter – Sep, Mon – Sat 1000 – 1700, Sun 1300 – 1700
£
Nineteenth-century prisons are brought to life with reconstructions of cells complete with realistic models in contemporary costumes. The jail is on the site of the original Castle of Jedburgh and is the only remaining example of a Howard Reform Prison.

Museums

MELROSE MOTOR MUSEUM
Annay Road, Melrose
200 yards from Melrose Abbey, towards Newstead
Tel: (089682) 2624
Open: Mid May – mid Oct, daily 1030 – 1730
£
P: Available
Disabled access
Car enthusiasts will enjoy a couple of hours looking at the collection of vintage and more modern vehicles. There are also old motorcycles and bicycles as well as toy cars.

TEDDY MELROSE
The High Street, Melrose
Tel: (089682) 2464
Open: Mon – Sat 1000 – 1700, also Sun 1400 – 1700 Apr – Oct
£; children free if accompanied by their teddy bear
Tea-room
Disabled access and facilities including braille panels
'The most complete teddy museum in the world today' covering character bears like Rupert, Paddington and Winnie the Pooh. Lots of bears to touch – cuddly, threadbare, large and small as well as old trikes and other toys that parents might remember. Children can have fresh fruit juices from Pooh glasses and teddy bear biscuits (with no E additives) in the tea-room. School visits welcome.

CLAPPERTON DAYLIGHT PHOTOGRAPHIC STUDIO

The Studio, 28 Scotts Place, Selkirk
Tel: (0750) 20523
Open: Apr – Oct, Sat – Sun only 1400 – 1630

The art of photography has changed a great deal over the past 120 years as you will see in one of the oldest original daylight photographic studios.

THE TRIMONTIUM TRUST

Ormiston Institute, The Square, Melrose
Tel: (089682) 2463
Open: Easter – Oct, Mon – Sat 1000 – 1230, 1400 – 1630, Sun 1400 – 1630
£

An opportunity to see daily life as it was at the time of the Roman Empire. There is an exhibition of a Roman frontier post which is currently being excavated with scale models of forts, aerial photographs, audio-visual room, children's corner, blacksmith's workshop with tools and weapons, and a pottery. The shop sells miniature soldiers.

HALLIWELL'S HOUSE MUSEUM

Halliwell's Close, Selkirk
Entrance to Close can be seen from Market Place
Tel: (0750) 20096
Open: Apr – Oct, Mon – Sat 1000 – 1700, Sun 1400 – 1600; Nov – Dec, Tue – Sun 1400 – 1600
Free
P: Available

The building was once used as a home and an ironmonger's shop. Some of the rooms have been furnished and decorated in the original style.

KELSO MUSEUM TURRET HOUSE

Abbey Court, Kelso
Tel: (0573) 23464
Open: Easter – Oct; Mon – Sat 1000 – 1200, 1300 – 1700, Sun 1400 – 1700
£

What were schools like in Victorian times? Find out at the Turret House where children (and adults) can experience a school lesson. Other displays include a reconstructed skinner's workshop and a 19th-century market-place.

EYEMOUTH MUSEUM

Auld Kirk, Market Place, Eyemouth
Tel: (0890) 50678
Open: Easter – Oct, Mon – Sat 1000 – 1200, 1330 – 1700; extended hours in Jun – Aug
£
Disabled access

In 1881, 189 fishermen were drowned in one day off the coast of Eyemouth. The museum is a memorial to those men. There is a fisherman's cottage kitchen, a lifesize boat's wheelhouse and a huge tapestry illustrating the tragedy, displays on farming, milling, sailmaking, boatbuilding and smuggling as well as a natural history section.

THE CORNICE MUSEUM OF ORNAMENTAL PLASTERWORK

31 High Street, Peebles
Down close next to eletricity showroom
Tel: (0721) 20212
Open: Apr – Sep – phone for opening hours
£
Disabled facilities

Re-creation of a plasterer's casting shop illustrating methods of creating ornamental plasterwork. Try plastering for yourself – wellies and aprons are provided.

ROBERT SMAIL'S PRINTING WORKS (NTS)
9 High Street, Innerleithen
Tel: (0896) 830206
Open: Apr – Oct, Mon – Sat 1000 – 1300, 1400 – 1700, Sun 1400 – 1700
£
This is a working printing museum with vintage machinery, including a 100-year-old press. Visitors can try manual typesetting.

Parks and Playgrounds

WILTON LODGE PARK
Wilton Park Road, Hawick
Off A7 near town centre
Tel: (0450) 75991
P: Available
Café, picnic area
Disabled access
Roxburgh District often wins awards in the Britain in Bloom competition and the park is full of beautiful and dazzling flowers. Walk by the river or around the walled gardens and greenhouses. There is even a scented garden for the blind. Summer activities include putting, tennis, trampolines, crazy golf and table-tennis while the children's play area and trim track are open all year. There is also a museum and art gallery.

SHEDDON PARK
Kelso
A pleasant park with play areas for young children and flat paths for cycling or tricycling. Older children can play tennis, putting, swingball or table-tennis.

EYEMOUTH SEAFRONT
Play on the bouncy castle or have a game of giant chess or draughts during the summer.

HAY LODGE PARK
Peebles
Putting, trim track, boating on the River Tweed, paddling pool, play area, gold course and museum

Riding

HAWICK CIRCULAR HORSE RIDING ROUTE
Hawick
Tel: (0835) 23301
A 27-mile long route of connected cross-country tracks. The route is extensively waymarked.

WESTERTOUN RIDING CENTRE
Westruther, by Gordon nr Lauder TD3 6NW
B6456 to Duns
Tel: (057 84) 270/202
From £
Lessons for those under 6 last for 30 mins. Older children can have lessons, half-day hacks or residential riding holidays.

BOWHILL RIDING AND TREKKING CENTRE
Selkirk TD7 5ET
Tel: (0750) 20192/21432
From ££
Tuition is in an outdoor, all-weather arena. Experienced riders can follow the trail rides which last for between 1 and 3 hours. Less experienced riders can hack through woodland tracks. Half-hour lead rein rides for small children and complete beginners. STRA approved.

WHISGILL RIDING CENTRE
Newcastleton TD9 0TQ
Tel: (03873) 75675
From £
STRA approved. Families and unaccompanied children over 10 welcome. Outdoor manege, picnic rides, forest treks.

HAZLEDEAN HOLIDAY AND RIDING CENTRE
Hassendeanburn, nr Hawick
Tel: (045 087) 373
£
Children's one-hour rideouts from the centre. Also lessons and jumping.

PEEBLES HYDRO STABLES
Innerleithen Road, Peebles EH45 8LX
Tel: (0721) 21325
From ££
Pony-trekking for beginners and novice riders, trail riding for the more experienced. Half-hour pony walks in the forest for children from 6 years. Each pony is led by someone on foot.

Scotland at Work – Past and Present

SELKIRK GLASS
Selkirk TD7 5EF
Tel: (0750) 30954
Open: Mon – Fri 0900 – 1630
Coffee shop
Toilets
Watch glass paperweights being made. A good visit for children aged 3 or more.

Sport and Leisure Centres

TEVIOTDALE LEISURE CENTRE
Mansefield Road, Hawick

Tel: (0450) 74440/75644
Open: Daily
Various charges
P: Available
Cafeteria
Leisure pool and warm baby pool with water sprays and palm trees. If it's too hot outside, cool off with some ice-skating in the summer. Phone for details of special pool events, children's summer shows, and the annual fireworks concert. Play area. Swim parties can be arranged with food and cartoons to round off the treat. Family changing-rooms.

JEDBURGH SPORTS CENTRE
Pleasance, Jedburgh
Tel: (0835) 62566
Open: During term time, Mon – Fri 1800 – 2000, Sat 0900 – 1200, Sun 1400 – 2000
Various charges
Table-tennis, all-weather tennis courts, dry ski slope, rock-climbing tower.

Swimming

GALASHIELS SWIMMING POOL
Livingstone Place, Galashiels
Tel: (0896) 2154
Open: Mon – Fri from 1200, Sat/Sun from 0900
£
Refreshments available
Disabled access
A modern pool with family changing-rooms. Mother and toddler sessions, canoeing, snorkelling and fun sessions. Swimming parties arranged.

SELKIRK SWIMMING POOL
Victoria Park, Selkirk
Tel: (0750) 20897

Open: Mon – Fri from 1200, Sat/Sun from 0930
£
Refreshments available
Special sessions for mothers and toddlers as well as fun sessions and lessons for older children. You can also learn canoeing and snorkelling.

KELSO SWIMMING POOL
Inch Road, Kelso
Tel: (0573) 24944
Open: Daily
£
Cafeteria
A 25m swimming pool with fun sessions and a giant inflatable spider. The soft play area has a bouncy jungle, slides, rocking horses and sit 'n' ride toys.

WATERSIDE FITNESS CENTRE
Oxnam Road, Jedburgh
Tel: (0835) 63430
Open: Daily
£
Cafeteria
The walls round the 25m swimming pool are decorated with bright tropical scenes. Look out for the huge inflatable spider which must live on one of the desert islands.

TEVIOTDALE CENTRE – *see* SPORT
AND LEISURE CENTRES

Walks

LINDEAN RESERVOIR
nr Selkirk
3 miles E of Selkirk on minor road linking A7 and A699
Tel: (0835) 23301
Open: All year
P: Available

Take a circular walk round the reservoir or go on a ranger-led walk through the wildlife reserve and look for interesting birds from the hide.

WAVERLEY WALK
Hawick
Picnic area
No disabled access
A 4.5 mile walk along the line of the old railway returning via a footpath on the north side of the River Teviot. Local children cleared the route of rubbish and overgrown vegetation to create the walk.

ABBEY ST BATHANS
nr Duns
Tel: (03614) 242/251
Open: Daily
Picnic area, tea-room (weekends and public hols Apr – Sep, daily Jun – Aug)
Walks through natural oak woodland along the riverside and up to open moorland and Edinshall Broch (*see* FISH).

GLENTRESS, CARDRONA, LINDINNY AND THORNYLEE FORESTS
nr Innerleithen
Tel: (0434) 250209
These forests are between Peebles and Galashiels off the A72
P: Available
Picnic areas at Cardrona and Thornylee
Details of the various waymarked walks are available in a leaflet from local tourist centres or the Forestry Commission (Peebles: 0721 20448; Hawick 0450 77001). Some of the routes are suitable for mountain bikes and pony-trekking, while at Glentress there is a wheelchair route round picturesque ponds.

PLACES TO EAT

Restaurants and Hotels

CRINGLETIE HOUSE
Eddleston, Peebles EH45 8PL
On A703, 2 miles N of Peebles
Tel: (072 13) 233
Open: Mar–Dec, daily
Lunches between 1300–1345 with both vegetarian dishes and children's helpings available. Afternoon teas. Recommended in the Good Food Guide.

EDNAM HOUSE HOTEL
Bridge Street, Kelso
Tel: (0573) 224168
Good for lunch on a hot day when children can play on the lawns.

FLOORS CASTLE
Kelso TD5 7RW
Tel: (0573) 23333
On the A699 W of Kelso
Open: May–Sep (not Fri or Sat), daily in Jul/Aug.
A reasonably priced restaurant with tables set in the courtyard in good weather. Recommended in the Taste of Scotland guide.

KINGSMUIR HOTEL
Springhill Road, Peebles EH45 9EP
Tel: (0721) 20151
On S side of Peebles
A country house in wooded grounds. Children welcome and may be served smaller portions. Featured in the Taste of Scotland guide.

KIRKLANDS HOTEL
West Stewart Place, Hawick TD9 8BH
Tel: (0450) 72263
200 yds off A7, half a mile N of High Street
The children's play area is set in a very large garden. Featured in the Taste of Scotland guide.

MARMION'S
Buccleuch Street, Melrose
Beside Melrose Abbey
Tel: (089682) 2245
Very French atmosphere and food to match. A place for a special treat.

MELROSE STATION RESTAURANT
Melrose
Tel: (089682) 2546
Open: All year, daily 1000–1800 (1700 Nov–Mar)
Partial disabled access
The station has been described as 'the handsomest provincial station in Scotland'. Look around the heritage centre and craft workshops.

THE ROB ROY
Dock Road, Berwick-upon-Tweed
Tel: (0289) 306428
Really fresh fish for lunch.

THE SMOKERY
Teviot Smokery, Crailing, nr Kelso
Very good lunches at moderate prices. Lovely water garden between the conservatory and the River Tweed.

SUNLAWS HOUSE
Sunlaws by Kelso TD5 8JZ
Tel: (05735) 331
Children's menu.

WHEATSHEAF HOTEL
Main Street, Swinton TD11 3JJ
Tel: (089 086) 257

Open: Tue – Sun 1145 – 1400, 1800 – late
Disabled access and facilities
A smart pub/restaurant serving home-made rolls and other good food. Children's portions. Garden to relax in. Very popular, so it is advisable to book.

Quick Meals and Snacks

KAILZIE GARDENS
Kailzie, nr Peebles EH45 9HT
Tel: (0721) 22807
Open: 1215 – 1400, 1500 – 1700
Border tarts, meringues and the best pastry for miles.

TEDDY'S COFFEE SHOP
Part of 'Little Ones', 8 High Street, Galashiels
Tel: (0896) 3308
Nice, comforting children's food like banana or chocolate spread sandwiches.

Pubs

HERGIE'S WINE BAR
Iron Street, Galashiels

Tel: (0896) 50400
A bistro where children are made very welcome through the day.

TRAQUAIR ARMS
Innerleithen EH44 6PD
Tel: (0896) 830229
Very 'child-friendly'.

Fish and Chips

FISH AND CHIP CAFÉ
Castlegate, Berwick
Good food and quick service.

Bakeries

HOSSACK'S BAKERY
42 Market Place, Selkirk
Tel: (0750) 20977
Delicious Selkirk bannocks – a local speciality.

SHIRRA BAKERY
14 Market Place, Selkirk
Tel: (0750) 20690
Good bread and baking, especially the gourmet shortbread.

PLACES TO STAY

Hostels

SYHA – KIRK YETHOLM
Kelso TD5 8PG
Tel: (057382) 631
Family rooms are available. Bikes may be hired locally.

SYHA – MELROSE
Priorwood, Melrose TD6 9EF
Tel: (089682) 2521
Book in advance to be sure of family rooms. Tennis courts, golf, putting, craft centre and motor museum are all close by. The swimming baths at Galashiels are only 3 miles away.

Caravan and Camping Sites

RHODES CARAVAN SITE
Lime Grove, North Berwick EH39 5NJ
Tel: (0620) 2197
Open: mid Mar – Sep
£
Grassy site with access to the beach. Good play area.

Hotels

PEEBLES HOTEL HYDRO
Innerleithen Road, Peebles EH45 8LX
Tel: (0721) 20602
£££
Indoor swimming pool, playroom and games room. There are 30 acres of ground with a challenging adventure playground plus a less demanding play area for toddlers, tennis, pitch and putt, and riding. Listed in the Taste of Scotland guide.

EDINBURGH AREA

Local pressure groups and the District Council have done a great job in raising the status of families with young children and Edinburgh is well on the way to becoming Britain's most child-friendly city. The District Council's publication, *Child Friendly Edinburgh*, and the National Childbirth Trust's *Edinburgh for Under-5s*, contain a mass of useful information about the city and its facilities. Look out, too, for 'We Welcome Small Children' stickers in shops, restaurants and so on. And, unlike any of the other tourist boards in Scotland, Edinburgh has compiled details of hotels and guest houses which have facilities and a warm welcome for families with children.

In spite of all this activity, there is a distinct lack of shoppers' creches in the city centre. Some appear at Christmas, but for year-round shopping there is nothing available. However, there are baby-changing facilities at the public toilets in Waverley Market, the Mound, West Princes Street Gardens, Canonmills, Tollcross, Taylor Gardens, Bath Street in Portobello and the High Street in South Queensferry. Littlewoods (90–91 Princes Street) also has changing space while Mothercare (84 Princes Street), Boots (101 Princes Street), Debenham's (109–112 Princes Street), John Lewis (St James Centre), John Menzies (107 Princes Street), 'The Terrace' at Cameron Toll Shopping Centre, and Ingliston Market all have mother and baby rooms.

All in all, Edinburgh is a good place for families. It has all the usual big city attractions like excellent museums (watch the press for details of special exhibitions like 'Dinosaurs Alive') and leisure centres, as well as a number of exciting festivals which take place in the spring and late summer. If you are hungry there is plenty of choice as Edinburgh has more restaurants per head of the population than any other part of Britain.

Although the city centre is always busy, the peace of the countryside is only a few minutes away by car. Going east along the coast will take you to some beautiful beaches (but avoid Portobello as it does not reach EC standards for water quality), and the Pentland hills are immediately south of the city. There are also a number of very attractive country parks which are delightful oases in the midst of old mining areas.

Edinburgh is well served by roads and rail links. Whichever way you choose to travel, there is easy access to Glasgow in the west, and Fife is just to the north, across the River Forth. If you are coming to Edinburgh for the day, it is often more fun – and more convenient – to travel by train as the station is in the city centre and you can avoid the traffic.

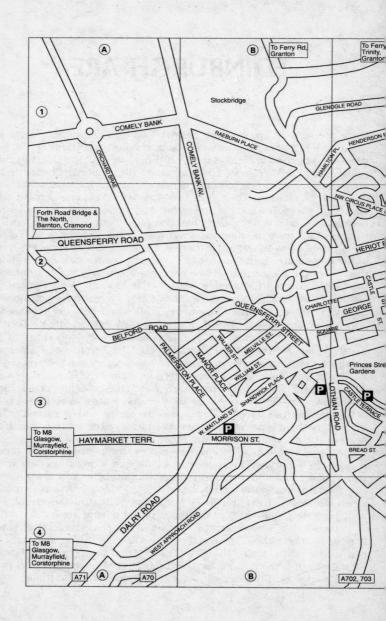

MAP A: Edinburgh City Centre

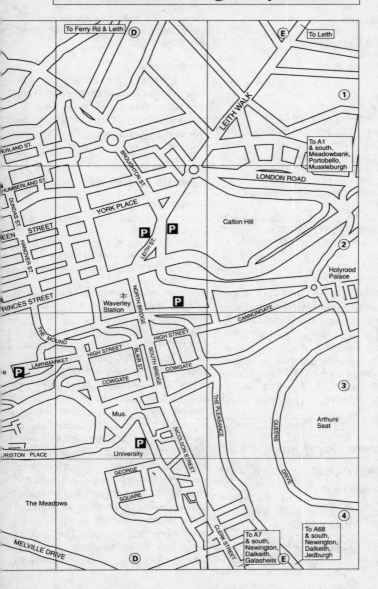

PLACES TO VISIT

Aeroplanes

EDINBURGH AIRPORT
Off the A8
Tel: (031) 333 1000
Free
P: Charge
Cafeteria
Toilets and baby-changing area
You can see planes landing and taking off from the viewing gallery or the cafeteria. A noisy outing.

MUSEUM OF FLIGHT
East Fortune Airfield, North Berwick
EH39 5LF
Off B1347, 1.5 miles S of North Berwick
Tel: (062088) 308/031 225 7534
Open: Easter–end Sep, 1030–1630
Free
P: Free
Tea-room and picnic area
A wide variety of aircraft are on display at the airfield which was used by the RAF during World War II. There is a supersonic Lightning Fighter, a Comet 4, a Spitfire, and a 1930 Puss Moth. Exhibitions show the development of fighter aircraft from 1914 to 1940. The R34 airship flew from East Fortune to New York in 1919.

Adventure Playgrounds

DALKEITH COUNTRY PARK—
see COUNTRY PARKS

Ancient Monuments

CAIRNPAPPLE HILL (HS)
nr Bathgate
On B792, 1.5 miles E of Torphichen
Open: Apr–Sep, Mon–Sat 0930–1900,
Sun 1400–1900
£
No disabled access
It is always a bit creepy to see how people buried their dead. This neolithic cairn dating from 1800 BC has a grave burial from the Copper Age and a cist burial from the Bronze Age on display.

Animals and Birds

EDINBURGH ZOO
Corstorphine Road, Edinburgh EH12 6TS
Tel: (031) 334 9171
Open: Daily, Mon–Sat 1900–1800 (or
dusk), Sun 0930–1800 (or dusk)
£££; free for Blue Peter badge wearers
P: Charge
Full catering and ice-cream kiosks
Limited disabled facilities
Toilets
One of the biggest attractions at the zoo is the new penguin house which has a glass-sided pool so you can see the penguins swimming underwater. A suspension bridge gives an aerial view and there is even a creche pool for the chicks. Apart from the penguins there are over a thousand rare and beautiful mammals, birds and reptiles to see, ranging from polar bears to South American tree frogs. Special attractions include the animal-handling sessions during holidays and at weekends, and a reconstructed steading with small domestic animals. The zoo is on a steep hillside so it is worth taking or hiring a pushchair for

toddlers whose legs may soon tire. There is a playground near the chimps' compound but it is not clear whose antics inspire whom! With all this, it is not surprising that the zoo is amongst the 10 most popular tourist attractions.

DUDDINGSTON LOCH
Arthur's Seat, Edinburgh
Tel: (031) 557 5262
Free

The loch is only a few minutes from the city centre. There are plenty of ducks, geese and swans as well as rare birds. The Scottish Wildlife Trust runs special events and guided walks in the summer for those keen to find out more. For permission to use the hide, phone (031) 220 3713. Try combining a visit to the loch with an energetic walk up ARTHUR'S SEAT – *see* WALKS.

LOTHIAN AND BORDERS POLICE STABLES AND DOG-HANDLERS
Police Headquarters, Fettes Avenue, Edinburgh
Tel: (031) 331 3131
Open: Nov – May by request

Clubs and groups can meet the horses and dogs. Interesting talks; activity sheets.

EDINBURGH BUTTERFLY AND INSECT FARM
Dobbies Gardening World, Lasswade EH18 1AZ
Between Gilmerton and Eskbank on A7
Tel: (031) 663 4932
Open: Mar – Oct, daily 1000 – 1730
££
P: Free
Tea-room
Toilets

Masses of tropical butterflies and moths are free to fly around a huge glasshouse filled with exotic plants, ponds and pools of bubbling mud. Caterpillars, chrysalises and emerging butterflies are kept in the breeding room. Don't take children into the insect rooms if they are afraid of spiders, but braver souls like looking at tarantulas, ants, stick insects and scorpions. A recent addition to the complex is a bee garden complete with an aviary containing a million bees. The butterfly house can become unbearably hot in mid-summer, so it is best to go on a cloudy day. Also has a children's playground, tropical fish shop and garden centre.

EDINBURGH BIRD OF PREY CENTRE
beside EDINBURGH BUTTERFLY AND INSECT FARM (see above)
Tel: (031) 654 1720
Open: Summer, Mon – Fri 1000 – 1700; Winter Sat – Sun 1100 – 1600
£

A collection of birds of prey including a barn owl and buzzard which you can handle.

BEECRAIGS – *see* COUNTRY PARKS

Arts and Crafts

NATIONAL GALLERY OF SCOTLAND
The Mound, Edinburgh
Tel: (031) 556 8921
Open: Mon – Sat 1000 – 1700, Sun 1400 – 1700 and longer during the Festival
Free
Disabled access
Toilet

Although the art gallery is rather too staid for a long visit, many children enjoy the freshness of the Impressionists on the second floor.

SCOTTISH NATIONAL GALLERY OF MODERN ART
Belford Road, Edinburgh
Tel: (031) 556 8921
Open: Mon – Sat 1000 – 1700, Sun 1400 – 1700
Free except for special exhibitions
P: Available
Café – see **PLACES TO EAT**
Toilet
There are large pieces of sculpture on the lawn and in most of the rooms. Be sure to have a good supply of paper and paint at home as a visit can be inspirational.

ROYAL MILE LIVING CRAFT CENTRE
12 High Street, The Royal Mile, Edinburgh
Tel: (031) 557 9350
Open: Mon – Sat 1000 – 1800, Sun 1000 – 1730
£
Coffee shop
Small children love to watch adults playing with clay and getting dirty. It's even better if they can join in and 'throw' a pot themselves. Take a look at the other crafts too – there

are demonstrations of hand and power weaving, knitting, kiltmaking, bagpipe-making and jewellery-making.

BRASS RUBBING CENTRE

Trinity Apse, Chalmers Close, Royal Mile
Tel: (031) 556 4364
Open: All year, Mon – Sat 1000 – 1700 (1800 Jun – Sep), Sun during Festival
£

No experience needed to make a rubbing. Choose from a brass commemorating Robert the Bruce and the Burghead Bull, ancient Pictish stones or rare Scottish brasses. There is a small charge for materials.

ST MARY'S CHURCH

Sidegate, Haddington EH41 4BZ
Tel: (062 082) 5111
Open: Easter – Jun, Sat 1300 – 1600; Jul – Sep, Thu – Sat, Mon 1300 – 1600
£ for materials

You don't need to be artistic to make a lovely brass rubbing from one of the replica brasses.

Beaches

It is a sad fact that some of the most attractive beaches in this area are spoiled by sewage and litter. Vote with your feet and avoid DUNBAR EAST, NORTH BERWICK BAY, FISHER-ROW, PORTOBELLO and SILVER-KNOWES as these failed to meet standards set by the EC according to the 1992 Good Beach Guide. DUNGLASS, THORTONLOCH, BEL-HAVEN BEACH, WHITESANDS BAY, PEFFERSANDS, SEACLIFF, MILSEY BAY, YELLOWCRAIG, GULLANE, GOSFORD SANDS, LONGNIDDRY, SETON SANDS and CRAMOND are listed as having met the grade.

THORTONLOCH

off A1 S of Dunbar
P: Available

A very clean, sandy beach with shallow dunes behind. A good bird-watching area. Swimming is not advisable as there is a fairly strong undertow. There are toilets and a small shop at the nearby caravan site.

GULLANE BAY

Gullane village
P: Available
Picnic area, refreshment stand and nearby village shops
Toilet block inland from the centre of the beach

A mile and a half of sand, which is cleared of litter each day in summer. 15ft-high sand dunes give lots of shelter from the wind so children can still play in the sand on days when parents would usually be huddled indoors. Another alternative to the main beach is to walk along the coast path to a series of tiny sandy bays to the east. The beach is safe for bathing and wind-surfing. There is also a riding track round the bay and a small play area off a path through the dunes.

JOHN MUIR COUNTRY PARK – *see* COUNTRY PARKS

Bike Hire and Cycle Routes

Cycling in Edinburgh is no fun if you have to stick to the streets, but there are many miles of quiet and attractive cycleways bordered by birches, rowans and brambles. Most of the routes have been developed from the network of disused railway lines. For further information on the cycle routes and their access points, tel: (031) 225 2424 or write to Spokes, 232 Dalry Road, Edinburgh EH11 2JG.

Boats and Boat Trips

THE EDINBURGH CANAL CENTRE

27 Baird Road, Ratho, Edinburgh EH28 8RA
Follow signs from Dalmahoy on A71 or Newbridge roundabout on A8
Tel: (031) 333 1320/1251/1629
From ££
Restaurant
Disabled facilities and access

Hire a boat or sit back and enjoy a trip on a 12-seater boat on the canal (don't forget the Santa cruises at Christmas). The canal boats may be hired for children's parties. The watery theme continues on land with a boat-shaped play area and walks along the towpaths. There is also a wildfowl reserve and a putting green. Meals can be eaten while cruising on a canal boat but the award-wining BRIDGE INN RES-TAURANT and POP INN BISTRO (*see* PLACES TO EAT) are probably a better bet with small children.

MAID OF THE FORTH

Watson Marine Ltd, Hawes Pier, South Queensferry
Tel: (031) 331 4857
Open: May – mid Sep
£££
Café on board, tea-room on the island

A boat trip across the Firth of Forth to Inchcolm island will appeal to all ages. Wrap up warmly for the crossing if you plan to sit on deck. The hour or so on shore gives you time to explore the small beach, the ruined abbey and the WWI fortifications which include a tunnel right through the hill-top. There are often grey seals basking on the rocks.

SPIRIT OF FIFE

1c West Harbour Road, Granton, Edin-burgh
Open: Daily
££
P: Free
Refreshments

The water-bus between Edinburgh and Fife takes 25 minutes to cross the River Forth. There are connecting buses to central Edinburgh. At lunch-times the ferry cruises under the bridges.

BASS ROCK TRIP

Mr Marr, North Berwick
Tel: (0620) 2838
Open: Summer
£££

Take a boat trip to the 350ft-high rock. Pirates once used it as a strong-hold. It has also been used as a prison and as a hermit's retreat in years gone by. There is a manned lighthouse though nowadays the main inhabitants are thousands of seabirds including the third largest gannetry in the world.

NORTH BERWICK LIFEBOAT

North Berwick
Free (donations)

The lifeboat was bought with funds raised by *Blue Peter* viewers.

VICTORIA AND JANET TELFORD CANAL BOATS

Canal Basin, Union Canal, Linlithgow
Tel: (0506) 842575
Open: Weekends from Easter – Sep, 1400 – 1700
£

Have a 30-minute trip on a diesel-powered replica of a Victorian steam-packet boat, or hire a rowing boat. There is also a small museum.

Bus Trips

EDINBURGH CLASSIC TOURS
Waverley Bridge, Edinburgh EH1 1BB
Tel: (031) 220 4111
Open: All year, Mon – Sat
££
Travelling on an open-top bus is a great way to see the sights. Tickets are valid all day so passengers can get off to visit various attractions on the route.

GUIDE FRIDAY
Waverley Bridge, Edinburgh EH1 1BB
Tel: (031) 556 2244
Open: Daily 0900 – 1800
£££
More open-top buses. Children never seem to object to sight-seeing when they are sitting on the front seat of the top deck.

Camera Obscura

OUTLOOK TOWER AND CAMERA OBSCURA
Castle Hill, Royal Mile, Edinburgh
Between the Castle and Lawnmarket
Tel: (031) 226 3709
Open: Daily, Apr – Oct 1000 – 1800, Nov – Mar 1000 – 1700
££
No disabled access
An amazing Victorian optical device like a giant revolving periscope which projects a live image of the city on to a viewing table. Children love to 'catch' pedestrians in their hands or make buses 'drive' up vertical slopes! As you climb up to the top floor you pass through displays of holography and pin-hole photography.

Castles

EDINBURGH CASTLE (HS)
Castle Rock, top of Royal Mile, Edinburgh
Tel: (031) 225 9846
Open: Apr – Sep, Mon – Sat 0930 – 1700, Sun 1100 – 1700; reduced hours Oct – Mar
££
P: Available
Partial disabled access
One of the most famous castles in the world. Be prepared to talk about volcanoes and eruptions once the children find out that it is built on an ancient volcanic plug. Distract any tendency to weepiness at the dog cemetery with a visit to the crown jewels and the cannon called Mons Meg.

CRAIGMILLAR CASTLE (AM)
Craigmillar Castle Road, Edinburgh
2.5 mile SE of city centre, signposted off A68
Tel: (031) 661 4445
Open: Summer, Mon – Sat 0930 – 1830, Sun 1400 – 1830
£
Mary Queen of Scots came here after her secretary, Rizzio, was murdered at Holyrood, and it was here that her nobles plotted the murder of her husband, Darnley. Nowadays the ruins have nothing worse to offer than dark staircases and echoing rooms.

PALACE OF HOLYROOD HOUSE
At the foot of the Royal Mile, Edinburgh
Tel: (031) 556 7371

*Open: Apr – Oct, Mon – Sat 0930 – 1715,
Sun 1030 – 1630; Nov – Mar,
Mon – Sat 0930 – 1545. May be closed in
May – Jul*
££
Toilets

The state rooms used by the royal family are open to the public, as are the apartments where Mary Queen of Scots lived. Interesting for over-9s. One of the top Scottish tourist attractions.

LAURISTON CASTLE

2 Cramond Road South, Cramond, Edinburgh
Tel: (031) 336 2060
Open: Castle from Apr – Oct; Grounds open all year 0900 – dusk
Castle – ££; grounds – free
Picnic area
Disabled facilities
Toilet

To see the secret room you need to go on a 40-minute tour. There are walks in the wooded grounds which are at their best in spring. Check for holiday activities.

HOPETOUN HOUSE

South Queensferry
12 miles W of Edinburgh
Tel: (031) 331 2451
Open: Easter, end Apr – Sep, daily 1000 – 1730
P: Available
House – ££; gardens – £
Restaurant, picnic areas
Disabled facilities

The extensive grounds include a ha-ha, a deer park with fallow and red deer, woodland walks, a walled garden, nature trails and a wildlife centre. Visitors to the mansion can get panoramic views over the Forth

Bridges from a viewing platform on the roof.

LUFFNESS

nr Aberlady
1 mile E of Aberlady on A198
Tel: (087 57) 218
Open: By arrangement
Free
P: Available
No disabled access

Lots of ruined fortifications, an old moat and gardens to run round.

TANTALLON CASTLE (HS)

nr North Berwick
On A198, 3 miles E of North Berwick
Tel: (031) 244 3101
Open: Mon – Sat 0930 – 1900, Sun 1400 – 1900; Oct – Mar 1600, closed Wed/Thur morning
£
P: Available
Partial disabled access

A large ruined stronghold built 500 years ago from red sandstone on the top of a cliff.

DIRLETON CASTLE (NTS)

nr North Berwick
7 miles W of North Berwick
Tel: (0620) 85330
£

The ruins of a 12th-century castle with lots of stone steps to climb and rooms to explore. The flower gardens are well worth a visit too.

BLACKNESS CASTLE (HS)

Blackness nr Linlithgow
Tel: (0506) 834807
Open: Apr – Sep, Mon/Thu – Sat 0930 – 1900, Tue 0930 – 1200, Sun 1400 – 1900
£

The fortress is built right on the edge of the Forth and, if you look from the east, it looks a bit like a battleship ready to set sail. It was used as a state prison in medieval times.

ROUGH CASTLE (HS)
nr Falkirk
Off B816, 6 miles W of Falkirk
Tel: (031) 244 3101 (HS, Edinburgh)
Open: All reasonable times
Free
No disabled access

The Romans must have thought Scotland a chilly place after Italy. This is the best preserved of the forts on the Antonine Wall and you can still see the ramparts and ditches easily.

Country Parks

BONALY COUNTRY PARK
Bonaly Road, Ediburgh
Tel: (031) 445 3383
Open: All year
P: Available
Picnic and barbecue area
Toilets

There are 3 walks into the Pentlands from here though the path to the left is too severe for small children. The middle path is a pleasant walk through fir trees to Bonaly Reservoir and it is possible to get along with pushchairs. The right-hand path goes up through heather on to the hill-tops.

HILLEND COUNTRY PARK
Hillend, Edinburgh
Off the ring-road
Tel: (031) 445 3383
P: Available
Picnic area
Toilets at the ski centre

Access to the hills is easy if you use the chairlift. There is a viewfinder to help identify the landmarks. *See also* **WINTER SPORTS**.

JOHN MUIR COUNTRY PARK
Dunbar
Tel: (0368) 63434
Open: All year
P: Free
Picnic and barbecue area
Toilets at carpark

With 8 miles of coastline including the sandy beach of Belhaven Bay, this is a wonderful spot for building sandcastles. There are inland and coastal walks where you can see lots of wildflowers, butterflies and, in the autumn, migrating birds. Those with horses can ride on the bridle paths and the beach. Don't forget to explore the ruins of Dunbar Castle and the old harbour. There is a small play area as well.

ROSSLYN GLEN COUNTRY PARK
by Roslin nr Penicuik
Off A701
P: Available
Picnic and barbecue area

There are woodland walks by a river with caves, weirs and waterfalls. Look out for the ruined mill, the bleachfield and Rosslyn Castle and Chapel. The undisturbed woodland is classified as a Site of Special Scientific Interest.

VOGRIE COUNTRY PARK
Vogrie Estate by Gorebridge EH23 4NU
Off B6372 nr Gorebridge
Tel: (0875) 21990
Open: All year
Picnic and barbecue areas

A very attractive park with a nature trail, woodland walks, a walled garden dating from last century, a small adventure playground and a 9-hole golf course. Special events for children aged 8 to 12 in Jul/Aug.

DALKEITH PARK
High Street, Dalkeith
Tel: (031) 663 5684
Open: Easter – end Oct daily 1100 – 1800
£
P: Free
Picnic areas, refreshment kiosk
Partial disabled access

The main attraction for children is the superb adventure play area with a fort, aerial walkways, huge slides, gorilla swings and commando nets. If they can be persuaded to leave, there are lovely woodland walks beside the river to a huge weir, an old amphitheatre, a huge orangery and a couple of very dark tunnels. The grounds are especially attractive in the late spring when the woods are filled with daffodils, bluebells and wild garlic.

ALMONDELL AND CALDERWOOD COUNTRY PARK
East Calder
On B7015 (A71) at East Calder, or off A899 at Broxburn
Tel: (0506) 882254
Open: Centre, Mon – Thu 0900 – 1700, Sun 1030 – 1800 (1630 Oct – Mar)
P: Available
Picnic and barbecue areas (book ahead)
Disabled parking and partial disabled access
Toilets

There is a great variety of wildlife in Calderwood which you may see while walking along the rough tracks through the woodland. It is especially attractive in spring when the bluebells are flowering. There is easier walking around Almondell where well-made paths run by the river and through woodland. Rangers are available to help with school visits (or other organised groups) and they also lead a series of walks during the summer. The visitor centre has large freshwater aquaria as well as displays of local and natural history.

BEECRAIGS COUNTRY PARK
nr Linlithgow
From Linlithgow take Preston Road S for 2 miles, signposted on left
Tel: (0506) 844516
Open: Centre Mon – Fri 0900 – 1700, reduced hours at weekends and in winter
Charges for some facilities
P: Free
Restaurant, picnic and barbecue areas
Limited disabled access

A beautiful country park with woodland walks and trails. Try walking to the top of Cockleroy if you are feeling energetic – on a clear day you can see as far as Arran. Look out for foxes and roe deer but if you aren't lucky you can still see red deer from a walkway and viewing platform. It's fun watching the water 'boil' as you feed the trout at the fish farm. Test your fitness on the trim trail or just have fun playing on the equipment, especially the 9m-high 'space net'. Sports enthusiasts can learn how to sail or fish, follow orienteering courses or take part in canoeing and archery courses for children during the summer. Bring your own horse and ride on the bridle paths. Look out for craft workers on Sundays in summer when they demonstrate pottery, woodcarving, weaving and other skills.

POLKEMMET COUNTRY PARK
nr Whitburn
From Whitburn take B7066 W for 2 miles, signposted on right-hand side

Tel: (0501) 43905
Open: All year
P: Available
Restaurant, picnic areas

The park was once a family estate with its own golf course, bowling green and tennis courts. Nowadays, the 9-hole golf course and putting green are open to the public as are some new attractions including a play area for children and toddlers, and woodland walks. School groups can learn about the environment with the rangers.

MUIRAVONSIDE COUNTRY PARK
nr Whitecross
On B825 W of Whitecross, 3 miles W of Linlithgow
Tel: (0506) 845311
Open: Grounds – all year; Centre – Apr – Sep, Mon – Fri 1000 – 1400,
Oct – Mar 1000 – 1600 weekend only
Barbecue and picnic areas
Toilets

Walk through the 170 acres of woodland and parkland or visit the centre. Look out for relics of local industry including a disused mine shaft, water adit, mill lade and lime kilns. The model farm has pigs, sheep, ponies and goats as well as chickens and ducks. There is a dovecot and a children's play area. The ranger service organises seasonal walks for groups and school parties.

Farms

GORGIE CITY FARM
51 Gorgie Road, Tynecastle Lane, Edinburgh EH11 2AL
Tel: (031) 337 4202

Open: All year, including public holidays
0900 – 1630
Free
P: Free
Picnic area

This 2.5-acre farm is tucked away in the middle of the city. There are a variety of animals to see as well as a farm kitchen, workshop and craft facilities. Play area.

LIVINGSTONE MILL FARM – see
SCOTLAND AT WORK (ALMOND VALLEY HERITAGE CENTRE)

Festivals

EDINBURGH BOOK FESTIVAL
Charlotte Square, Edinburgh
Tel: (031) 225 1915
Open: August of 'odd' years ie. '91, '93
Various charges

Colourful tents spring up in the gardens in the middle of Charlotte Square. Authors read aloud and tell stories in the children's book tent and sometimes there are visits from book characters. Creche.

THE SCOTTISH INTERNATIONAL CHILDREN'S FESTIVAL
Inverleith Park, Edinburgh
Tel: (031) 554 6297
Open: End May
Various charges
Mothers' room

Some 30,000 children come to the 6 days of open-air and tented shows and workshops. These include theatre, mime, puppetry and dance. Get your face painted, learn some circus skills, browse through books and have fun! Creche.

INTERNATIONAL FESTIVAL OF SCIENCE AND TECHNOLOGY

Dome in Princes Street Gardens plus lots of other venues in Edinburgh
Open: early April
Various charges

Fascinating demonstrations and 'hands-on' experiments for children. You can spend hours in the Dome watching cakes explode and frozen daffodils shatter or making boomerangs.

EDINBURGH INTERNATIONAL FRINGE FESTIVAL

Various venues throughout the city
Open: August – during the International Festival
Some free street entertainment; various charges for shows

Edinburgh has lots of festivals but when people talk about 'the Festival' this (and its more cultured partner) is the one they mean. There are lots of shows especially for children including theatre, puppetry and music. A favourite haunt is the area around the Art Gallery where street entertainers juggle with fire and wobble on unicycles alongside bands, choirs and busking bagpipers.

Fish

NEWHAVEN FISHMARKET

Newhaven Harbour, Edinburgh
Tel: (031) 552 1355
Open: Thu from 0630
Free

The fishmarket makes an unusual pre-breakfast outing for early risers. The harbour and village are worth looking round at other times too.

Gardens

ROYAL BOTANIC GARDEN

Inverleith Row or Arboretum Road, Edinburgh
Tel: (031) 552 7171
Open: Daily 0900 (Sun 1100) till 1 hr before sunset (sunset in winter)
Free (donation for hothouses)
P: Street
Café
Disabled facilities
Toilets

Youngsters love to feed the grey squirrels and chase the pigeons in a dog-free environment. They even appreciate the wonderful displays of flowers! The 11 glasshouses full of exotic plants like banana trees, carnivorous plants and giant water lilies are great for wet, wintry afternoons. Exhibitions and educational activities.

PRINCES STREET GARDENS

Princes Street, Edinburgh
Open: All year
Disabled facilities and limited access
Toilets

Watch trains passing under the glass-sided footbridge and chase the pigeons. Climb the SCOTT MONUMENT (**MONUMENTS**), marvel at the floral clock, have a game of putting or play on the swings and roundabout in the east gardens. Don't miss the street entertainment at the foot of the Mound during the FESTIVAL.

Graveyards and Gruesome Places

GREYFRIARS BOBBY

Churchyard, Candlemaker Row, Edinburgh

Corner of George IV Bridge and Candle-maker Row
Open: All times
Free
Disabled access

A life-size statue of a Skye Terrier called Greyfriars Bobby. After his master's death in 1858, the wee dog watched over his grave in the nearby churchyard for 14 years.

EDINBURGH DUNGEON

18 Shandwick Place, Edinburgh
Tel: (031) 225 1331
Open: Daily, 1000 – 2000
£££

Not for young children or the faint-hearted. The advertising blurb calls it a 'historical torture museum' with realistic executions by guillotine, witches burning at the stake and other horrors.

THE WITCHERY WALKING TOURS

1 Upper Bow, Royal Mile, Edinburgh EH1 2JN
Meet outside The Witchery Restaurant, Castlehill
Tel: (031) 225 6745
Open: Tours at 1100, 1900, 2000 May – Sep
£££

Walking tours include 'Old Town/Graveyard Tour' and 'Ghosts and Gore Tour' for those aged 10 or more.

ROBIN'S EDINBURGH TOURS

Waverley Market, Princes Street, Edinburgh
Meet outside Tourist Information Centre
Tel: (031) 661 0125/7722
Open: Daily
££
Disabled access

Walking tours including 'Ghosts and Witches' and 'Dr Jekyll's Horror Walk' and are suitable for over-10s.

MERCAT WALKING TOURS

Mercat Cross, St Giles, Royal Mile, Edinburgh
Tel: (031) 661 4541
Open: Daily
££

Tours include 'Ghosts and Ghouls' and 'The Ghost Hunter Trail' and are suitable for over-10s.

GHOST WALKS

Mr Bruce Jamieson, 121 Baronshill Ave, Linlithgow
Tel: (0506) 843087
£££

Book a place on one of the group tours during the summer or try a more spooky walk at Hallowe'en. Good fun for over-10s.

Heritage Centres

THE EDINBURGH EXPERIENCE

Calton Hill, Edinburgh
East end of Princes Street
Tel: (031) 556 4365
Open: May – Oct, Mon – Fri 1400 – 1730, Sat – Sun 1030 – 1730
£
P: Available
Disabled access

A short 3-D slide-show of Edinburgh and its history. Under-5s like wearing the special glasses. Also on Calton Hill is the Nelson Lookout Tower with a spiral staircase and lookout platform. The one o'clock Time Ball is dropped from here at the same time as the Edinburgh Castle gun is fired.

Indoor Fun

WAVERLEY MARKET
Princes Street, Edinburgh
Adjacent to Waverley Station
Tel: (031) 557 3759
Open: Mon – Sat 0830 – 1830 (1930 Thu),
Sun 1100 – 1700
Free
Various cafés, restaurants and take-
aways
Toilets with nappy-changing facilities
Forget about shopping and enjoy the atmosphere. Children love the glass elevator, fountains, statues, escalators and mirrors. Most of the shops are of no interest to children but there is a wonderful wooden toy shop where staff do tricks and toys can be touched, a chocolate shop with a mouth-watering selection of upmarket goodies at toddler height, and a handcart selling novelty hair-clasps and ribbons.

Monuments

THE SCOTT MONUMENT
Princes Street Gardens, Edinburgh
£
Those with a head for heights and strong legs will enjoy climbing up this Victorian Gothic spire.

Museums

MUSEUM OF CHILDHOOD
42 High Street, Royal Mile, Edinburgh
EH1 1TG
Tel: (031) 225 2424 x 6645
Open: Mon – Sat 1000 – 1800 (Oct – May
1700), Sun (during Festival)
1400 – 1700
Free
Partial disabled access
Toilets

A fine collection of toys, dolls and doll's-houses, costumes and nursery equipment. Some working models such as a haunted house peep show and a nickleodeon. Parents and grandparents keep spotting things they used to play with. The shop sells small 'old-fashioned' toys.

THE PEOPLE'S STORY MUSEUM
Canongate Tolbooth, Royal Mile, Edinburgh
Near the foot of the Royal Mile
Tel: (031) 225 2424 x 6638
Open: Mon – Sat 1000 – 1700 (Jun – Sep
1000 – 1800) and Sundays during Festival
1400 – 1700
Free
Disabled facilities and access
Toilet
The sights, sounds and smells of the past including reconstructions of a prison cell, a 1940s' kitchen, a steamie, a pub and a tea-room. Video. School groups welcome. Excellent for over-7s.

ROYAL MUSEUM OF SCOTLAND
Chambers Street, Edinburgh
Tel: (031) 225 7534
Open: Mon – Sat 1000 – 1700, Sun 1400 –
1700
Free
P: Meters
Tea-room
Disabled access and facilities
Toilets
The most interesting sections for under-5s are the stuffed birds and animals, and the working model engines operated by push-buttons. Older children are fascinated by the dinosaurs, fish and insects, and the mineral section where there are

stones that glow in ultraviolet light and real gold found by someone whilst walking in Perthshire. Phone for details of special events such as quizzes, drama sessions and workshops.

SCOTTISH AGRICULTURAL MUSEUM
Ingliston, nr Edinburgh Airport
Tel: (031) 333 2674
Open: All year during termtime
Free
P: Available
Teas
Disabled access and facilities
The museum is used a lot by schools to add interest to project work. Displays relating to farming, old trades and skills, social and home life are supplemented by an audio-visual show.

THE FIRE MUSEUM
Central Fire Station, Lauriston Place, Edinburgh
Tel: (031) 228 2401
Open: By arrangement, Mon – Fri 0900 – 1300, 1400 – 1630
Free
A large selection of old fire engines and equipment. Visits can be arranged to the working fire station under the Community Education Programme.

SCOTTISH WHISKY HERITAGE CENTRE
Castlehill, The Royal Mile, Edinburgh EH1 2NE
Beside Edinburgh Castle
Tel: (031) 220 0441
Open: Daily, 1000 – 1700
££
Disabled access
Take a trip back in time on an overturned whisky barrel and find out about Scotland's national drink. The tour and displays are really interesting, even if you are too young to drink.

MYRETON MOTOR MUSEUM
nr Aberlady
Off A918, 6 miles SW of North Berwick
Tel: (087 57) 288
Open: May – Oct, daily 1000 – 1800; Nov – Apr, daily 1000 – 1700
££
P: Available
Disabled facilities
Some of the motor cars, cycles, World War II military vehicles and automobilia date back almost 100 years. Don't forget the children's quiz book.

KINNEIL MUSEUM
Kinneil Estate, Bo'ness, West Lothian
Tel: (0506) 824318
Open: Apr – Sep, Mon – Sat 1000 – 1700; Oct – Mar, Sats only 1000 – 1700
Free
Visit the Kinneil Roman Fortlet which is close to the museum. Guides in period costume describe local history during the summer season.

FALKIRK MUSEUM
Callendar House, Falkirk
Tel: (0324) 24911 x 2202
Open: All year, Mon – Sat 1000 – 1230, 1330 – 1700
Free
Guides in historical costume will answer your questions about the old-fashioned kitchen implements.

Parks and Playgrounds

A city the size of Edinburgh has many parks and open spaces (*see* ADVENTURE PLAYGROUNDS, COUNTRY PARKS,

GARDENS, WALKS), so only a few of the best are described here.

FORT SAUGHTON
Saughton Park, Balgreen Road, Edinburgh
Tel: (031) 557 1265
Open: All year
Picnic area
Toilets
Edinburgh's most exciting playground (no dogs) full of helter-skelters and seesaws for toddlers, gorilla swings, aerial runways and a monster climbing net for older children. There is a putting green, hothouses and a scented garden for the blind nearby.

SIGHTHILL PARK
Broomhouse Road, Edinburgh
Open: All year
Another dog-free adventure playground with a fort theme with equipment suited to toddlers as well as teenagers.

LAUDERDALE PARK
Dunbar, East Lothian
Tel: (0368) 63518
Facilities from Apr–Sep
Try skittles or giant draughts as well as the usual summer facilities like table-tennis, trampolines, swingball, putting, crazy golf and paddling pool.

LODGE GROUNDS
North Berwick
Tel: (0620) 3104
Facilities from Apr–Sep
Table-tennis, skittles, crazy golf, swingball, trampolines, good swing park, aviary. Fun for toddlers to 10-year-olds.

THE PEEL
Linlithgow
nr Linlithgow Palace
Picnic area

Large children's play area with swings, climbing frame and paddling pool. Remember to bring some stale bread to feed the ducks.

DOLLAR PARK
Camelon Road, Falkirk
Half a mile from town centre
Open: Facilities, Easter–Sep; Park: all year
Toilets
Putting, tennis, paddling pool, pets' corner, bouncy castle, play area, giant chess and draughts, table-tennis, glasshouses and lots of space for ball games.

CALLENDAR PARK
Callendar Road, Falkirk
Off A803
Tel: (0324) 24911 x 2395
Open: Daily, dawn–dusk; facilities, May–Sep from 1200
P: Available
Kiosk
The park is only a few minutes from the town centre. The two play areas include Fort Callendar adventure playground which is by the boating pond. Try pitch and putt or crazy golf, bounce on the inflatable castle, or have a drive in a mini car. Woodland walks, bird sanctuary.

Picnic sites

LEADBURN STATION PICNIC SITE
nr Penicuik
A6094
P: Available
Eat your picnic on the old railway platforms and imagine how it would have been when trains still ran between Edinburgh and Peebles.

Railways

WAVERLEY STATION
tel: (031) 556 2477
Visit – free; train trip £ – ££

It is fun to take a short trip to Haymarket (2 minutes) or, better still, across the Forth Bridge to North Queensferry. Contact the Duty Officer for free guided tours tailored to suit groups of children from playgroup-age upwards.

BO'NESS AND KINNEIL RAILWAY
Union Street, Bo'ness, West Lothian EH51 9AQ
Off A993
Tel: (0506) 822298
Open: End Mar – Oct, Sat and Sun; mid Jul – mid Aug daily 1100 – 1630
From ££
P: Free
Buffet car on platform and trains

Working steam railway system with historic locomotives and rolling stock. Combine a train trip with a visit to BIRKHILL CLAY MINE (*see* SCOTLAND AT WORK). Annual events include a Teddy Bear's Picnic, a visit from Santa and a Thomas the Tank Engine weekend.

Riding

TOWER FARM RIDING STABLES
85 Liberton Drive,
Edinburgh
Tel: (031) 664 3375
Lessons from £££

Under-5s can try a short pony ride but lessons are for older children. Indoor school. BHS, ABRS and STRC approved.

WESTMUIR RIDING CENTRE
Totley Wells Grange, nr South Queensferry
Tel: (031) 331 2990
From £

Riding from age 3. Indoor school. ABRS and BHS approved.

APPIN EQUESTRIAN CENTRE
Drem, North Berwick
Tel: (062088) 366/519
From ££

Indoor arena, lessons, residential courses.

EDINBURGH AND LASSWADE RIDING CENTRE
Kevock Road, Lasswade EH18 1HX
Tel: (031) 663 7676
£££

ABRS, STRA approved. Indoor and outdoor tuition, evening classes, jumping lessons, 'tiny tots' starting classes, hacking and trekking. Birthday parties a speciality.

BEECRAIGS – *see* COUNTRY PARKS

Science and Technology

FORTH ROAD AND RAIL BRIDGES
North and South Queensferry
10 miles W of Edinburgh
Tel: (031) 331 1699
Free
Disabled access

For over 800 years travellers were ferried across the Firth of Forth. Queensferry was named for Queen Margaret who regularly used this passage between Dunfermline and Edinburgh in the 11th century. The ferry ceased in 1964 when the

Queen opened the road bridge (2,753 yds long).

The rail bridge was completed in 1890 and was one of the greatest engineering feats of its time. Following the centenary celebrations it is now floodlit at night. There is a bridge exhibition at the Queensferry Lodge Hotel on the other side of the Forth.

ROYAL OBSERVATORY
Blackford Hill
Tel: (031) 668 8405
Open: Daily, Mon–Fri 1000–1600, Sat, Sun and public holidays 1200–1700
£
P: Available
Partial disabled access

The exhibition about our solar system has some spectacular photographs of deep space. There are videos and computer games to try out as well as Scotland's largest telescope. Astronomy shop.

INTERNATIONAL FESTIVAL OF SCIENCE AND TECHNOLOGY –
see FESTIVALS

Scotland at Work – Past and Present

FOUNTAIN BREWERY
Gilmore Park, Edinburgh EH3 9YY
Off Fountainbridge near the west end of Princes Street
Tel: (031) 229 9377 x 3015
Open: Tours 1015 and 1415, Mon–Thu; advance notice required
£
P: Available

The breweries in Edinburgh can give a distinctive odour to the air. At Fountainbridge you can go on an educational tour of one of Europe's most automated breweries and watch cans being filled at the rate of 1500 a minute on the High Speed Can Line. Minimum age 8.

PRESTON MILL AND PHANTASSIE DOOCOT (NTS)
nr East Linton
Off A1 at East Linton, 6 miles W of Dunbar
Tel: (0620) 860426
Open: Apr–Oct, Mon–Sat 1100–1700 (Oct 1630, Sun 1400–1700 (Oct 1600)
£
P: Available
Disabled facilities

Children are fascinated by water so a visit to a working water-mill should appeal. The doocot once contained 500 birds which would have been used to make pigeon pies. There are ducks and geese on the pond.

SCOTTISH MINING MUSEUM
Lady Victoria Colliery, Newtongrange
10 miles S of Edinburgh on A7
Tel: (031) 663 7519
Open: All year, Tue–Fri 1000–1630, Sat–Sun 1200–1700
£
P: Free
Picnic area and tea-room
Limited disabled access

Put on a coal-miner's hat, turn on the winding gear and go to the pit-head. See what it was like for children working in the mines a hundred years ago – try to pull a coal sledge while crawling on your hands and knees. Good hands-on exhibits and interesting village scenes with life-size models. A good educational outing for 9 to 12-year-olds. After visiting the Newtongrange colliery you can drive along the heritage trail which links it with the museum's other site at PRESTON-GRANGE on B1384 between Mussel-burgh and Prestonpans.

COUSLAND SMIDDY
Cousland by Dalkeith
On A68, 1.5 miles past Fordell filling station
Tel: (031) 663 1058
Free
Open: Phone to arrange a visit
Experience the atmosphere of a working smiddy; perhaps see a farrier at work shoeing horses. The museum is still being developed and improved. School parties welcome by arrangement.

ALMOND VALLEY HERITAGE CENTRE
Millfield, Livingston, West Lothian
Off A705
Tel: (0506) 414957
Open: Easter–Oct, daily 1000–1700; Nov/Feb/Mar, weekends 1000–1700
£
Picnic and barbecue areas, café (see **PLACES TO EAT***)*
Partial disabled access
A working 18th-century water-mill with life-size models including the miller at work. There are small farm animals which children can handle, a play area, nature trail and cart rides. A small classroom can be used for school visits. Don't forget to visit the countryside museum and venture down the shale mine.

BIRKHILL CLAY MINE
nr Upper Kinneil Farm, nr Bo'ness, West Lothian
A706 to Linlithgow, right at crossroads, 2 miles to farm, follow signs
Tel: (0506) 825855
Open: Sat/Sun Easter–Oct 1230–1600; mid Jul–Aug, Mon–Sat 1130–1600
£
P: Available
Refreshments
Mine tour not accessible to disabled visitors
Travel to the mine on a steam train from BO'NESS (*see* **RAILWAYS**). Visit the underground tunnels where fireclay was mined. Learn how miners worked the clay and see 300-million-year-old fossil trees. Above ground there is a meadow walk, and walks through the ancient woodlands. Look round the miner's cottage which is furnished in the style of the 1920s.

Sport and Leisure Centres

LITTLE MARCO'S
Marco's Leisure Centre
51 Grove Street, Haymarket, Edinburgh
Tel: (031) 228 2341
Open: Daily 0930–2000
£££ (reductions for members)
Café and lounge
An indoor adventure playground with a bouncy castle, slides, soft play area, ball pool, tunnels to crawl through and more. Children must be between 31–55 inches tall. Parties are really well organised and slickly managed.

KOKO'S CHILDREN'S LEISURE CENTRE
Craig Park, Newcraighall Road, Edinburgh
Tel: (031) 669 0082
Open: Daily 1000–1900
££–£££
Cafeteria

Soft play areas, bouncy castles, ball pools, mirror maze, tube chutes and bumpy chutes, aerial walkway. Only for under-10s or children less than 55 inches tall though toddlers may prefer a less daunting play area near the café. Boisterous parties can be arranged for up to 35 children.

CORSTORPHINE LEISURE CENTRE
9 High Street, Corstorphine, Edinburgh
Tel: (031) 316 4939
Open: Mon–Fri 1000–2100, Sat–Sun 1000–1700
££
A small 'fun-world' for under-8s with a bouncy castle, ball pool, trampolines and small slides. Toddlers play area. Private parties can be arranged.

AINSLIE PARK LEISURE CENTRE
92 Pilton Drive, off Ferry Road, Edinburgh Quarter of a mile E Crewe Toll roundabout, on left after Northern General Hospital
Tel: (031) 551 2400
Open: All year, Mon–Fri 1000–2200, Sat–Sun 1000–1800
Various charges
P: Available
Cafeteria
Disabled access and facilities
The centre has a large pool, a teaching pool, a spa pool and a flume. Parent and child sessions, lessons for all ages. The changing-rooms have some family cubicles. Also badminton (over-5s), table-tennis, dance (5 to 8s), judo (over-5s), football (over-5s), tae-kwon-do (over-5s), karate (over-5s). Creche. Football and swimming parties can be arranged.

JACK KANE CENTRE
208 Niddrie Mains Road, Edinburgh
Tel: (031) 669 0404
Open: Daily 0900–2230
P: Available
Vending machine
Disabled access and facilities
After-school session with a bouncy castle, summer play sessions with entertainers like Mr Boom, pre-school gymnastics, soft play sessions, 5-a-side football. Under-5s like the bouncy cake which is available for parties. Creche.

MEADOWBANK SPORTS CENTRE
139 London Road, Edinburgh
Tel: (031) 661 5351
Open: Tue and Thu (may also be booked for parties)
£
Cafeteria
Disabled access and facilities
Soft play area for under-10s and handicapped children. Creche.

MURRAYFIELD ICE RINK
Riversdale Crescent, Murrayfield
Tel: (031) 337 6933
Open: Daily 1430–1630, check for evening sessions
££
Café
Open sessions, lessons, skate hire (size 8 shoe upwards)

KENNEDY FUN CENTRE
3 Windsor Place, Portobello, nr Edinburgh
Tel: (031) 669 1075
Open: Mon–Sat
From £
Snack bar
Toddler sessions, trampolining, ball pool, bouncy castle, pirate ship, chutes and soft play area for 2 to 12-year-olds. The centre can be booked for private parties.

THE LOCH CENTRE
Well Wynd, Tranent
Tel: (0875) 611081
£
Swimming pool, lessons. Badminton, squash, trampolines (under-8s), Saturday Morning Club and Friday Afternoon Club (primary children). Soft play area for parties. Creche facilities available at certain times.

KARTING INDOORS
Upper Diamond, Gladsmuir nr Haddington
Off A1 on B6363
Tel: (0875) 53550
From £££ for 6 minutes
Children aged 8 upwards can try driving a fun-kart round the track. Even the de-tuned versions of pro-racer karts feel very fast when the seat of your pants is only an inch off the ground.

NORTH BERWICK SPORTS CENTRE
Grange Road, North Berwick EH39 4QS
Tel: (0620) 3454
Open: All year, 1400 – 2200
£
Badminton, trampolines, table-tennis, roller-skating, bouncy castle, Primary Play Day (first Saturday of each month). Creche facilities available at certain times.

KNIGHTSRIDGE TEN-PIN BOWLING COMPLEX
Deer Park Golf and Country Club, Livingston
Tel: (0506) 31037
Open: Daily from 1000
From £££ for 3 games
Lots of indoor fun. Bumpers are available during the day to help beginners.

BATHGATE SPORTS CENTRE
Balbardie Park, Bathgate
Tel: (0506) 634561
£
Café
The soft play area is open all day (under-8s). Older children enjoy the badminton, 5-a-side football, archery, trampolining, international BMX track and skateboard ramp. There is a Saturday club for those aged 6 or more. There are 'Try-A-Sport' sessions each day during the holidays.

MARINER LEISURE CENTRE
Glasgow Road, Camelon, Falkirk
A803, 1 mile W of High Street
Tel: (0324) 22083
Open: Daily 0900 – 2200
P: Available
£
Coffee lounge
Disabled facilities including changing-rooms and showers
Palm trees grow around the lagoon-shaped pool which has underwater lighting and a wave machine, as well as an elephant chute. Parent and toddler sessions, family swim discos, and swim parties are available. Badminton, squash, dance (ballet, tap, disco), mini-aerobics, trampolining and pre-school activity classes. One of the top 20 tourist attractions in Scotland.

GX SUPERBOWL
Redbrase Road, Camelon, Falkirk
Tel: (0324) 613933
Open: Daily, 1000 – 2300
From £
Restaurant
Ten-pin bowling centre with computerised scoring.

Swimming

AINSLIE PARK LEISURE CENTRE —
see **SPORT AND LEISURE CENTRES**

LEITH WATERWORLD
Foot of Leith Walk, Edinburgh
Open: Mon — Fri 1200 — 2200, Sat — Sun
0900 — 1700
££
P: Available
Café
A brand new pool with waterfalls, rainfall, water mushrooms, waves, cannons, geysers, bubble beds, water chutes and a river-run for inflatable rides. Crash barriers make the children's lagoon almost calm. Creche. The pool may be hired for private use on weekend evenings.

ROYAL COMMONWEALTH POOL AND NAUTILUS FLUME COMPLEX
Salisbury Road, Edinburgh
1 mile from North Bridge
Tel: (031) 667 7211
Open: Mon — Fri 0900 — 2100, Sat — Sun
1000 — 1600 (weekends end May — Aug
0800 — 1900)
£
P: Available
Cafeteria
Disabled access and facilities
A 50-metre swimming pool, diving pool, teaching pool with playpens alongside. The flumes (the largest complex in Europe) have names like 'Twister', 'Black Vortex' and 'Stingray'. Swimming lessons, parent and baby sessions, pre-school gymnastics. Creche. Play sessions with magicians, stilt walkers, face-painting, entertainers and water play sessions.

DUNBAR LEISURE POOL
Castle Park, Dunbar
Tel: (0368) 65456
Open: Daily from 1000
£
One of East Lothian's main attractions. The brand new leisure pool has a flume, wave-maker, bubble bed, water geysers and fan spray. Swim parties can be arranged.

BONNYRIGG LEISURE CENTRE
King George V Park, Bonnyrigg
Tel: (031) 663 7579
Open: Daily 0900 — 2200
£
A brand new leisure pool with a bubble bed, water cannon and a water umbrella. Young children like the soft play area while older kids can play tennis as long as they are supervised.

Theatres and Cinemas

THEATRE WORKSHOP
34 Hamilton Place, Edinburgh
Tel: (031) 225 7942
Open: Mon — Sat 0930 — 1730; evenings
as per theatre programme
From £ for workshops; £££ for shows
Cafeteria
Disabled facilities
Many shows for school children and under-5s. Youth theatre where those aged 10 or more can attend training sessions and workshops.

THE NETHERBOW
43 — 45 High Street, Edinburgh
Tel: (031) 556 9579
Café
A very small theatre with shows for children including puppet shows at Easter and a Christmas pantomime.

FILMHOUSE
88 Lothian Road, Edinburgh
Tel: (031) 228 2688
Restaurant
Matinees on Saturday afternoons during term-time for over-3s.

UNITED CINEMAS (UCI)
Craig Park, Edinburgh
Tel: (031) 669 0777/0771
Kiosk
12-cinema American-style complex with children's film club at weekends. Good ice-cream.

BRUNTON THEATRE
Musselburgh
Tel: (031) 665 2240
P: Available
Disabled access and facilities
Regular children's shows in February, July and October as well as the Christmas pantomime.

Toys

WIND THINGS
11 Cowgatehead, Grassmarket, Edinburgh
Tel: (031) 220 6336
Open: Mon – Sat 1000 – 1700 (Sun during Festival and before Christmas)
Kites, stunt kites and kite-making materials, parachuting bears. Juggling equipment – free introductory lessons.

BUGSY'S
28 King's Stables Road, Edinburgh EH1 2JY
Tel: (031) 228 6669
Open: Daily from 1000
From £££ per 30 minutes for track and car hire

An American-style diner – but you don't have to eat anything to have a go with Scalectrix tracks and cars.

WAVERLEY MARKET – *see* INDOOR FUN

Walks

HERMITAGE OF BRAID AND BLACKFORD POND
Braid Road, Edinburgh
Tel: (031) 447 7145
P: Available near pond
Picnic areas
Disabled access and facilities
Toilets
Feeding ducks on the pond is always popular with tiny tots. The best woodland walks are around the Hermitage but it is exhilarating to climb to the top of Blackford Hill. The hill is also a good place for sledging. Visitor centre, ranger service, children's nature club and conservation group.

CRAMOND
5 miles NW of city centre on the Firth of Forth
Tel: (031) 336 2163
Open: All year
Free
P: Available
Assisted disabled access
Picturesque 18th-century village with a Roman fort and medieval tower, old schoolhouse and iron mills. A causeway is exposed at low tide and leads to an island in the Forth. A very small ferry takes you across the river to a beach walk and Dalmeny House (£).

ARTHUR'S SEAT
Holyrood Park, Edinburgh
Start from Dunsapie Loch
Open: All year
Arthur's Seat is the remains of an extinct volcano which erupted 325 million years ago. The route is quite steep but it is worth the effort when you see the views of the city and surrounding country from the top.

TRAPRAIN LAW
nr Dunbar
Off A1, 5 miles W of Dunbar
Open: All times
No disabled access
A good pair of legs and some determination will get most people to the top of the 734ft high whale-backed hill. There is a 2000-year-old Iron Age fortified site at the summit.

NORTH BERWICK LAW
North Berwick
Open: All times
No disabled access
The 613ft volcanic rock is slightly smaller than TRAPRAIN LAW. Three-year-olds have been known to trudge doggedly to the top when bribed with chocolate biscuits. There is a Napoleonic watch tower and an archway made from the jawbone of a whale at the summit.

YELLOWCRAIG NATURE TRAIL
(see BEACHES)
North Berwick
Access road from the B1345, 2 miles W of North Berwick
Tel: (031) 226 4602
P: Available
Barbecue area
An interesting and varied nature trail through woodland, sand dunes and along the seashore. There is a Tarzan area with a tree-house, and guided walks in summer.

FLOTTERSTONE VISITOR CENTRE
Easter Howgate, nr Edinburgh
Off A702
P: Free
Picnic area, restaurant nearby
Limited disabled access
Toilets
Gentle walks along the paths and very quiet roads. Suitable for prams and wheelchairs. The small visitor centre has displays of natural history and lucky visitors sometimes get a conservation poster to colour in. There are more energetic walks up the Pentland Hills for enthusiasts.

MOORFOOT HILLS
Access from Gladhouse Reservoir, off B5372 at Upper Side
Like the better known Pentland Hills, the Moorfoots are rough walking country but quite suitable for fit family outings.

UNION CANAL
Tel: (0506) 856624
Access at Ratho, Linlithgow and Falkirk
The canal, 31.5 miles long, was opened in 1822 and originally flowed from Edinburgh to lock 16 on the Forth and Clyde Canal. It runs through attractive countryside and excursions by canal boat are available – *see VICTORIA* and *JANET TELFORD* CANAL BOATS and EDINBURGH CANAL CENTRE – BOATS AND BOAT TRIPS. There are ranger-led walks along the canal as well as boating and canoeing (Tel 0324 612415). Take a torch and look for stalactites in the Falkirk Tunnel.

Watersports

PORT EDGAR
South Queensferry EH30 9SQ
9 miles E of central Edinburgh
Tel: (031) 331 3330
£££
Cafeteria
Watersports courses include dinghy sailing, canoeing, windsurfing for over-8s. Also hire of dinghies, sailboards.

LEVENHALL LINKS LEISURE PARK
Musselburgh
Tel: (031) 229 5887
Various charges
Windsurfing courses or board hire (over-8s). The small pond is ideal for beginners, but more experienced windsurfers go to LOCHORE MEADOWS COUNTRY PARK in Fife. Children on the courses must be able to swim.

LINLITHGOW LOCH
Linlithgow
Tel: (0506) 843121
Open: Mon – Sat from 0900, Sun from 1245
Various charges
Learn windsurfing, canoeing and sailing. Permits for those using their own equipment are available from the Tourist Office.

BEECRAIGS – *see* **COUNTRY PARKS**

UNION CANAL – see **WALKS**

Winter Sports

HILLEND
Biggar Road
Off A703 S of ring-road
Tel: (031) 445 4433
Open: Apr – Sep, Mon – Fri 0930 – 2100;
Oct – Mar, daily 0930 – 2200
From ££ for skiing; £ for the chairlift to the summit – see HILLEND – **COUNTRY PARKS**
P: Free
Refreshments and picnic area
Disabled facilities
The largest artificial ski slope in Britain. Facilities include chairlift, 'T' bar and tow, ski hire, tuition, showers and changing-rooms. Fine views from the top of the chairlift (available to non-skiers) of the Pentland Hills, over Edinburgh and beyond.

MEADOWMILL SPORTS CENTRE
Tranent, East Lothian EH33 1LZ
Tel: (0875) 810232
££
A dry ski slope with equipment for hire. Get into shape in the summer and be ready for the real snow when it comes.

POLMONT SKI-SLOPE
nr Falkirk
Tel: (0324) 711660
Open: Mon – Fri, 0900 – 2100
££
Dry ski slope with ski tow. Instruction and ski hire.

PLACES TO EAT

Hotels and Restaurants

L'AUBERGE
56 St Mary's Street, Edinburgh EH1 1SX
Tel: (031) 556 5888
Open: Tue – Sun 1215 – 1400
Disabled access
Very smart French restaurant with set lunches under £9. Children's helpings available.

THE BEECRAIGS
Beecraigs Country Park
nr Linlithgow
Tel: (0506) 670099
see **COUNTRY PARKS**

BEHIND THE WALL CAFÉ
Backshop Bistro, 14 Melville Street, Falkirk
Tel: (0324) 33338
Café, bar, bistro, conservatory and beer garden with food available all day.

CAPRICE PIZZERAMA
327 Leith Walk, Edinburgh
Tel: (031) 554 1279
Pizzas are the speciality. Watch them being made to order. A good place for a bargain lunch.

CAVALIERE RESTAURANT
124 High Street, Dalkeith
Children can make their own pizzas at quiet times (phone to check). Any uneaten portions can be taken home.

CHINESE HOME COOKING
21 Argyle Place, Edinburgh EH9 1JJ
Open: Daily 1730 – 2300
A converted shop with the atmosphere of a working man's café but with delicious Cantonese food at low prices. Recommended in the Good Food Guide.

DARIO'S RESTAURANT
85/87 Lothian Road, Edinburgh
Tel: (031) 229 9625
Another cheap and cheerful pizza house with small portions available for small appetites.

DUNCAN'S LAND
8 Gloucester Street, Edinburgh
Tel: (031) 225 1037
Open: Tue – Sat 1230 – 1400, 1830 – 2200
Moderately priced lunchtime menu. Soft spot for children.

FAIRMILE INN
Biggar Road, Fairmilehead
Open: Daily
High-chairs, imaginative food and small, snack-size meals.

FAT SAM'S AMAZIN' PIZZA PIE FACTORY
The Old Meat Market, Fountainbridge, Edinburgh
Tel: (031) 228 3111
Open: Daily 1200 – late
Lots of pizzas and pasta dishes. Children enjoy the action as well as the food – automated puppets hanging from the ceiling, piranha fish in huge tanks, a pianola, a jazz band from Mon – Thu and an electronic board for birthday messages. The children's menu doubles as a gangster mask. Cakes and puddings come with sparklers for birthday celebrations.

GARFUNKEL'S RESTAURANT
31 Frederick Street, Edinburgh
Tel: (031) 225 4579
Handy location in town centre. Fast food. Under-10s are automatically given a goody bag with crayons etc.

HARDING'S
2 Station Road, North Berwick EH39 4AU
Tel: (0620) 4737
Open: Wed – Sat 1200 – 1400
Disabled access and facilities
Set lunches under £8, children's helpings. Recommended in the Good Food Guide.

HELIOS FOUNTAIN
7 Grassmarket, Edinburgh
Tel: (031) 229 7884
Open: Mon – Sat 1000 – 1800, Sun in Aug and Dec
A small self-service restaurant with vegetarian dishes and wholefoods. Baskets of toys to keep children amused.

HENDERSON'S SALAD TABLE
94 Hanover Street, Edinburgh
Tel: (031) 225 2131
One of the first wholefood restaurants in the city with a huge range of salads, hot dishes and puddings. Counter service means that children can see the food before they choose. It can be very busy at lunchtimes and the queue seems to go on forever if you have small children in tow.

KALPNA
2 – 3 St Patrick Square, Edinburgh
Tel: (031) 667 9890
Open: Mon – Sat (not Sat lunch) 1200 – 1430, 1730 till late
Disabled access
Vegetarian Indian food. Set lunches start at £3. Children's helpings. Recommended in the Good Food Guide.

KAVIOS RESTAURANT
1 Commercial Street, Edinburgh
Tel: (031) 554 5272
A lively continental café where children have great fun preparing the pizzas before eating them. Pasta eaters are catered for too. Birthday messages are displayed on an electronic message board.

KWEILIN RESTAURANT
19 – 21 Dundas Street, Edinburgh
Tel: (031) 557 1875
Freshly cooked Cantonese food. A bit pricey but nice for a treat. Patient and friendly staff.

LADY NAIRNE HOTEL
Willowbrae Road, Edinburgh
Tel: (031) 661 3396
Good food and quick service. Highchairs, children's menu and small portions available.

LAURISTON FARM RESTAURANT
Lauriston Farm Road, Silverknowes, Edinburgh
Open: Daily 1100 – 2200
Lots of room, loads of toys, garden and children's menu.

LOONTOWN
28 William Street, Edinburgh
Tel: (031) 220 1688
Delicious Chinese food, though fairly expensive.

LORENZO'S
5 Johnstone Terrace, Edinburgh
Tel: (031) 226 2426
Open: Daily 1200 – 2300
Interesting Italian dishes. Eat outside in fine weather. Quite pricey.

MAMMA'S AMERICAN PIZZA COMPANY

30 The Grassmarket, Edinburgh
Open: Daily

Twin of PAPPA'S (below) in Victoria Street. Gourmet pizzas in a variety of sizes to suit all appetites. Lovely ice-creams.

MR MARIO'S

103/105 Dalry Road, Edinburgh
Open: Daily

Small restaurant and takeaway with mini minestrone and baby pizzas or small portions off the adult menu. Clip-on chairs for babies.

OMAR KHAYYAM

1 Grosvenor Street, Haymarket, Edinburgh

Tandoori restaurant with omelettes and chicken for those who don't like curry. Friendly and helpful staff.

PAPPA'S GREAT AMERICAN EATS

7 Victoria Street, Edinburgh

Serves burgers and traditional American food. Half portions and doggie bags for those whose appetite is defeated by the portion size.

PIERRE VICTOIRE

10 Victoria Street, Edinburgh
Tel: (031) 225 1721
and
38/40 Grassmarket, Edinburgh
Tel: (031) 226 2442
and
8 Union Street, Edinburgh
Tel: (031) 557 8451

French restaurants recommended in the Good Food Guide. Great with 'foodie' children.

RATHO PARK

Brewer's Fayre, Dalmahoy Road, Kirknewton

Same owners as LAURISTON FARM. Spacious interior, good food and wonderful outdoor play area for under-12s.

RICHARD'S PIZZARAMA

11/12 Seafield Road, Portobello
Nr Portobello roundabout
Open: Evenings from Tue – Sat

Toys to play with between courses. Sparklers, puppets, fish in tanks and lots more to keep children entertained.

RICHMOND PARK HOTEL

26 Linlithgow Road, Bo'ness
Tel: (0506) 823213

Children's menu or small portions off the main menu. High-chairs available.

SHAMIANA

14 Brougham Street, Edinburgh EH3 9JH
Tel: (031) 228 2265
Open: Daily 1200 – 1400 (not Sat – Sun); 1800 – late
Disabled access

Children's helpings. Recommended in the Good Food Guide.

THE STAR AND GARTER RESTAURANT

1 High Street, Linlithgow
Tel: (0506) 844445

Old coaching inn.

THE TIFFIN

Easter Road, Edinburgh

Italian restaurant with great value lunches.

Quick Meals and Snacks

MR BONI'S RESTAURANT
4 Lochrin Buildings, Edinburgh
Tel: (031) 229 5319
Open: Daily from 1030 (1230 on Sun)
Cheap and cheerful. Burgers and sandwiches followed by delectable ice-creams with all the trimmings. There are high-chairs and booster seats. Ice-cream cakes can be made to order. You can also buy ice-cream cones and ice-cream gateaux to take away too.

SPUD-U-LIKE RESTAURANT
18A Brougham Street, Tollcross, Edinburgh
Tel: (031) 229 2910
and
Kiosk 2, Cameron Toll, Edinburgh
Tel: (031) 664 9040
and
Waverley Market, Princes Street, Edinburgh
Tel: (031) 557 1546
Steaming hot baked potatoes with a great variety of fillings.

JOHN LEWIS – THE PLACE TO EAT
St James Centre, Edinburgh
Top of Leith Walk
Tel: (031) 556 9121
Mother and baby room
A good spot to refuel after a busy shopping trip. The food is well presented and small portions or a children's menu are available. The staff are willing to warm bottles and process food for babies.

GALLERY OF MODERN ART
Belford Road, Edinburgh
Recommended in the Good Food Guide. Clip-on chairs for toddlers – *see* ARTS AND CRAFTS.

DR JEKYLL'S COFFEE HOUSE
9A Castle Street, Edinburgh
Tel: (031) 220 3675
Down a long flight of stairs but once inside it is spacious with high-chairs and good baby-changing facilities. Run by the Chest, Heart and Stroke Association.

THE COFFEE SHOP
Almond Valley Heritage Centre – see
SCOTLAND AT WORK.
Tel: (0506) 414957

Pubs

THE ABERCORN
42/46 Portobello Road, Edinburgh
Next to Piershill Safeway
Open: Daily
Large, friendly pub with a beer garden complete with play area. Try a pub lunch after doing the shopping.

THE BRIDGE INN
Ratho, Midlothian
Tel: (031) 333 1320
Award-winning pub with first-class food for adults and children at a very reasonable price. Children can stay in the pub till 2000. There's lots to do here apart from eating – *see* EDINBURGH CANAL CENTRE (BOATS AND BOAT TRIPS).

CITY CAFÉ
Blair Street, off High Street, Edinburgh
Open: Daily
Trendy café/bar where children are welcome till 2000. Sweetie counter behind the bar! Milkshakes for under-age drinkers.

FLOTTERSTONE INN
Milton Bridge, nr Penicuik
Tel: (0968) 76853
Good selection of bar snacks and a garden to play in. Pleasant walks around the Pentlands (*see* WALKS).

THE LAW HOTEL
Grange Road, North Berwick
Tel: (0620) 2793
A welcoming pub at the foot of North Berwick Law. Lots of well-maintained toys, prams and trikes and a paddling pool. Burgers and bar snacks.

Ice-Creams

MR BONI'S
Cockburn Street, Edinburgh
see also QUICK MEALS AND SNACKS.
Choose between single, double or triple scoops of delicious ice-cream with dark or white chocolate flakes.

MARGIOTTA
102 Marchmont Road, Edinburgh
Tel: (031) 452 8584
and
115 Bruntsfield Place, Edinburgh
and
Colinton Village, Edinburgh
and
Craiglockhart Road, Davidsons Mains, Dalkeith
Has 20 mouth-watering flavours.

Fast Food Chains

LITTLE CHEF
Dreghorn, Edinburgh
On the N side of A720 ringroad on the Dreghorn link
Tel: (031) 441 3497
Disabled facilities

Baby-changing area
Fast food for fast travellers.

BURGER KING
10 Princes Street, Edinburgh
Tel: (031) 557 4575
and
118 Princes Street, Edinburgh
Tel: (031) 220 1644

PANCAKE PLACE
130 High Street, Edinburgh
Tel: (031) 225 1972
and
35 – 37 Shandwick Place, Edinburgh
Tel: (031) 228 6322

PIZZA HUT
34/36 Hanover Street, Edinburgh
Tel: (031) 226 3652
and
46 North Bridge, Edinburgh
Tel: (031) 226 3038
and
113/117 Lothian Road, Edinburgh
Tel: (031) 228 2920
Voted Egon Ronay's fast food restaurant of 1990.

McDONALD'S
137 Princes Street, Edinburgh
Tel: (031) 226 3872
and
48 High Street, Falkirk
Tel: (0324) 20006

Bakeries

MATHIESON'S
Howgate Centre, High Street, Falkirk
Tel: (0324) 35364
Local baker with lots of branches.

PLACES TO STAY

Hotels

BRUNTSFIELD HOTEL
69/75 Bruntsfield Place, Edinburgh
Tel: (031) 229 1393
£££
Swimming pool, babysitting, meals all day.

ELLERSLY HOUSE HOTEL
Ellersly Road, Edinburgh EH12 6HZ
Tel: (031) 337 6888
£££
Children of all ages welcome. Cots and high-chairs. Beautiful walled gardens.

LADY NAIRNE HOTEL
228 Willowbrae Road, Edinburgh
Tel: (031) 661 3396
£££
Every convenience available.

MALLARD HOTEL
East Links Road, Gullane EH3 12AF
Tel: (0620) 3288
£££
There are 5 golf courses including a children's course nearby. Baby listening service, high teas, garden and games room.

NORTON HOUSE HOTEL
Ingliston, Edinburgh EH28 8LX
Tel: (031) 333 1275
£££
Children's menu and high-chairs. Outside play area with bark chippings. Children's packs for overnight stays.

SCANDIC CROWN HOTEL
80 High Street, Edinburgh EH1 1TH
Tel: (031) 557 9797
£££
Family rooms, babysitting service. Children's menu with picture to colour in. Access to supervised leisure pool. Check on what is available as the hotel is being refurbished following a fire in 1992.

TRAVELODGE
Dreghorn, Edinburgh
On N side of A720 ringroad on the Dreghorn Link
Tel: (031) 441 3497
Part of the LITTLE CHEF chain. Basic family accommodation for people *en route* to somewhere more interesting. Double bed, sofa bed, child's bed, cots on request all in one fixed-price room. Rooms have an *en suite* bathroom, central heating and TV, alarm clock and tea/coffee making facilities. The rooms are available from 1500 till 1200 the next day.

Bed and Breakfasts

BELLEVUE GUEST HOUSE
8 East Claremount Street, Edinburgh EH7 4JP
Tel: (031) 556 4862
From £
Family rooms, high-chairs, cots.

GUEST HOUSE, 34 LIBERTON BRAE
Edinburgh EH16 6AF
Tel: (031) 658 1980
From £
Attic made into a playroom, swings in the garden, toys and high-chairs.

SHARON GUEST HOUSE

1 Kilmaurs Terrace, Edinburgh EH16 5BZ
Tel: (031) 667 2002
From £
High-chairs, cots, children's meals.

CAMERON TOLL GUEST HOUSE

299 Dalkeith Road, Edinburgh EH16 5JX
Tel: (031) 667 2950
From £
High-chairs, cots, books, children's meals, play corner, baby listening.

THE LAIRG GUEST HOUSE

11 Coates Gardens, Edinburgh EH12 5LG
Tel: (031) 337 1050
From £
Family room, high-chair, cot and children's books.

GUEST HOUSE, 17 CRAWFORD ROAD

Edinburgh EH16 5PQ
Tel: (031) 667 1191
From £
Rocking horse, high-chair, babysitting facilities.

CRIOCH GUEST HOUSE

23 East Hermitage Place, Edinburgh EH6 8AD
Tel: (031) 554 5494
From £
Cots, babysitting, play park opposite house.

GUEST HOUSE, 33 COLINTON ROAD

Edinburgh EH10 5DR
Tel: (031) 447 8080
From £
Very family-orientated guest house with high-chairs, cots, toys, books and babysitting if required.

GUEST HOUSE, 6 DEAN PARK CRESCENT

Edinburgh EH4 1PN
Tel: (031) 332 5017
From £
Cots, children's games.

GUEST HOUSE, 2A DOVECOT ROAD

Edinburgh EH12 7LF
Tel: (031) 334 4651
From £
Plenty of toys, big garden, babysitting.

'NO 22', THE DICKIE GUEST HOUSE

East Claremont Street, Edinburgh EH7 4JP
Tel: (031) 556 4032
From ££
Children welcome. High-chairs, cots and other baby equipment, babysitting.

HERALD HOUSE

Grove Street, Edinburgh EH3 8AP
Tel: (031) 228 2323
From £
Guests have free use of the facilities at LITTLE MARCO'S (*see* **SPORT AND LEISURE CENTRES**) which is situated opposite. High-chairs, cots and babysitting.

BEN DORAN GUEST HOUSE

11 Mayfield Gardens, Edinburgh EH9 2AX
Tel: (031) 667 8488
From £
Families welcome. High-chairs, story books. No charge for babies, minimal charge for toddlers.

Caravan and Camp Sites

YELLOWCRAIGS CARAVAN CLUB SITE

Dirleton, North Berwick EH39 5DS
Tel: (062085) 217
Open: Apr – Sep
££

A Caravan Club site for touring caravans only. There is a good play area and access to the beach. A new baby room with baby bath and excellent disabled washing facilities are thoughtful additions to the usual facilities.

SETON SANDS

Longniddry EH32 0QF
Tel: (0875) 813333
£££

An award-winning caravan site with a heated outdoor swimming pool, a play area for small children and bike hire.

GREATER GLASGOW

Glasgow did not have a good reputation in the past, but there has been a remarkable turnaround in recent years, to the extent that Glasgow became Europe's 'City of Culture' in 1990. The smiling cartoon character of Mr Happy and the promotional slogan, 'Glasgow's Miles Better', say it all — Glasgow is now a great place for families.

More people live here than in all the rest of Scotland put together but there are plenty of open spaces as Glasgow has more acres of parkland than any comparable European city. These range from big country parks with nature trails, watersport facilities and assault courses to city parks with butterfly houses and play areas for those with special needs. If you want a change from cycling in the parks, try out the network of long-distance off-road cycle routes which is being developed around the west of Scotland.

There is a good range of indoor activities on offer — leisure centres where you can skate along tree-lined trails, or in the company of a woolly mammoth, and swimming pools which resemble primeval swamps. The museums cover a wide variety of fascinating topics and include Haggs Castle, a history museum specifically for children.

Getting around the city is made easy by the underground and overground rail networks. And bus travel can be a bargain if you use a Family Day Tripper Ticket or a Super Mum/Dad card. For information contact the Travel Centre, St Enoch Square, Glasgow (Tel: 041-226 4826).

Going further afield is straightforward too as Glasgow is at the centre of good road and rail networks. If you are travelling by car you can reach Loch Lomond and the Trossachs, or Edinburgh, in less than an hour. ScotRail operate a frequent service to Edinburgh, and there are regular departures for the Ayrshire coast and Stranraer, as well as Carstairs which is on the western edge of the Border country.

If you are coming to Scotland from abroad, both Prestwick and Glasgow airports receive transatlantic flights and there are regular connections with the major cities in Britain and Europe.

There is a high level of afterschool care provided at recreation centres throughout Greater Glasgow but only 3 shoppers' creches — at the Sauchiehall Street Centre, East Kilbride Shopping Centre and an in-store creche at the Newlands Safeway on the south side of the city. Boots (33

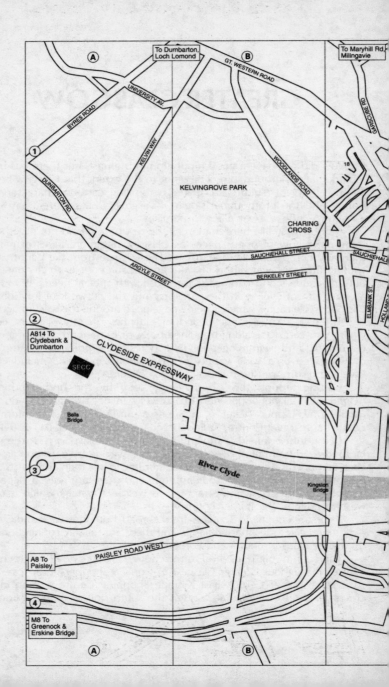

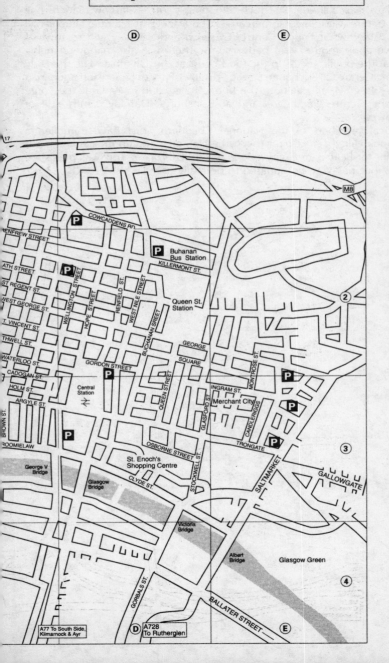

Map B: Glasgow City Centre

The Plaza, East Kilbride; St Enoch Shopping Centre, Glasgow; Sauchiehall Street Centre, Glasgow), Mothercare (9 The Plaza, East Kilbride; Sauchiehall Street, Glasgow; St Enoch Centre, Glasgow) and Safeway at Crossmyloof all have good mother and baby rooms. There are also nappy-changing areas at the public toilets in the food court at the Olympia Mall, the Early Learning Centre (26 Buchanan Street, Glasgow), Princes Square (off Buchanan Street, Glasgow), and at both the public toilets and in Asda at the Forge Shopping Centre (Parkhead), and at Sainsburys (Darnley, south side of Glasgow).

Local members of the National Childbirth Trust have compiled a handbook called *Let's Go* for the Rutherglen area and another is being put together for Bearsden. A citywide guide called *Tots in Tow* was published in 1987 but needs to be updated to be really useful.

PLACES TO VISIT

Animals and Birds

GLASGOW ZOO
Calderpark, Uddingston, Glasgow
Off A74 (M74)
Tel: (041) 771 1185/6
Open: Daily 0900 – 1700 (winter 1000 – 1700)
££
P: Free
Café, picnic areas
An award-winning zoo specialising in big cats and reptiles. See many rare breeds of animals including white tigers, giant tortoises, black bears and porcupines.

LOCHWINNOCH (RSPB)
Largs Road, Lochwinnoch
Off A760, 9 miles SW of Paisley
Tel: (0505) 842663
Open: All year, Fri – Wed 1000 – 1715
£
P: Available
Partial disabled access
A Scandinavian-style nature centre with an observation tower and exhibitions. Walk round the nature trails and look over the marshes from the bird hides.

DALZELL COUNTRY PARK AND BARON'S HAUGH NATURE RESERVE (RSPB)
nr Motherwell
Free
Picnic areas
This is the RSPB's most urban nature reserve. Look out for peregrine falcons while walking through the woods or taking a break in the secluded picnic areas.

EASTWOOD BUTTERFLY KINGDOM
by Rouken Glen Park, nr Clarkston
Between East Kilbride and Paisley
Tel: (041) 620 2084
Open: Daily end Mar – early Nov
£
Disabled access and facilities
Butterflies and moths fly round the banana trees and other exotic plants in the tropical garden. Some of the butterflies are very large and can frighten small children. Avoid the insectarium if your children have an aversion to large insects – there are scorpions, tarantulas, preying mantis and stick insects. Small children prefer the pets' corner where you can see rabbits, budgies, fish and hamsters. Education packs and guided tours are available for school groups.

DRUMPELIER COUNTRY PARK
PALACERIGG COUNTRY PARK –
see **COUNTRY PARKS**

Bike Hire and Cycle Routes

GLASGOW/LOCH LOMOND CYCLEWAY
Tel: (041) 552 8241
A safe 21-mile route for cyclists and pedestrians from the centre of Glasgow to Loch Lomond. It starts at the SECC and makes its way via Clydebank, Dumbarton to Balloch and Loch Lomond. The cycleway now connects with routes through the Trossachs as far north as Killin.

PAISLEY/IRVINE CYCLE AND WALKWAY
Tel: (041) 552 8241
Fifteen miles of disused railway line have been converted into a shared pedestrian/cycle path. There are two main routes – Paisley to Kilbirnie via Johnstone, Kilbarchan and Lochwinnoch, and Paisley to Kilmacolm via Linwood and Bridge of Weir.

STRATHCLYDE COUNTRY PARK – *see* COUNTRY PARKS

Boats and Boat Trips

RIVER CRUISES
Broomielaw landing stage, Jamaica Street, Glasgow
Under railway bridge at Jamaica Street
Tel: (041) 221 8702
Open: Daily Easter – Oct with departures approx every hour
P: Available
Light refreshments
Disabled facilities
Modern fully enclosed vessel offering views of docks and ships working cargo, shipyards and new ships being built including warships.

PS WAVERLEY
Waverley Excursions, Anderston Quay, Glasgow
Tel: (041) 221 8152
Write or phone for details of departure points and times
From ££
Meals, refreshments
Disabled facilities
The *Waverley* was the last paddle steamer to be built for service on the Clyde, and is now the last sea-going paddle steamer in the world. A variety of cruises from Glasgow and Ayr, along the Clyde coast.

MV GIPSY PRINCESS
Auchinstarry Bridge nr Kilsyth
B802, 1 mile S of Kilsyth
Tel: (0236) 721856/822437
Open: May – Sep, Sun afternoons, 1400, 1500
£
The *Gipsy Princess* is a new (1900) custom-built, 36-seater passenger boat with open-air and covered accommodation. Trips through the Kelvin Valley.

Bus Trips

DISCOVERING GLASGOW TOURS
George Square (W side), Glasgow
Tel: (041) 942 6453
Open: May – early Oct, 1000 – 1600
£££
Ticket valid all day. Nine stops at places of interest where passengers may disembark.

Castles and Stately Homes

COLZIUM HOUSE AND GROUNDS
nr Kilsyth
Turn left 1 mile E of Kilsyth on A803
Tel: (0236) 823281
Phone for opening hours
Free
P: Available
Tea-room, picnic areas
Eighteenth-century mansion house with a courtyard and walled garden. There is a children's zoo in the grounds as well as a curling pond, a loch, woodland walks, and an arboretum where children could learn the names of different trees.

BOTHWELL CASTLE (HS)

Bothwell
W of Motherwell, off B7071 overlooking
River Clyde
Tel: (031) 244 3101 (HS, Edinburgh)
Open: Apr–Sep 0930–1900, Sun 1400–
1900; closes at 1600 Oct–Mar, also
closed Thu afternoons and all day Fri
£

The massive ruins of one of the finest 13th-century castles in Scotland which the English and Scots battled over many times. The interpretive centre has life-size models of people at work including a boy gardener and a miner.

Country Parks

MUGDOCK COUNTRY PARK

Craigend Visitor Centre, Craigallian Rd,
nr Milngavie, Glasgow G1 4RE
Off A81, 1 mile S of Strathblane
Tel: (041) 956 6100
Open: Park daily; Centre daily 1300–
1630
P: Available
Tea-room, barbecue and picnic areas

There are two main play areas in the park. One is for under-10s while the other has no age limits so parents can join in the fun (if they feel up to it). The centre has displays of insects and pond life, a touch table and an observation beehive. There is a small play area where children can do stencil drawings and other activities related to wildlife. With 500 acres of moors, wood, pasture and marshland there are plenty of walks and a bridle path which may be used for riding or mountain biking. There is fishing at Mugdock Loch and Craigend Pond and a permanent orienteering course.

PALACERIGG COUNTRY PARK

Palacerigg Road, Cumbernauld G67 3HU
A80 Glasgow/Stirling
Tel: (0236) 720047
Open: Park, daily, dawn–dusk; centre,
summer 1000–1800 except Tue
P: Free
Café, picnic areas and barbecues

The emphasis is on wildlife native to northern lands. Lots of Scottish wildlife to see including roe deer, badgers, foxes and stoats as well as bison, wolves, lynx, chamois and deer. The centre has an excellent museum and facilities. Other activities include pony-trekking and golf.

CASTLE SEMPLE COUNTRY PARK

Off Largs Road, Lochwinnoch
9 miles SW of Paisley
Tel: (0505) 842882
Open: Daily except Christmas and New
Year's Day, 0900–dusk
Various charges for use of the loch
Picnic areas
Limited disabled access
Toilets

200-acre country park based on Castle Semple Loch. Bring your own boat or hire canoes, rowing boats or sailboards. (No motor boats or keel boats allowed.) Bank fishing. Next to RSPB visitor centre.

FINLAYSTONE ESTATE AND COUNTRY PARK

Langbank PA14 6TJ
A8 at Langbank
Tel: (047554) 505/285
Open: Daily 1030–1700
£
Picnic and barbecue areas, tea-room
(summer weekends)
Disabled facilities at Eye Opener

A great place for children of all ages. There are detective trails and children's assault courses, a maze and a play area with a fort for younger children. The visitor centre has a slide show, games and quizzes, and is the starting point for ranger-led walks. Pick soft fruit in season. A special collection of dolls from around the world can be seen on Sundays (Apr – Aug, 1430 – 1630). The beautiful gardens have woodland walks, waterfalls, a smelly garden and a pond.

GLENIFFER BRAES COUNTRY PARK
Glenfield Road, Paisley
Tel: (041) 884 3794
Open: Dawn – dusk
P: Available
Picnic areas
An upland park of 1300 acres with an adventure play area. There is a fine nature trail and many miles of waymarked paths across moorland. Rangers organise guided walks and activities on conservation and educational themes. The park also hosts motocross championships, sheep dog trials, equestrian, orienteering and cross-country events.

STRATHCLYDE COUNTRY PARK
nr Motherwell
M74 Junct 5 or 6 from the north, west or south; A725 from the east
Tel: (0698) 266155
Open: All year
Free entry but charges for facilities
P: Available
Cafeteria (Easter – Oct), picnic areas
Disabled facilities
The large man-made loch is ideal for all sorts of watersports. Equipment available for hire includes broncos, wave bobs, bumper boats, Canadian canoes, rowing boats and water skis.

There are 2 sandy beaches and a nature trail with bird hides which younger children enjoy, while older children can play tennis or putting, or hire a bike to ride around the park. The visitor centre is the starting point for seasonal guided walks.

Bored with the healthy outdoor activities? Then pay a visit to the fairground which has all the usual stomach-churning rides. Look out for details of major events such as circuses and firework displays.

DRUMPELIER COUNTRY PARK
nr Airdrie
M8 from Glasgow, junct 8 to A89, left at B8752, then right at 'T' junct
Tel: (0236) 22257
Open: Apr – Oct, daily 0900 – 2000; Nov – Mar, Wed – Sun 1200 – 1700
P: Available
Disabled facilities
One of the lochs has a crannog – an artificial island home made by prehistoric man. Hire a boat and take a closer look, do a bit of fishing or walk round the loch and Monkland Canal. Orienteering course, ranger-led walks, play areas, peace garden, butterfly house, glasshouse complex.

CALDERGLEN COUNTRY PARK
Strathaven Road, East Kilbride
On A726, East Kilbride – Strathaven Road
Tel: (03552) 36644
Open: Park open daily
Picnic areas
Limited disabled access, enclosed play area for disabled children and toddlers
Park consists of over 300 acres of wooded gorge and parkland with a network of paths, a nature trail and large waterfalls on the Rotten Calder river. The visitor centre includes an

imaginative natural history display on 'hidden worlds'. There are rabbits, an arctic fox, owls, parakeets, ponies and goats in the children's zoo, an adventure playground and enclosed toddlers' play area.

CHATELHERAULT COUNTRY PARK
Carlisle Road, Ferniegair, Hamilton ML3 7UE
On A72, 1.5 miles S of Hamilton town centre
Tel: (0698) 426213
Free entry to park, £ entry for house and visitor centre
Go on a ranger-led walk (from Apr – Oct) through the woods or by the 200ft-deep cleft of the Avon Gorge and dredge up some 'water-weirdies' or try the foods that cavemen might have eaten when they'd had no luck catching mammoths. Look out for the ruins of Cadzow Castle where Mary Queen of Scots once stayed, an Iron Age fort and the herd of white Cadzow cattle.

Fairgrounds

STRATHCLYDE COUNTRY PARK – *see* COUNTRY PARKS

Farms

LAMONT CITY FARM
Barrhill Road, Erskine
Tel: (041) 812 5335
Open: Daily 1030 – 1700
Free
Picnic area
Community project farm with typical animals and smaller pets. Play areas and donkey rides (small charge).

Gardens

GLASGOW BOTANIC GARDENS
Great Western Road, Glasgow
Tel: (041) 334 2422
Open: Gardens 0700 – dusk; glasshouses from 1000
Free
Disabled facilities
The glasshouses contain a wide range of tropical and temperate plants. The warm temperatures make them especially attractive when you have pre-school children to entertain on a cold, wet winter's day. Outside is a herb garden full of lovely smells and a play area for small children, as well as lots of paths to explore and space to run.

FORMAKIN ESTATE
Bishopton
2 miles W of Bishopton on B789
Tel: (0505) 863400
Open: All year, daily 1100 – 1800
£
P: Available
Restaurant
Disabled facilities
The mansion house is an unfinished shell set in landscaped grounds and gardens (over-grown but being restored) with bothy/stableblock court-yard, craft workshops, towerhouse, gatelodges, derelict mealmill. Exhibition area, rare breed farm, shop.

GREENBANK GARDEN (NTS)
Off Old Mearns Road, Clarkston
Tel: (041) 639 3281
Open: All year, daily 0930 – sunset
£
Garden for the disabled
A large walled garden and woods with regular walks and events. Good for toddlers whose parents are keen gardeners.

Indoor Fun

THE FORGE SHOPPING CENTRE
Parkhead, Glasgow
Tel: (041) 556 6661
Open: Mon – Sat 0900 – 2000, Sun 1000 – 1700
P: Available
Disabled access and facilities
Mother and baby room
Have a no-shopping trip and ride the escalators or go up and down in the glass lift. Look out for special seasonal entertainments. Play area.

Markets

THE BARRAS
Glasgow Cross, Glasgow
Quarter mile E of Glasgow Cross
Tel: (041) 552 7258 (Wed – Sun)
Open: All year, Sat and Sun 0900 – 1700
Free
Cafés
Disabled facilities
World-famous weekend market, with an amazing number of stalls and shops. Founded 100 years ago, the Barras is now home to over 800 traders each weekend. Look out for the Barras archways, children's creche and buskers. All markets are covered.

Museums

MUSEUM OF TRANSPORT
Kelvin Hall, Bunhouse Road, Glasgow G3 8DP
Follow signs to Kelvin Hall
Tel: (041) 357 3929
Open: Daily, Mon – Fri 1000 – 1700 (Thu 2100), Sun 1200 – 1800
Free
P: Street
Café with high-chairs
Disabled facilities
A museum covering the history of transport, including a reproduction of a typical 1938 Glasgow street and a subway station. Children of all ages (and their parents) will enjoy looking at the trams, buses, fire engines, horse-drawn vehicles and railway locomotives. Other features include a large display of ship models and a walk-in motorcar showroom with cars from the 1930s right up to modern times.

SCOTLAND STREET SCHOOL MUSEUM OF EDUCATION
225 Scotland Street, Glasgow
Tel: (041) 429 1202
Open: Wed 1400 – 1600; closed during school holidays
Free
Toilets
School-age children love to see how their predecessors were taught. The school, which was designed by Charles Rennie Mackintosh, opened in 1906. It served as an elementary school and then as a primary school until 1979. It now houses a Museum of Education with two reconstructed classrooms.

THE TENEMENT HOUSE (NTS)
145 Buccleuch Street, Glasgow
Tel: (041) 333 0183
Open: Apr – Oct, daily 1400 – 1700; Nov – Mar, Sat – Sun 1400 – 1600
£
A Victorian tenement house with 2 rooms, kitchen and bathroom complete with original boxbeds, kitchen range, sink and coal bunker. Better for older children as toddlers get frustrated when they are not allowed to touch anything.

HUNTERIAN MUSEUM AND ART GALLERY

University of Glasgow, University Ave,
G12 8QQ
Tel: (041) 330 4221/5431
Open: Mon – Sat 0930 – 1700
Free
Refreshments
Disabled access

Look at curiosities from the South Seas, and at the fossil collection. Practical classes for school groups include Romans, Celts, Egyptians, Dinosaurs and Captain Cook (museum); Mackintosh and Whistler (art gallery).

HAGGS CASTLE

100 St Andrew's Drive, Glasgow G41 4RB
Tel: (041) 427 2725
Open: All year, Mon – Sat 1000 – 1700,
Sun 1200 – 1800
Free
P: Street
Access to ground floor only for disabled visitors

The Castle is now a museum of history for children with lots to touch. Historical displays change regularly and quiz sheets add interest. It is a good idea to book ahead for summer holiday activities as they are very popular. The gardens have been landscaped and include herb and vegetable plots, and a knot garden.

ART GALLERY AND MUSEUM

Kelvingrove, Argyle Street, Glasgow
Tel: (041) 357 3929
Open: Mon – Sat 1000 – 1700 (Thu 2100),
Sun 1200 – 1800
Free
Café with high-chairs
Disabled access and facilities

One of the most popular tourist attractions in the city. Children are fascinated by the display of dinosaurs and stuffed animals.

PEOPLE'S PALACE

Glasgow Green, Glasgow
Tel: (041) 554 0223
Open: Mon – Sat 1000 – 1700 (Thu 2100),
Sun 1200 – 1800
Free
Café

Find out about the history of Glasgow. Topics include trade unions, women's suffrage, entertainment and sport. Younger children prefer the Winter Gardens and everyone enjoys the baking in the wholefood café.

SMA' SHOT COTTAGES

11/17 George Place, Paisley
Tel: (041) 812 2513/889 0530
Open: May – Sep, Wed/Sat 1300 – 1700
Free
Tea-room

The damp atmosphere of the west coast doesn't appeal to everyone, but it was good for the cotton weaving industry and as a result there are a number of old restored weavers' cottages in the area. Victorian millworkers once lived in this restored artisans' house. There is also an 18th-century loom shop and exhibition.

WEAVER'S COTTAGE (NTS)

Shuttle Street, Kilbarchan
Tel: (05057) 5588
Open: Daily, Jun – Aug 1400 – 1700,
limited Apr/May and Sep/Oct
£

Another typical 18th-century weaver's cottage containing the last of the village's handlooms. Watch a skilled weaver at work.

DAVID LIVINGSTONE CENTRE

Station Road, Blantyre, Glasgow G72 9BT
A74, Blantyre Station 400yds
Tel: (0698) 823140
Open: Mon – Sat 1000 – 1800, Sun 1400 –
1800
£
P: Free
Tea-room (Apr – Sep), picnic area

David Livingstone, the famous explorer and missionary, was born here in 1813. He lived in a 'single-end' in Shuttle Row – an 18th-century block of mill tenements, and worked in the cotton mill by the time he was 10. He studied after work each night and eventually became a doctor. Much of his adult life was spent exploring Africa where he crossed the Kalahari desert and discovered the Victoria Falls. While exploring Africa he met H. M. Stanley who greeted him with the famous words, 'Dr Livingstone, I presume?' There are relics of the Industrial Revolution and of his travels in Africa, a social history museum and a play area.

HAMILTON MUSEUM

129 Muir Street, Hamilton
Tel: (0698) 283981
Open: Mon – Sat 1000 – 1700 (closed
Wed/Sat 1200 – 1300)
Free

The museum used to be a staging-post for horse-drawn carriages travelling to London. See a 4-in-hand coach and a reconstructed Victorian kitchen as well as costumes of that era.

Novelties

HAMILTON MAUSOLEUM

Hamilton
Tel: (0698) 66155

Open: Easter – Sep, daily tours at 1500
(also 1900 on Sat/Sun in Jul/Aug)
£

The mausoleum was built by the Tenth Duke of Hamilton so that he would be remembered after his death. It has a tremendous echo that lasts for 15-seconds – the longest echo of any building in Europe.

Parks and Playgrounds

VICTORIA PARK AND FOSSIL GROVE

Victoria Park Drive North, Glasgow
Facing Airthrey Avenue
Tel: (041) 959 2128
Open: Mon – Sat 0800 – dusk, Sun 1000 –
dusk; Fossil Grove open by arrangement
Snacks kiosk
Disabled access

Play area, crazy golf, tennis courts, boating pond and a bouncy castle in the summer. The stumps and roots of trees that grew 330 million years ago can be seen in 'fossil grove' which was discovered in 1887.

KELVINGROVE PARK

Argyle Street/Kelvin Way, Glasgow

There are attractive play areas in the park. The Kelvin Walkway runs along the river and leads up to the BOTANIC GARDENS – see GARDENS.

LINN PARK

Between Clarkston Road and Carmunnock Road, Cathcart, Glasgow
Picnic areas
Disabled facilities

Play areas (including a new special needs play area), assault course and children's zoo. Nature trail, woodland walks and paths to the falls on the River Cart.

112

TOLLCROSS PARK
Tollcross Road, Parkhead, Glasgow
A pets' corner, exotic birds, and fish tanks. A stream flows through the wooded glen. Nature trail.

GARNETHILL PARK
Rose Street, Garnethill, Glasgow
A very new park with play areas in the centre of the city.

CASTLETOWERS
Machrie Road, Castlemilk, Glasgow
The play park, which opened in the autumn of 1992, has a castle and moat.

WOODHEAD PARK
Lenzie Road, Kirkintilloch
Tel: (041) 776 2151
A large park with putting green, aviary and trampolines

BARSHAW PARK
Glasgow Road, Paisley
Tel: (041) 889 2908
Boating pond, playground and a model railway to ride on. Summer facilities include trampolines, bowling, tennis, putting and crazy golf. Those with bikes can play bicycle polo, go on the BMX track, or try out their road skills in the model traffic area. There is also a nature corner with goats and ponies.

ROBERTSON PARK
Inchinnan Road/Paisley Road, Renfrew
Tel: (041) 886 2807
Picnic area
The model traffic area, with traffic lights and roundabouts, is fun for young cyclists (small charge for bike hire). Play in the playground and look at the animals in the pets' corner.

JUNIPER ROAD
Viewpark, Motherwell
Open: Daily 0900 – 1730 (2200 in summer)
Supervised playground with lots of apparatus including a trapeze. Suitable for 3 to 13-year-olds. Fenced, and locked at night.

HOULDSWORTH PARK
Wishaw
Open: Daily 0900 – 2300
Toilets
Supervised play area for toddlers complete with climbing ropes, slides and 'springies'. The space net and other equipment appeals to over-7s.

STRATHAVEN PARK
Strathaven
Tel: (03552) 71332
A lovely park with lots of open space for ball games. Hire boats on the boating pond or try canoeing.

ROUKEN GLEN
Rouken Glen Road, Thornliebank, Giffnock
Open: All reasonable times
Free
P: Available
Tea-room, picnic areas
Partial disabled access
Toilets
One of Glasgow's most attractive parks with a walled garden, lovely shaded walks and a waterfall. Ranger service. The dog-free playground is designed for toddlers and young children. Boating, bouncy castles and putting in the summer. Look at butterflies and creepie-crawlies at the EASTWOOD BUTTERFLY KINGDOM – *see* ANIMALS AND BIRDS.

Playschemes and Creches

SAUCHIEHALL STREET SHOPPING CENTRE CRECHE
Sauchiehall Street, Glasgow
On lower floor
Open: During centre hours
A well thought-out creche with a security entrance. Under-8s can be left with qualified nursery nurses for a couple of hours while Mum or Dad does the shopping.

SHOPPERS' CRECHE
East Kilbride Shopping Centre, East Kilbride
££ per hour
A good creche for 2 to 7-year-olds.

STRATHKELVIN PLAYSCHEME
Various venues
Tel: (041) 772 3210
Open: Summer
£
Archery (over-7s), athletics (over-9s), basketball (8 to 12-year-olds), canoeing (over-9s), cycling proficiency (8 to 12-year-olds), football (7 to 12-year-olds), golf (over-8s), marine cadet course (7 to 12-year-olds), mountain biking (over-10s), netball (9 to 12-year-olds), pony-riding (over-8s), rambling (over-8s), sailing (over-8s), tennis (over-8s), treasure hunts (over-8s), volleyball (over-10s), windsurfing (over-8s).

SUNBUSTERS
Various venues, Motherwell
Tel: (0698) 267515
Open: Jul – Aug
Toddlers enjoy the puppet shows and entertainers while older children can have fun with the arts and crafts, sweet-making, reading, computer competitions, playing board games or learning circus skills. At other times of the year the Community Arts Programme runs workshops in visual arts, dance, drama and music.

Riding

DALZELL RIDING SCHOOL
Manse Road, Dalzell Estate, Motherwell
Tel: (0698) 268771
££ per hour
Thirty-minute walks on a lead-rein for under-4s.

Science and Technology

THE DOME OF DISCOVERY
South Rotunda, 100 Govan Road,
Glasgow G51 1JS
Tel: (041) 427 1792
Open: Tue – Sun (and Bank Holidays) 1000 – 1730
££
'Hands-on' exhibits make science fun. There is nothing boring about the 60 or so exhibits and demonstrations covering aspects of physics, biology, chemistry and the environment. Audience participation is invited at the science shows which take place at weekends. There are special events during school holidays as well.

COATS OBSERVATORY AND WEATHER STATION
Oakshaw Street, Paisley
Tel: (041) 889 2013/3151
Open: Mon/Tue/Thu 1400 – 2000, Wed/-Fri/Sat 1000 – 1700
Free
The observatory has been recording astronomical and meteorological information since 1882. It has a

satellite picture receiver and is one of the best equipped stations in the country.

Scotland at Work – Past and Present

SUMMERLEE HERITAGE TRUST
West Canal Street, Coatbridge ML5 1QD
Tel: (0236) 31261
Open: All year (not Christmas) 1000–1700
Free
P: Available
Tea-room, picnic area
Disabled facilities
This part of Scotland was hailed as 'the workshop of the world' during the Industrial Revolution. The clatter of belt-driven Victorian machinery and the hiss of gas engines takes you back to those times. Look round the award-winning archaeological excavations of 1835 ironworks and take a trip on an electric tram. Play area by the canal.

SMA' SHOT COTTAGES, WEAVER'S COTTAGE – *see*
MUSEUMS

Sports and Leisure Centres

LITTLE MARCO'S
Marco's Leisure Centre
62 Templeton Street, Glasgow
Nr Glasgow Green
££
Ball swamp, bouncy castle, chutes and so on for 4 to 8-year-olds. Children can be left while parents use the other facilities in the centre.

HOLLYWOOD BOWL
Elliot Street, Finnieston, Glasgow
Tel: (041) 248 4478
Open: Daily 1000–2400
££
Computerised 10-pin bowling.

BELLAHOUSTON SPORTS CENTRE
Bellahouston Drive, Glasgow
Tel: (041) 427 5454
Open: Daily, 0920–2230
£
Indoor sports including badminton, judo and trampolining.

BISHOPBRIGGS SPORTS CENTRE
147 Balmuildy Road, Bishopbriggs, Glasgow
Tel: (041) 772 6391
Open: Daily 0900–2200
£
Cafeteria
Disabled access and facilities
Summer activity programme includes badminton, videos and bouncy castle. Fun sessions with inflatables in the swimming pool. Creche.

HUNTERSHILL OUTDOOR RECREATION CENTRE
Crowhill Road, Bishopbriggs, Glasgow
Tel: (041) 772 8592
£
Wide range of outdoor activities including archery.

NEW ACTION SPORTS ACTIVITIES
Low Moss Go-Kart Track, Low Moss Road, Bishopbriggs, Glasgow
Tel: (041) 945 4949
Open: Daily 1000–2130
Picnic area
From £
Rally, karting, paintball, speedball,

buzzboard. Safety equipment supplied. Kiddies karts, 2-seater trainers.

SUMMIT ICE RINK
Finnieston, Glasgow
Tel: (041) 204 2215
Open: Wed – Sun; skating on Sat 1430 – 1730 and 2000 – 2300; Sun 1400 – 1700 and 1930 – 2200
£

Cool off through the summer at a skating party or a disco. Skate hire available.

ALLANDER SPORTS COMPLEX
Milngavie Road, Bearsden, Glasgow G61 3DF
Tel: (041) 942 2233
£
Cafeteria

Parent and toddler swimming sessions, lessons and canoeing. Badminton, gymnastics, hockey, archery, cricket, fencing, basketball, netball, martial arts, table-tennis, snooker. Playaway scheme and roller-skating. Birthday parties.

LAGOON LEISURE CENTRE
off Mill Street, Paisley
Tel: (041) 889 4000
Open: Mon – Fri 1000 – 2200, Sat – Sun 1000 – 1700
P: Available
Cafeteria
Disabled facilities

Fun pool with waves which break over coloured artificial rocks. A 55yd waterslide passes through a jungle of plants. The learner pool is good for families with young children. Family changing-rooms. The ice-rink can be used for ice dancing, curling, hockey, figure skating, discos and ice pantos. Birthday parties can be arranged.

LINWOOD SPORTS CENTRE
Brediland Road, Linwood
Tel: (0505) 29461
£
Picnic area

There is a BMX track, a fitness trail, a playground and tennis courts outside. Indoor facilities include badminton, squash, table-tennis, roller-skating, trampolining and 5-a-side football. Saturday morning fun sessions (under-11s). Take the stress out of birthday parties by booking a trampoline, football or roller-skating party here. Creche.

GX SUPERBOWL
21 – 23 Walneuk Road, Paisley
Tel: (041) 848 1442
Open: Daily, 1000 – 2400
££

Ten-pin bowling with computerised scoring. Young children can find it difficult to hit the pins so bumpers are available to make the lane narrower.

SHOTTS LEISURE CENTRE
Benhar Road, Shotts
Tel: (0501) 23333
Open: Daily, 0900 – 2200 (except 25/26 Dec and 1/2/3 Jan)
P: Available
£
Cafeteria
Disabled facilities and access

A 25m pool with water cannons, bubble beds and waterfalls. The children's lagoon has water spouts and bubble bursts. Learn to swim or practise your sporting skills. There are plenty of sports to choose from including squash, judo, gymnastics, badminton, 5-a-side football, boxing, carpet bowls, gym joey (pre-school), table-tennis, volleyball, basketball

and netball. Bouncy castle parties can be arranged. Family changing-rooms.

AQUATEC
Menteith Road, Motherwell ML1 1TW
Tel: (0698) 276464
Open: Daily 1000 – 2200
P: Available
£ – ££
Café

Disabled access and facilities
Tropical leisure pool with flumes, wild water channel, water cannons, water beds, waterfall and outdoor hot springs. The children's pool has fountains and a Tommy Turtle slide. The pools are quite shallow so they are more suitable for younger children than the pool at the nearby

TIME CAPSULE. Skate through tree-lined alpine trails complete with snowstorms to the ice cavern which has fibre optics lighting and rest area with log fire. Competent skaters can go to an ice disco. Swimming or skating parties can be arranged.

WISHAW BOWL
Caledonian Centre, Glasgow Road, Wishaw
Tel: (0698) 350060
From £
Café
Strike it lucky—go 10-pin bowling. Children only on Saturdays. Book ahead to be sure of getting bumpers.

THE TIME CAPSULE
Buchanan Street, Coatbridge ML5 1EK
Tel: (0236) 441444
Open: Daily 0900—2200
£££
Café
Go back in time and try ice-skating with a woolly mammoth or swim in a primeval swamp. There is a tropical wave pool beside a volcano, water chutes, a high-speed glacier run, tidal waves and a rubber ring ride. This fantasy world is one of Scotland's top attractions.

THE ICEBOWL
The Olympia, East Kilbride
Tel: (03552) 44065
£££
It is hard work to keep your footing on the ice so you'll keep warm even if you can't skate like Torville and Dean. The 9-screen cinema in the same complex has at least 2 children's films on at any time.

Swimming

GOVAN FUN POOL
Harthill Street, Glasgow
Tel: (041) 445 1899
£
Pool with flume.

POLLOK LEISURE POOL
27 Cowglen Road, Glasgow
Tel: (041) 881 3313
Daily 1000—1700, Sat—Sun 1000—1600
£
Café
Fun pool with a 54m water slide and wave machine.

DOLLAN BATHS
Brouster Hall, Town Centre Park, East Kilbride
Tel: (03552) 21357
£
An olympic-size pool and a learners' pool decorated with seaside murals.

BISHOPBRIGGS SPORTS CENTRE, ALLANDER SPORTS COMPLEX, LAGOON LEISURE CENTRE, SHOTTS LEISURE CENTRE, AQUATEC and THE TIME CAPSULE—*see* SPORT AND LEISURE CENTRES

Theatres and Cinemas

MOTHERWELL CONCERT HALL THEATRE COMPLEX
Motherwell
Tel: (0698) 267515
Children's programmes includes the latest films, puppet shows, appearances by popular Scottish singing acts like the Singing Kettle and Mr Boom, and children's theatre productions like *Charlie and the Chocol-*

ate Factory and *Bugsy Malone.* Aspiring actors (aged 5 to 13) can audition for parts in the annual children's show.

MOTHERWELL MOVIE HOUSE
Motherwell
Tel: (0698) 267515
Children's films on Saturdays.

THE ICEBOWL – *see* SPORT AND LEISURE CENTRES

Walks

CLYDE WALKWAY
Stretches from SECC in central Glasgow via Glasgow Green to Cambuslang, following the course of the Clyde.

FORTH AND CLYDE CANAL
Tel: (041) 332 6936
Walk along the towpath at Anniesland and Maryhill.

KILMARDINNY LOCH
Thomson Drive, Bearsden, Glasgow
A short walk round the loch.

Toddlers like to feed the ducks, swans and geese with old crusts of bread.

MOTHERWELL
Tel: (0698) 832117
Walks between Apr – Oct
Free
A programme of guided walks around the industrialised area of Motherwell showing some of the unspoilt places. Look for badgers, make woodland sculptures, or go on a fungal foray. Phone for dates and times.

MONKLAND CANAL
Glasgow
There are towpaths between Calderbank and Drumpelier with plans to link up with SUMMERLEE HERITAGE PARK – *see* SCOTLAND AT WORK.

Watersports

CASTLE SEMPLE COUNTRY PARK – *see* COUNTRY PARKS

PLACES TO EAT

Hotels and Restaurants

BALBIR'S VEGETARIAN ASHOKA
141 Elderslie Street, Glasgow
Tel: (041) 248 4407
Open: Daily 1200–1400, 1700–2300
Disabled access
Big portions of inexpensive, simple Indian vegetarian food. Children get scaled-down portions. Carry-outs available.

CAFE GANDOLFI
64 Albion Street, Glasgow
Tel: (041) 552 6813
Open: Mon–Sat 0930–2330
Disabled access
French-style café with a big selection of good food (including breakfast) and excellent coffee. Lunches and evening meals.

THE CANAL STREET STATION
Beefeater Restaurant, Stow Brae, Paisley
Tel: (041) 887 9110
Children have a choice of pizza, burger, mini sausages or fish stars on the 3-course Mr Man menu. Kids' meals are also served in the no-smoking area of the bar. In good weather you can eat outdoors in the beer garden. Nappy-changing facility.

CHICAGO MEAT PACKERS
Hope Street, Glasgow
An American-style restaurant with burgers, etc.

COPTHORNE HOTEL
George Square, Glasgow G2 1DS
Tel: (041) 332 6711
Good lunches, children's menu.

(Fridays are very busy.)

THE CROOKED LUM
Beefeater Restaurant, Brunel Way, The Murray, East Kilbride
Tel: (03552) 22809
Enjoy a bar snack in the beer garden while the children amuse themselves in the outdoor play area. A 3-course Mr Man menu is available in the dining-room and children's meals are also served in the family section of the bar. Nappy-changing facility.

Di MAGGIO'S PIZZA PLACE
1038 Pollokshaws Road, Glasgow
Tel: (041) 632 4194
and
42 Gateside Street, Hamilton
Tel: (0698) 891828
and
61 Ruthven Lane, Glasgow
Tel: (041) 334 8560
Pizza and pasta restaurant with a carry-out and delivery service. Highchairs available.

THE DOVECOTE
Beefeater Restaurant and Bar
4 South Muirhead Road, Cumbernauld
Tel: (0236) 725339
Families with young children are made very welcome. Watch the children having fun in the modern play area (set on bark chippings) while relaxing in the beer garden. Children can have a bar snack outside, a light meal in the family section of the bar or a more substantial 3-course meal from the Mr Man menu available in the dining-room. Nappy-changing facility.

GARFUNKLES
Bath Street, Glasgow
Burgers, pizzas and fun for all the family.

GLENSKIRLIE
Banknock, nr Cumbernauld
Tel: (0324) 840210
A pleasant family hotel with a garden where you can eat in fine weather. Can be very busy.

GOURMET HOUSE
19 Ashton Lane, Glasgow
Tel: (041) 334 3229
Open: Mon–Sat 1200–1400, 1700–2400
Children are treated as VIPs. Tasty and moderately priced Cantonese cooking.

JANSSEN'S
1355 Argyle Street, Glasgow
Tel: (041) 334 9682
A brasserie where children are genuinely welcome. Close to Kelvingrove Art Gallery.

LOON FUNG
417 Sauchiehall Street, Glasgow
Tel: (041) 332 1477
Open: Daily, 1200–2330
Children are treated like little emperors. Large portions of Cantonese food at reasonable prices.

PJ'S PASTARIA
Maryfield House, Ruthven Lane, Glasgow
and
Food Court, Princes Square, Glasgow
Tel: (041) 339 0932
Open: Daily 1200–1430, 1700–2400
Disabled access
Very basic, cheap and cheerful for all the family. Half-price pasta at certain times. Huge ice-creams. Children's menu.

Quick Meals and Snacks

COMESTIBLES AND BESPOKE SANDWICH SHOP
Basement Courtyard, Princes Square, Glasgow
Tel: (041) 226 4309
A staggering array of sandwiches made to order.

COFFEE POT
Gourock, near ferry terminal
Good home-baking and tasty snacks.

FAMOUS COFFEE HOUSE
Findlay Clark Garden Centre, Boclair Road, Milngavie, Glasgow
Tel: (0360) 20721
Open: Daily 0900–2100 (1800 in winter)
Recommended by Egon Ronay. Good food, children's menu. Can be busy at weekends.

OCTOBER CAFÉ
The Rooftop, Princes Square, Buchanan Street, Glasgow
Tel: (041) 221 0303
Open: 1200–1800
A wonderful setting. The bar serves simple food and sandwiches all afternoon. Vegetarian dishes. Recommended in the Good Food Guide.

LA PÂTISSERIE FRANÇOISE
138 Byres Road, Glasgow
Tel: (041) 334 1882
Open: Mon–Sat 0930–1830
Almost like being in France–lots of tarts and cakes to revive flagging spirits.

WINTERGREEN CAFÉ
People's Palace, Glasgow Green
Tel: (041) 554 0195
Open: Daily 1000–1615 (later on Thurs)
Inexpensive wholefood to refresh

weary children before or after a visit to the PEOPLE'S PALACE – *see* MUSEUMS.

Pubs

BAY HORSE (BAR AND LOUNGE)
39 Bothwell Road, Hamilton ML3 0AS
Tel: (0698) 285910
Beer garden with play equipment including sandpits, playbus, chute, netball, swings, scribble wall. Bar lunches.

THE HORSE SHOE BAR
17–21 Drury Street, Glasgow
Tel: (041) 221 3051
Open: Meals served Mon–Sat 1200–2000
The bar is over 104ft long and is listed in the Guinness Book of Records. School-dinner food at bargain prices.

Fish and Chips

HARRY RAMSDEN'S
251 Paisley Road, Glasgow G5 8RA
Tel: (041) 429 3700
Open: Daily
P: Available
Disabled access
Great fish and chips, indoor and outdoor play areas.

JIMMY'S
1 Victoria Road, Glasgow
Tel: (041) 423 4820
Open: Daily from 1100 (closed 1500–1700 Mon–Fri)
Disabled access and facilities
Unprepossessing decor but wonderful fish and chips, including salmon in batter. Babies and toddlers positively welcomed and accommodated in state-of-the-art high-chairs.

Ice-Creams

COLPI'S
38 Main Street, Milngavie, Glasgow
Tel: (041) 956 2040
Open: Daily 0930–2100
A variety of flavours of mouth-watering Italian ice-cream.

FAZZI BROS
64 Cambridge Street, Glasgow
Tel: (041) 332 0941
Open: Mon–Sat 0830–2100, Sun 1100–1900
Delicious Italian ice-cream and aniseed wafers.

Fast Food Chains

BURGER KING
80–84 Argyle Street, Glasgow
and
74 Sauchiehall Street, Glasgow
and
304–306 Sauchiehall Street, Glasgow
and
27/29 Southgate, East Kilbride
and
5A High Street, Paisley

LITTLE CHEF
Cumbernauld
On A80, 10 miles E of Glasgow (N bound)
Tel: (02367) 22507
Baby-changing and disabled facilities
and
Baillieston
7 miles E of Glasgow, 1 mile W of M73 (E bound)
Tel: (041) 771 8710

McDONALD'S
101–105 Sauchiehall Street, Glasgow G2 3DD
Tel: (041) 332 6009
and
165 Trongate, Glasgow

Tel: (041) 552 5830
and
209 – 215 Argyle Street, Glasgow
Tel: (041) 248 3909
and
40 St Enoch Square, Glasgow
Tel: (041) 226 2299
and
11 Queensway, East Kilbride
Tel: (03552) 66336
and
3 Brandon Parade South, Motherwell
Tel: (0698) 76055
and
Unit 6/7 Regional Centre, Clydebank
G81 2UA
Tel: (041) 951 1947/1952

DRIVE-THROUGH McDONALD'S

Forge Shopping Centre, Gallowgate, Parkhead, Glasgow G31 4EB
Tel: (041) 556 4767
and
Pollockshaws Road, Glasgow
Tel: (041) 424 1655
and
Springburn, Glasgow
Tel: (041) 557 1950

OLIVERS COFFEE SHOP AND BAKERY

55 Union Street, Glasgow G1 3RB
Tel: (041) 221 0195
and
28A – 30 High Street, Paisley PA1 2BZ
Tel: (041) 889 0751

THE PANCAKE PLACE

91 Union Street, Glasgow G1 3TA
Tel: (041) 248 2562
and
22/24 Cambridge Street, Glasgow
and
58 – 59 The Plaza, East Kilbride
Delicious hot pancakes with a variety of sweet and savoury fillings.

SPUD-U-LIKE

306 Sauchiehall Street, Glasgow G3 3HL
Tel: (041) 333 9485
and
Olympia Food Court, East Kilbride
Tel: (03552) 45677
Both restaurants serve baked potatoes with a wide range of fillings.

PLACES TO STAY

Caravan and Camping Sites

STRATHCLYDE PARK CARAVANNING AND CAMPING SITE
nr Motherwell
Tel: (0698) 266155
££
A high-quality campsite for touring caravans and tents (no statics). All the amenities of the Country Park are within walking distance – *see* **COUNTRY PARKS.**

Hotels

THE BLACK BULL HOTEL
Main Street, Milngavie, Glasgow G62 6BH
Tel: (041) 956 2291
£££
Only 6 miles from the city centre. Has 2 family rooms with double beds and bunks. Baby listening service.

WICKETS HOTEL
52 Fortrose Street, Glasgow G11 5LP
Tel: (041) 334 9334
£££
Walled garden, family rooms.

LOCH LOMOND, THE TROSSACHS, STIRLING AND PERTHSHIRE

Mountains, wooded glens, beautiful lochs and the more sophisticated pleasures of high-quality leisure centres, modern playgrounds and street theatre are all to be found in this area. Even better – Loch Lomond is only 30 minutes by car from central Glasgow, while Perth and Stirling are about an hour from Edinburgh. This is a real point in its favour as children, especially very young ones, are not keen on travelling. They would much rather forget the scenery and get on with the action – be it water-skiing, canoeing and board sailing on Loch Lomond or at the big watersports centres at Lochearnhead, admiring the big game animals at Blair Drummond Safari Park, or braving the flumes at Perth Leisure Pool.

A guide to Perth for families with pre-school children has been put together by local childminders, while Stirling District Council produces a really useful booklet called *Stirling with Kids*. The Council's attitude towards families and children has been exemplary in recent years. Their range of activities and facilities for handicapped children is particularly impressive and includes holiday playschemes designed to encourage integrated play, and a new play area with access and equipment for wheelchair users at Polmaise Park. The excellent shoppers' creche is threatened with closure, however, which would be a blow to many parents.

Stirling Festival takes place in early August each year and could make a good focal point for a holiday in the area. But make a note of the date of the Glasgow holiday fortnight, better known as the Glasgow Fair, as the Trossachs and Loch Lomond become extremely busy then.

PLACES TO VISIT

Ancient Monuments

CAMBUSKENNETH ABBEY (HS)
Stirling
1 mile E of Stirling off Causewayhead
Road, or on foot from Abbey Road
Open: Apr–Sep, Mon–Sat 0930–1900,
Sun 1400–1900
£

The monastery ruins make a nice backdrop for a picnic. Robert the Bruce held his parliament here in 1326.

INCHMAHOME PRIORY
Access from Port of Menteith nr Aberfoyle
Open: Apr–Sep, Mon–Sat 0930–1900,
Sun 1400–1900
£ for ferry, free entry

The ferry trip on its own would be fun as you have to put up a flag to attract the ferryman. Combine this with the thrill of imagining Mary Queen of Scots being held prisoner here when she was only 5 years old and you've got a great outing.

Animals and Birds

BLAIR DRUMMOND SAFARI AND LEISURE PARK
Blair Drummond nr Stirling FK9 4UR
M9/A84 exit 10 then 4 miles towards
Callander
Tel: (0786) 841456
Open: End Mar–early Oct, 1000–1630
£££
P: Free
Cafeteria
Award-winning disabled facilities
Facilities for nursing mothers

One of the top tourist attractions in Scotland. Drive through wild game reserves and see the collection of Siberian tigers, lions, zebras, camels, monkeys, young elephants etc. Attractions especially for children include the pets' farm, penguin pool and waterfall, performing sealion shows and a boat safari round chimp island. Have some fun on the giant astraglide, splashcats, pedal boats and adventure playground.

DOUNE PONDS
Access from Moray Street, Doune nr Dunblane
Tel: (0786) 79000 x 72153
Disabled access to trails and hide

40-acre nature reserve with walks and bird-watching hide.

THE SCOTTISH WOOL CENTRE
Off Main Street, Aberfoyle
Tel: (08772) 850
Open: All year
££ for sheep show; £ for farm
P: Available
Coffee shop
Disabled facilities
Toilets

Follow the story of Scottish wool from the sheep's back to the final garment. Feed the lambs, watch sheep being sheared, see spinning and weaving. Watch sheepdogs demonstrate their skills. There is a play area and a children's farm too.

BEN LAWERS NATIONAL NATURE RESERVE (NTS)
nr Killin
Bridge of Balgie road off A827, 4 miles
NE of Killin
£

Open: End Mar–Sep, 1000–1700
P: Available

A lovely part of the country but don't go out of your way to visit the reserve as the nature trail on the lower slopes of Ben Lawers is suffering from erosion due to the huge numbers of visitors to the area. Visitor centre.

INCHCAILLOCH NATIONAL NATURE RESERVE
nr Balmaha
Ferry from Balmaha Boatyard
Tel: (0389) 58511

Permits are required to walk the 2-mile nature trail around the wooded island. *See* MACFARLANE & SON – **BOATS AND BOAT TRIPS.**

FAIRWAYS HEAVY HORSE CENTRE
Walnut Grove, Kinfauns by Perth
2 miles E of Perth off A85
Tel: (0738) 32561
Open: Daily, Apr–Sep 1000–1800
£
Disabled facilities

There are 40 brood mares during the summer months, 2 premium stallions and lots of new-born foals. Enjoy a ride on a wagon pulled by a team of Clydesdales. A video show features the heavy horses at work throughout the year and shows the blacksmith shoeing horses.

GLENGOULANDIE DEER PARK
nr Aberfeldy
9 miles from Aberfeldy on B846 to Kinloch Rannoch
Tel: (08873) 261/306
Open: Daily, 0900 to 1 hour before sunset
£ on foot, £3 per car
P: Available
Picnic area

Partial disabled access

Native animals in a natural habitat. Many endangered species are kept and there are also fine herds of red deer and Highland cattle. No dogs.

LOCH OF THE LOWES
nr Dunkeld
Off A923, 2 miles NE of Dunkeld
Tel: (035 02) 337
Open: Daily; visitor centre Apr–Sep
Free
P: Available
Disabled access

The area is managed by the Scottish Wildlife Trust. From the observation hides in the woodland around the loch you can see various waterfowl and ospreys. Visitor centre has wildlife displays and a slide programme.

MONARCH DEER FARM
Naemoor Road, Crook of Devon, nr Kinross
Off A977
Tel: (05774) 310
Open: Daily, dawn–dusk
£
P: Available
Farmhouse teas, picnic area
Disabled facilities
Toilets

See red deer and various rare animals. On the riverside walk to the waterfall you will see waterfowl. Play area.

VANE FARM NATURE RESERVE (RSPB)
nr Kinross
On S shore of Loch Leven on B9097, 1 mile E of Junct 5, M90
Tel: (0577) 62355
Open: Apr–Oct 1000–1700, Nov–Mar 1000–1600
£
P: Free

Picnic and barbecue area, tea-shop
Partial disabled access, disabled facilities
Toilets

Some 15,000 spend overwinter here and there are guided walks round the farms where you might see newly hatched geese or swans. Join in the fun at a botanical barbecue or pretend to be a Red Indian on a family fun day. Use the binoculars and telescopes in the nature centre or test your ornithological knowledge with the interactive displays. There are jigsaws and other activities for young children too. A nature trail winds up through birch woods to the top of Vane Hill.

BUTTERFLY HOUSE AND CHILDREN'S FARM

Kinross KY13 7NQ
Next to services on M90, Junct 6
Tel: (0577) 64739
Open: Easter – Oct 1000 – 1800
££
P: Free
Café, picnic area
Disabled facilities

Butterflies fly round you as you walk through the hothouses. Remember to wear thin clothes as the air is very warm. It is fine for youngsters who have not already seen the wonderful BUTTERFLY FARM at Dalkeith in Edinburgh. There is an aviary and a children's farm too.

FALCONRY CENTRE

Kinross KY13 7NQ
Next to services on M90, Junct 6
Tel: (0577) 862010
Open: Daily 1030 – 1730 (dusk in winter)
££

Get close to birds of prey and watch them flying. Some will even return to land on your arm if you feel brave enough to volunteer to help.

Bike Hire and Cycle Routes

CYCLEWAY FROM CALLANDER TO STRATHYRE

The route is mostly cycletrack though there are some short stretches of very quiet road. A round trip is 9 miles but this can be halved by starting from the carpark at Ben Ledi which is right beside the cycletrack. The Strathyre Inn serves light meals like soup and rolls to boost energy for the return journey.

PEDALERS

Main Street, Killin FK21 8UH
Tel: (0567) 652201
A827
££ per half day

Cycle hire including children's bikes and a child seat.

TROSSACHS CYCLE HIRE

Trossachs Holiday Park by Aberfoyle FK8 3SA
Tel: (08772) 614
£ per day

Large range of bikes for hire from 5-speed to 21-speed. Child seats available. Route planning, maps.

ATHOLL ACTIVITY CYCLES

Folk Museum Park, Blair Atholl
Tel: (0796) 3553
Open: Easter and end May – Oct, daily 0900 – 1800 (Tue 1300 – 1800)
From £ per hour

Children's bikes and adult bikes with baby carriers available. Low season hires. Suggestions for routes given if required.

BCA WATERSPORTS – *see*
WATERSPORTS

Boats and Boat Trips

SS *SIR WALTER SCOTT*
Trossachs Pier, Loch Katrine
Pier at E end Loch Katrine, 9 miles W of Callander
Tel: (041) 355 5333
Open: May – Sep, Mon – Fri 1100, 1345 and 1515; Sat and Sun 1400, 1530
From £
P: Available
Cafeteria
Partial disabled access
Take a short cruise on one of the regular summer sailings from the pier to Stronachlachar. The old steamer was the winner of the Steam Heritage's Premium Prize for 1989. Visitor centre.

MacFARLANE & SON
The Boatyard, Balmaha, Loch Lomond G63 0JG
Tel: (036 087) 214
£ – £££
Open: Summer sailings
Join the mailboat trip in the morning and have coffee or lunch on one of the islands. There are cruises amongst the islands in the afternoons as well as ferry trips on the nature trail on Inchcailleach. Rowing boats and outboard motors may also be hired.

MV *KENILWORTH* CRUISES
Pier, Helensburgh
Tel: (0475) 21281
Open: May – Sep, Mon – Sat cruises from 1040
From ££
Carpark at the pier
Light refreshments
Disabled access at high tide
A 1930s' vintage passenger vessel with a distinctive red funnel. Sailings to Dunoon, Rothesay, Millport and other nearby resorts.

SWEENEY'S CRUISES
Riverside, Balloch Alexandria
Tel: (0389) 52376/51610
Open: All year
££
Boatyard tea-room; also refreshments on board
Cruises on Loch Lomond depart hourly.

Bus Trips

OPEN-TOP BUS
Stirling
Tel: (0786) 79901
Open: Jun – Sep, hourly departures from 1000
£
History is not dull if it is viewed from the upstairs front seat of a vintage 1940s' open-top bus.

Castles and Stately Homes

STIRLING CASTLE (HS)
Stirling
Tel: (0786) 50000
Open: Mon – Sat 0930 – 1715 (1620 Oct – Mar); Sun 1030 – 1645 (1230 – 1535 Oct – Mar)
££ including entry to visitor centre
P: Available
Cafeteria
Partial disabled access
Stirling Castle is built on the top of a 250ft-high rock. Children are impressed by the lifesize people resting in the barrack rooms and building the great hall. The visitor centre on Castle Hill (NTS) has a good video show. One of the top 20 Scottish visitor attractions and winner of a Scottish Tourism Oscar in 1991.

DOUNE CASTLE (HS)
Doune
8 miles S of Callander on A84
Tel: (0786) 841742
Open: Summer, Mon – Sat 0930 – 1900,
Sun 1400 – 1900; Winter, closed
Thu/Fri
£
Disabled access to grounds
Ruined medieval castle with spiral staircase, huge open fireplaces, a portcullis and a well.

CASTLE CAMPBELL AND DOLLAR GLEN (HS)
Dollar
Tel: (031) 244 3101 (HS, Edinburgh)
Open: Castle Apr – Sep daily, Oct – Mar closed Thu afternoon and Fri
£
P: Available
No disabled access to the walk
The castle, which is also known as Castle Gloom, is perched at the top of two burns named Care and Sorrow. There are spectacular walks by both burns as they cascade down narrow ravines. Take great care with young children after heavy rain and in the autumn as the paths, walkways and bridges can be slippery, and you may want to avoid the steeper side altogether.

SCONE PALACE
Perth PH2 6BD
2 miles NE of Perth
Tel: (0738) 52300
Open: Easter – mid Oct, Mon – Sat 0930 – 1700, Sun 1330 – 1700 (Jul/Aug from 1000)
Palace – £££; grounds only – £
P: Available
Restaurants, picnic area
The famous 'Stone of Scone' was brought here in the 9th century by Kenneth McAlpine, King of the Scots.

It was used as a coronation stone until it was stolen in 1296 and taken to Westminster Abbey in London. There is an aventure playground and an historic pinetum with giant sequoias.

LOCH LEVEN CASTLE (HS)
Kinross
Tel: (031) 244 3101 (HS, Edinburgh)
Open: Apr – Sep, Mon – Sat 0930 – 1900,
Sun 1400 – 1900
£
P: Available
No disabled access
The castle stands on an island which is reached by ferry from KIRKGATE PARK – *see* **PARKS AND PLAYGROUNDS**. Mary Queen of Scots was imprisoned here but managed to escape after 11 months.

BLAIR CASTLE
Blair Atholl, nr Pitlochry PH18 5TL
Off A9
Tel: (079 681) 207
Open: End Mar – Oct, Mon – Sat 1000 – 1800, Sun 1400 – 1800 (Apr/May/Oct 1400 – 1600)
£££
P: Free
Picnic areas, restaurant
Disabled facilities and access to ground floor.
The Duke of Atholl is the only person in the UK, apart from the Queen, with his own private army. Look around 32 furnished rooms in the 700-year-old castle. There are extensive parklands with peacocks, Highland cattle, a deer park, nature trails and pony-trekking – *see* **RIDING**.

DUMBARTON ROCK AND CASTLE (HS)
Dumbarton
1 mile SE of town centre

130

Tel: (0389) 32828
Open: Apr – Sep, Mon – Sat 0930 – 1900,
Sun 1400 – 1900,
Oct – Mar closes 1600
£
No disabled access

One of the oldest fortified sites in Britain was built on this great rocky outcrop. The castle which stands there now is linked with the legendary wizard Merlin. Imagine what it might have been like to man the gun emplacements and batteries when the castle was under attack.

Caves

ROB ROY'S CAVE
Inversnaid
Ferry from Inversnaid Hotel, Inveruglas
(Tel: 087786 223) on A82
Free

The famous cattle drover is said to have sheltered in this cave. It is 2 miles N of Inversnaid, and may also be reached from Aberfoyle (14 miles on B829).

Country Parks

GARTMORN DAM COUNTRY PARK AND NATURE RESERVE
by Sauchie, Alloa
2 miles NE of Alloa on A908
Tel: (0259) 214319
Open: All year at all times
P: Free
Picnic areas
Disabled facilities
Toilets

This is the oldest reservoir in Scotland. The dam has made a good winter roost for migrating ducks. Ranger-led walks are arranged through the attractive woodland,

and there is boat and bank fishing. The visitor centre has exhibits and slide shows, touch tables and games.

BALLOCH CASTLE COUNTRY PARK
Alexandria
Off A82, 15 miles NW of Glasgow
Tel: (0389) 58216
Open: Park daily sunrise – sunset; centre Easter – Sep, daily 1000 – 1800
Picnic and barbecue areas
Disabled facilities

A park with 200 acres of woodland and ornamental gardens on shores of Loch Lomond. Self-guided and ranger-led walks.

Farms

KILTYRIE FARM AND WILDLIFE PARK
Killin
Tel: (0567) 820580
Open: End May – Sep, 1000 – 1600; other times by arrangement
Free (donation)
Picnic areas

Youngsters love to help feed and stroke the animals in the children's corner. Special wildlife habitats have been developed for wilder creatures like foxes. Best in early summer when there are baby animals to see.

Festivals

STIRLING FESTIVAL
Stirling
Tel: (0786) 71588 (from mid July)
Open: Early Aug
Free

Family fun wherever you go in Stirling during the festival. Watch out for magic shows, street theatre, fire-eaters, jugglers, Punch and Judy shows, unicyclists, massive balloon release, story time, activity sessions etc. All library events and street theatre are free. Programmes are available at all the libraries.

Fish

SWANS WATER FISHERIES
Sauchieburn, Stirling
Tel: (0786) 814805
£
Spend a peaceful afternoon bank fishing in well-stocked ponds. Don't rely on catching your tea though, just in case you are unlucky!

DRUMMOND FISH FARM
Aberuchill, Comrie, nr Crieff
Tel: (0764) 70500
Open: Daily 1000–2200 (1700 May–Sep)
£ entry includes pellets to feed the fish
P: Available
Picnic area
Feed the fish or hire a rod (££) and try to catch them in the children's fishing pond. You pay extra for any fish you catch.

GLENDEVON FISH FARM
Crook of Devon, Kinross KY13 7UL
Tel: (05771) 840 297
Open: Mid Mar–Christmas, 1000–1800 (2000 in midsummer)
£–££
Restaurant
Disabled fishing
Feed 50,000 trout or catch your supper. Suitable for children and disabled anglers. There is also a commando-style adventure playground with aerial slides over water (so not for under-8s).

GARTMORN DAM – see COUNTRY PARKS

Forest Parks

QUEEN ELIZABETH FOREST PARK
nr Aberfoyle
Off A821, 1 mile N of Aberfoyle
Tel: (08772) 258
Open: Centre mid Mar–mid Oct, daily 1000–1800
P: Available
Picnic areas, cafeteria
Disabled facilities
There are lovely walks along the 3 well-signposted forest trails which begin from the visitor centre (which has exhibitions and an audio-visual show). Look out for brambles and blaeberries in the autumn along the 70 miles of waymarked forest trails. If you don't fancy walking, try hiring a bike and following the cycle trails, or go pony-trekking.

Gardens

UNIVERSITY OF STIRLING
Stirling
Free
Cafeteria
Pleasant walks around Airthrey Castle with its walled gardens, woodland. Don't forget some bread to feed the ducks and swans

MEGGINCH CASTLE GARDENS
nr Perth
A85, 10 miles E of Perth
Tel: (082 12) 222
Open: Apr/Jun/Sep, Wed only 1400–1700; Jul–Aug, Mon–Fri 1400–1700
£
P: Available
Partial disabled access

The gardens around the 15th-century castle have daffodils, rhododendrons and 1000-year-old yew trees. There is a double-walled kitchen garden and a golden yew trimmed in the shape of a crown.

BEATRIX POTTER GARDEN
Birnam
Off A9 between Perth and Pitlochry
Open: Gardens all year, Mon – Sat 1000 – 1200, 1400 – 1600,
Sun 1400 – 1600 (exhibition summer only)

For 12 years during her childhood, Beatrix Potter spent her holidays in Birnam. The area was the inspiration for *The Tale of Peter Rabbit* and the characters of Mrs Tiggywinkle and Mr Jeremy Fisher. Footpaths lead past Mr Tod's and Mrs Tiggywinkle's homes, by the stream and pond where Jeremy Fisher lived and on to Peter Rabbit's burrow.

BELL'S CHERRY BANK GARDENS
Arthur Bell Distillers Office, Glasgow Road, Perth
Tel: (0738) 27330
Open: Daily May – Oct 1100 – 1700
Free
P: Available
Café
Limited disabled access

The beautifully landscaped gardens have a huge range of heathers so there is always something to see in bloom. Good children's play area.

Graveyards and Gruesome Places

STIRLING HERITAGE WALKS
19 Irvine Place, Stirling
Meet at the Castle Hotel
Tel: (0786) 50945/75019

Family Ghost Walk: Jun – Sep, Tue – Sat 1900
£££

Family ghost walk in the early evening.

THE BEHEADING STONE
Gowan Hill, Upper Castlehill, Stirling
Free

It is thought that this stone was used for capital punishment in the 15th century.

Heritage Centres

BANNOCKBURN HERITAGE CENTRE (NTS)
Bannockburn nr Stirling
Tel: (0786) 812664
Open: Site all year; centre end Mar – Oct, daily 1000 – 1800
£
Restaurant

The famous Battle of Bannockburn, where Robert the Bruce defeated the English, took place here. Find out more about it by watching the video and looking round the exhibition. There are explanatory noticeboards around the battlefield. Try your hand at brass rubbing (extra charge).

GREAT SCOTS VISITOR CENTRE
off High Street, Auchterarder
Tel: (0764) 62079
Open: Easter – Jun 1300 – 1700, Jul – Oct Mon – Sat 1000 – 1700,
Sun 1300 – 1700
£
P: Available
Barrs Irn Bru Bar with Irn Bru on draught
Disabled facilities

Go back in time and imagine a world without TV, telephones, penicillin, golf, marmalade and Peter Pan. Find out about the discoveries and inventions of some great Scots in a special show complete with computerised lighting effects. See a remnant of the Industrial Revolution – the last working power loom in Scotland – and watch tartan cloth being made. Don't forget to try Scotland's other national drink, which is supposed to be made from girders.

Indoor Fun

ST JOHN'S CENTRE
Perth
Free
Open: During shopping hours
Cafeteria in BHS

Go on a no-shopping outing with toddlers and have some fun with the mirrors, fountains, unusual lights and automatic doors. Look out for the musical clock.

Monuments

THE WALLACE MONUMENT
Stirling
Leave M9 at junct 10 by Stirling
Tel: (0876) 72140
Open: Feb – Oct, Fri – Tue 1000 – 1800, daily Jul/Aug
£
Tea-room and picnic areas

A gory audio-visual show and William Wallace's huge sword are the main attractions. From the top of the tower there are good views over 7 battlefields. Those with energy left after the climb to the top can walk through the woodland nearby or play in the adventure playground at CAUSEWAYHEAD PARK – *see* PARKS AND PLAYGROUNDS.

Museums

DOUNE MOTOR MUSEUM
Doune FK16 6HD
8 miles NW of Stirling on A84
Tel: (0786) 841203
Open: End Mar – Oct, daily 1000 – 1700
£
P: Free
Self-service cafeteria, picnic areas
Toilets

A collection of vintage and post-vintage cars, including examples of Hispano Suiza, Bentley, Jaguar, Aston Martin, Lagonda, and the second-oldest Rolls Royce in the world. Rallies and motor racing hill climbs in Apr – Sep.

SMITH ART GALLERY AND MUSEUM
Dumbarton Road, Stirling
Tel: (0786) 71917
Open: Apr – Oct, Tue – Sat 1030 – 1700, Sun 1400 – 1700;
Nov – Mar reduced hours
Free
Café (with high-chairs)
Disabled access

Special children's programme includes art exhibitions, workshops and school education service. This is the contact point for Operation Skylark – a summer countryside play-scheme for 8 to 12-year-olds.

THE ROB ROY STORY
Visitor Centre, Ancaster Square, Callander
Tel: (0877) 30342
Open: Daily, Oct – May 1000 – 1700; Jun /Sep 0900 – 1800;
Jul/Aug 0900 – 2200
££
P: Available
Disabled access and facilities

Go back 300 years and rediscover

the daring exploits of Rob Roy MacGregor, Scotland's most colourful folk hero. Visit the multi-vision theatre, listen to Rob Roy's 'talking head' and find out more about his life from the exhibition. One of the most popular tourist attractions in Scotland.

WEAVER'S HOUSE AND HIGHLAND TRYST MUSEUM
64 Burrell Street, Crieff
On A822
Tel: (0764) 5202
Open: Summer 0900 – 1830 daily; winter 1000 – 1630 Mon – Sat
£
P: Available
Coffee shop, tea garden
Disabled facilities
Award-winning museum with a dressing-up chest and Victorian games. In a row of 18th and 19th-century weavers' cottages, visitors can see tartan cloth being woven on handlooms as well as spinners and cordwainers at work. Open-air activities too.

CHILDHOOD HERITAGE CENTRE
Cuil-an-Daraich, Logierait by Pitlochry
A827, 1 mile off A9, 5 miles S of Pitlochry
Open: Tue – Sat 1000 – 1800, Sun 1400 – 1800
£
Dolls, teddies, vintage playthings, a 1930s' nursery and school-room. World War II display.

PERTH MUSEUM
George Street, Perth
Tel: (0738) 32488
Open: Mon – Sat 1000 – 1700
Free
P: Nearby

Disabled access and facilities
An award-winning natural history exhibition – good for whiling away an hour on a rainy afternoon.

DENNY SHIP MODEL EXPERIMENT TANK
Castle Street, Dumbarton G82 1QS
Tel: (0389) 63444
Open: Mon – Sat 1000 – 1600
£
This was a secret establishment until recently. Now you can watch large hulls being tested in the experiment tank which is as long as a football pitch. The process of making wax hulls has remained unchanged for over 100 years. Try designing and testing a boat yourself.

Parks and Playgrounds

BEECHWOOD AND BIKE PARK
Off St Ninians Road, Stirling
Tel: (0786) 79000 x 72155
Disabled facilities
The bike part has a miniature road system with bridges and traffic lights. Bikes for hire. Putting, BMX track, play area and walks.

CAUSEWAYHEAD PARK
Alloa Road, Stirling
At the foot of the Wallace Monument
Disabled facilities
Toilets
New play equipment including aerial cableway, paddling pool.

KINGS PARK
Kings Park Road, Stirling
Disabled facilities
Mother and baby room
Toddler swings, putting green, giant draughts/chess, crazy golf and trampolines. A toddlers' play area

with sand and water is fenced off from dogs. A special 'wheels park' for skateboards, skates and BMX bikes opened recently.

POLMAISE PARK
Polmaise Road, Fallin
P: Available
Disabled access and play facilities
Stirling pays a great deal of attention to the needs of disabled children. The play area, which is designed for integrated play between able-bodied and disabled children, has a giant sandpit with ramps, platforms, slides and bridges. Also a 'teeter-totter', sand tables with sand chutes and pulleys 'springies', aerial runway, maypole swing, tyre swing, conventional swings and multi-unit. Good equipment for older children too.

LAIGHHILLS PARK
Dunblane
Barbecue area
Toilets
A small unique sand play area for young children. Dog-proof fencing in the shape of a ship with entry by way of a net cargo bridge. Sand play, multi-unit climber, whale 'springies', twisted slide, Dutch disc, helter-skelter, swings.

OCHLOCHY PARK
Dunblane
At roundabout, take road to Sheriffmuir as far as golf course
A pleasant place for a short walk with toddlers who enjoy the streams, bridges, ponds and waterfowl.

SOUTH INCH
Perth
Tel: (0738) 39911 x 3603/5
Open: Mon – Sat 1000 – dusk, Sun 1400 – dusk
Ice-cream kiosk in summer
Toilets
A large public park with toddlers' play area as well as a paddling pool, putting, crazy golf, trampolines, boating and tennis. At Lesser South Inch there is a skateboard ramp.

NORTH INCH
Perth
Tel: (0738) 39911 x 3603/5
Open: All year, some facilities summer only
The site of the famous 'Battle of the Clans' which was fought here in 1396. The park borders the River Tay and there is a play area, golf course and putting. Good for buggies and small bikes. Toilets and café at BELL'S SPORTS CENTRE – *see* **SPORT AND LEISURE CENTRES.**

QUARRYMILL WOODLAND PARK
Isla Road, Perth
Tel: (0738) 33890
Open: Park all year; centre summer 0900 – 1700
Barbecue and picnic areas
Disabled facilities and access to almost 2 miles of walks
Toilets
Attractive network of paths through woodland. Ideal for prams and buggies. Visitor centre.

LARGHAN VICTORIA PARK
Coupar Angus
Tel: (0738) 39911 x 3603/5
Open: Mon – Sat 1000 – dusk, Sun 1400 – dusk
Paddling pool, giant draughts, 9-hole pitch and putt, putting, bouncy castle.

MACROSTY PARK
Crieff
Tel: (0738) 39911 x 3603/5
Open: Apr – Sep, Mon – Sat 1000 – dusk,
Sun 1400 – dusk
Large, picturesque park with play areas, paddling pool, giant draughts, putting, tennis, trampolines.

KIRKGATE PARK
Kinross
By the shores of Loch Leven
Crazy golf, putting, trampolines, bouncy castle and giant draughts. The dog-free play area for toddlers and pre-school children is set in fine sand which can blow into their eyes. Boat trips to LOCH LEVEN CASTLE (*see* CASTLES) leave from here.

LEVENGROVE PARK
Dumbarton
Picnic areas by the water
Wooded parkland between the rivers Clyde and Leven with walks, bowling, tennis, trampolines, putting, children's play area, crazy golf.

HERMITAGE PARK
Sinclair Street, Helensburgh
On B832 to Loch Lomond
Tel: (0436) 72513
Tennis, children's play area, putting green.

Playschemes and Creches

SOFT PLAYROOM
Cowane Centre, Cowane Street, Stirling
Tel: (0786) 62367
Open: Tue 1300 – 1700, Thu 1000 – 1200
(other times for pre-booked groups)
£
Coffee, tea and juice, sitting area for parents
Disabled access and facilities

A padded room filled with soft shapes to climb and hide in, build with and roll on. Playpen, baby toys and high-chairs are available.

SHOPPERS' CRECHE
The Arcade, Stirling
Entrance by railway station
Tel: (0786) 65336
Open: Mon – Sat, 1000 – 1730 (1700 in school holidays);
closed 2 weeks in July
£ per hour
Disabled and handicapped children welcome
Go shopping in peace knowing that your children are well looked after in the excellent shoppers' creche. Varied activites including woodwork, dressing up, pets' corner, books, cars, slides and painting (18mths to 12yrs). At time of going to press this excellent creche is threatened with closure – so check whether it still exists before setting off on a shopping trip.

TOWDABOUT
Various venues in Stirling
Tel: (0786) 79000
Open: Summer holidays
A mobile playground for under-7s, with lots of equipment for climbing, hiding, sliding and rocking.

PLAYVAN
Tel: (0786) 79000 x 2084
Open: Summer holidays
A mobile play van with supervised play sessions for under-12s, visiting rural locations. Wet weather provision.

SUPERBUS
Various venues
Tel: (0786) 79000
Open: Summer holidays, Christmas

Organised activities in summer including art and crafts (5 to 12-year-olds). Christmas activities (under-6s). Sandpit, computer, books, art and craft materials, toys and an inflatable. May be booked for galas etc.

Railways

THE HEATHER CENTRE AND MINIATURE RAILWAY
Keltie Bridge, Callander
On A84
Tel: (0877) 31188
Open: Daily 1000 – 1800
£
P: Free
Coffee shop
Miniature railway carries children and adults round the grounds. There is an adventure play area with a rustic climbing frame, logs to balance on, wigwams and a sandpit. Aquarium.

Riding

STRATHEARN STABLES
Crieff Hydro, Crieff
In grounds of hotel
Tel: (0764) 2401 x 431
From £
One-hour rides and lessons. Advance bookings advisable. Donkey rides for tiny children for a small charge.

BORELAND RIDING CENTRE
Fearnan by Aberfeldy PH15 2PG
Tel: (08873) 212
£
BHS approved. Novice treks and lessons with horses and ponies for all ages and abilities.

BLAIR CASTLE TREKKING CENTRE
Blair Atholl, Pitlochry PH18 5SR
Tel: (079 681) 263
From £
Hourly rides for experienced children aged 9 and upwards. There is no road work as all riding is in the countryside. Hats for hire. STRA approved.

TULLOCHVILLE TREKKING CENTRE
Tullochville Farm, Coshieville by Aberfeldy PH15 2LE
Tel: (0887) 830559
£
Instruction, trekking, hacking. First-time riders welcome. STRA approved.

GLENISLA PONY TREKKING CENTRE
Glenisla Hotel by Alyth
Tel: (057582) 333
Open: Daily, Apr – Oct
££
Full-day and half-day treks; barbecue treks. Novices welcome.

STRATHARDLE PONY-TREKKING CENTRE
Mrs Todd, Ballintium Post Office by Blairgowrie
10 miles N of Blairgowrie
Tel: (025086) 201
Open: All year
££ per half day
Lessons, children's fun day with lunch and tea.

Science and Technology

PITLOCHRY POWER STATION AND DAM
Pitlochry
Off A9 at Pitlochry

Open: Late Mar – Oct, daily 0940 – 1730
£
P: Available
Disabled access
Toilets
Watch salmon leaping up the fish ladder (free). This is one of 9 hydro stations in the Tummel Valley. The dam created Loch Faskally where boating and fishing are available. You can visit the turbine hall and try the interactive displays on hydro-electricity in the exhibition centre.

Scotland at Work – Past and Present

CLOCK MILL
Upper Street, Tillicoultry
Tel: (0259) 52176
Open: Apr – Sep, daily 1000 – 1700
Free
An exhibition of old spinning wheels and looms in a restored water-mill. Even very young children find the 5-minute video interesting. There are also craftspeople busy machine knitting, weaving and silk screen printing. The mill is part of the Mill Heritage Trail.

CAITHNESS GLASSWORKS
Dunkeld Road, Inveralmond, Perth PH1 3TZ
Tel: (0738) 37373
Open: Mon – Fri 0900 – 1630
Free
P: Available
Cafeteria
Disabled access and facilities
Toilets
Children can watch glass being blown from behind a window in the viewing gallery. The tools and techniques of glass-making have remained unchanged for centuries.

CRIEFF VISITOR CENTRE
Muthill, Crieff
Tel: (0764) 4014
Free
Open: Daily Apr – Sep 0900 – 1800, Oct – Mar 0900 – 1700
P: Available
Restaurant (Taste of Scotland approved)
Disabled facilities and access
Watch craftsmen making French-style *mille-fiori* paperweights. You can also see potters at work.

MEAL AND FLOUR MILL
Blair Atholl Village
Off A9
Tel: (0796) 481321
Open: Apr – Oct, Mon – Sat 1000 – 1800, Sun 1200 – 1800
P: Available
£
Tea-room
Disabled facilities
Built in 1613, the water-mill produces 80 tonnes of oatmeal a year as well as flour which is sold to shops and used in the mill bakery.

LOWER CITY MILLS/THE OLD GRANARY (NTS)
West Mill Street, Perth PH1 5QP
Signposted from inner ring-road
Tel: (0738) 30572
Open: End Mar – Oct, Mon – Sat 1000 – 1700;
Nov – Mar, Tue – Sat, 1000 – 1600
£
P: Available
Tea-room
Disabled facilities and partial access
Toilets
An award-winning Victorian town water-mill, restored to full working order, produces flour and oatmeal

in the traditional manner. Oatmeal from the mill was once used to make porridge for the inmates of prisons all over Britain. The exhibition room covers 900 years of milling history. Educational visits welcome. Under threat of closure, so check before setting off on a visit.

ABERFELDY WATER MILL
Mill Street, Aberfeldy
Tel: (0887) 20803
Open: End Mar – Oct, Mon – Thu, Sat 1000 – 1730, Sun 1200 – 1730
£
Tea-room
Taste the oatmeal produced in this restored water-mill. Oats were once the staple diet of the Scottish Highlanders who were renowned for their size and fitness. Audio-visual show.

PORRIDGE PRESS PRINTERS
The Auld Police Hoose, Strathcluanie, Dunkeld Road, Bankfoot nr Perth
Tel: (0738) 87225
Open: Mon – Fri 1000 – 1800 (advance notice please)
Free
P: Available
See a letterpress printing machine producing cards, pictures and stationery.

GORDON & DURWARD
14 West High Street, Crieff
Open: Normal shop hours
Free
A wonderful sweet shop filled with different flavours of tablet, fudges and sugar mice. There is a window looking into the production area and, if you are lucky, you might see a batch of mice being made. A mouth-watering experience.

Sport and Leisure Centres

ANNFIELD LEISURE STADIUM
Stirling
Tel: (0786) 79000
From £
Football, jockey (junior hockey). Also summer programme (over-8s): football, volleyball, netball, handball, hockey, rounders, short tennis, bowls, quick cricket, American football, baseball (Tel: 0786 50982).

ICE-RINK
Williamfield, Stirling FK7 9HQ
Tel: (0786) 50389
Open: Aug – Apr, Sat 1230 – 2200, Sun 1000 – 1700
££
Cafeteria
Don't worry about the cold – you'll get hot and bothered trying to keep your balance. Skate hire.

HOLLYWOOD BOWL
22 Forth Street, Riverside, Stirling
Tel: (0786) 63915
Open: 1000 – 2400
From ££
With 28-lane 10-pin bowling and children's play area.

THE LEISURE BOWL
Park Way, Alloa
Tel: (0259) 723527
Open: Daily Mon – Fri 0900 – 1500, 1800 – 2045 (closed Thu eve), Sat – Sun closes 1645
£
Café
Disabled access and facilities
Leisure pool with flume. Fun sessions during the summer and swimming lessons all year round. Ballet classes and snooker (children can play during the day but must be accompanied by an adult). A playscheme

and creche operate during the summer.

CLACKMANNAN ROAD SPORTS CENTRE
Alloa
Tel: (0259) 213131
Open: Mon–Thu 1000–2200, Fri 1000–2100, Sat–Sun 1000–1800
£
Badminton (over-8s), boxing, football training, roller disco and gymnastics. All sorts of parties can be arranged.

DUMYAT LEISURE CENTRE
Menstrie
Tel: (0259) 213131
£
Special events include a Witches and Warlocks week with a bouncy red dragon, treacle scone contest and ducking for apples. The dragon can also heat up a birthday party. Judo (over-8s), table-tennis (over-8s).

SPIERS CENTRE
29 Primrose Street, Alloa
Tel: (0259) 213131
£
Soft room, gymnastic classes (for toddlers upwards and including classes for the disabled), badminton, short tennis, song and dance classes (over-3s). Special events include the chance to make Christmas presents at the 'Chocolate Factory'. Gymnastics, karaoke parties.

ABERFELDY RECREATION CENTRE
Crieff Road, Aberfeldy
Tel: (0887) 820922
Open: All year, daily from 0930 (swimming usually starts later)
£
Cafeteria
Splash around in the 25m swimming pool or improve your swimming skills with a series of lessons. The toddlers' pool has a slide. Sports available include squash, snooker, table-tennis, gymnastics and karate.

ATHOLL LEISURE CENTRE
West Moulin Road, Pitlochry PH16 5EA
Tel: (0796) 3866
Open: Daily, 1000–2200
£
Badminton, basketball, baby bounce sessions in soft play area, 5-a-side football, junior soccer, karate, roller-skating, table-tennis, trampolining. Special holiday activities include competitions, treasure hunts, balloon races and talent contests. Saturday morning club for 5 to 8-year-olds with a bouncy monster, games and stories. Birthday parties can be arranged.

DEWAR'S RINKS
Glasgow Road, Perth
by the Leisure Pool
Tel: (0738) 24188
Open: Daily, 1000–1800 (2230 Jul–Aug)
££
P: Available
Restaurant
Cool off during the summer with a session at the ice-rink. Skating is also available on alternate weekends in winter.

GANNOCHY TRUST SPORTS COMPLEX/BELL'S SPORT CENTRE
Hay Street, Perth PH1 5HS
Tel: (0738) 22301
Open: All year, Mon–Fri 0900–2300, Sat–Sun 0900–2200
From £
Cafeteria
Kindergym, badminton, short tennis,

tennis, table-tennis, 5-a-side football, volleyball, basketball, netball, squash. Holiday activity classes for children.

MEADOW SPORTS CENTRE
Meadow Road, Dumbarton G82 2AA
Tel: (0389) 34094
Open: Daily 0900 – 2300
From £
Cafeteria
Disabled access and facilities
Leisure pool with aqua slide and a machine which can make 6 different kinds of waves. Sports on offer include 5-a-side football, trampolining, badminton, basketball, indoor hockey, gymnastics and majorettes. Creche.

Swimming

RAINBOW SLIDES LEISURE CENTRE
Goosecroft Road, Stirling
Tel: (0786) 62521
Open: Daily from 0900
£
Café
Disabled facilities and access
Spacious pool, toddlers' pool, waterslides filled with lighting and sound effects. Swimming lessons for pre-school and older children. Fun sessions for 6 to 12-year-olds with inflatables and water games. Mother and toddler sessions. Free creche. Arion Swimming Club for the Disabled has assisted swimming sessions (Tel: 0786 813224).

LOCH LEVEN LEISURE CENTRE
Lathro, Milnathort, Kinross KY13 7SY
Tel: (0577) 863368
Open: Daily 1000 – 2200

Café
£
Disabled access and facilities
A brand new pool with a unique moving floor which allows the depth of the pool to be adjusted for disabled access, sub aqua, diving and so on. There are family changing cubicles with baby facilities, and playpens around the poolside.

PERTH LEISURE POOL
Glasgow Road, Perth PH2 0HZ
Tel: (0738) 3053
Open: Daily, all year
£
P: Available
Café
A very popular (and often crowded) leisure pool with giant flumes, a long stretch of wild water, bubble beds and an outdoor lagoon. Mother and toddler sessions take place in the shallow children's pool which has a slide. Children's parties, complete with water toys, can be held in the small teaching pool when it is not being used for lessons, water polo or canoeing.

MEADOW SPORTS CENTRE, THE LEISURE BOWL and ABERFELDY RECREATION CENTRE – *see* SPORT AND LEISURE CENTRES.

Theatres and Cinemas

THE MACBOB CENTRE
MacRobert Arts Centre, University, Stirling
Tel: (0786) 61081
Open: Some Sats, 1430
Puppetry, magic and film shows for children. Phone for details.

ROYAL STIRLING PLAYERS
Details of locations from TIC,
Dumbarton Road
Tel: (0786) 75019
Performances: Jun—Sep
Free
P: Available
The town's rich and ancient heritage is brought to life by actors dressed as colourful characters from Stirling's royal past.

YOUTH THEATRE WORKSHOPS
Glebe Hall, Mar Street, Alloa
Tel: (0259) 213131
Learn some theatre skills — anything from slapstick and singing to makeup and mime (over-12s)

PITLOCHRY FESTIVAL THEATRE
Pitlochry PH16 5DR
Tel: (0796) 2680
Phone for details of summer shows specifically for children aged 3 to 10.

PERTH THEATRE
High Street, Perth
Tel: (0738) 21031
Coffee bar, restaurant open during the day as well as during performances
Variety of children's shows and pantos throughout the year.

Walks

TOWN WALL AND BACK WALK
Stirling
Access from Corn Exchange, Upper Castlehill and Castle Esplanade
Suitable for pushchairs
Walk round the best surviving town wall in Scotland, some of it from 1547, with other parts dating from the 18th century.

WEST HIGHLAND WAY
Rowardennan, Loch Lomond
Off B837 on E side of loch
Waymarked woodland and lochside walk following the West Highland Way.

BALMAHA TRAIL
Balmaha Pier, Balmaha
B837
P: Available
Option of steep walk to viewpoint (1.5 miles) or stroll along lower forest slopes (1.75 miles).

THE PINEAPPLE (NTS)
Dunmore, Airth nr Stirling
7 miles E of Stirling
Open: Daily 1000—sunset
Picnic area
A strange 18th-century folly shaped like a pineapple. Woodland walks and a large walled garden.

DOLLAR GLEN — *see* CASTLES
(CASTLE CAMPBELL)

SILVER GLEN
nr Alva nr Alloa
1 mile E of Alva on A91
P: Available
Attractive walk up wooded glen once famous for its silver mine. Start from the Ochil Hills Woodland Park.

GLEN LEDNOCK CIRCULAR WALK
Crieff
No disabled access
Descriptive leaflet available from Tourist Information Centre
A 4-mile walk through woodland in a beautiful glen to the foaming Devil's Cauldron.

THE KNOCK
Knock Hill, Crieff

Open: All year
P: Available
A popular walk up the hill near Crieff Hydro.

BIRKS O' FELDY
Aberfeldy
From centre of Aberfeldy, or A826 Crieff Road
P: Available
Picnic area
Paths and nature trails through beautiful wooded den with views of the Moness Falls.

BUCKIE BRAE
Craigie Hill Golf Course, Low Road, Perth
Off Glasgow Road
Pleasant walk for active children — too steep for buggies and prams.

RIVER ERICHT
Wellmeadow, Blairgowrie
Picnic area
The path runs along the wooded west bank of the River Ericht to an impressive rocky gorge.

TUMMEL FOREST
nr Pitlochry
B8019 from Pitlochry to Kinloch Rannoch
P: Available
Picnic areas
Three marked walks through Forestry Commission plantation round the loch or uphill. Toilets.

KINLOCH RANNOCH
P: Available
B8109 to Kinloch Rannoch, walk starts at Allt Mor Crescent
A 3-mile walk follows the bank of the River Tummel then on to the hillside. Return by the same route or follow the road. Toilets.

RANNOCH FOREST
nr Kinloch Rannoch

B8019 to Kinloch Rannoch, right on to B846 for 3 miles, park after Carie
P: Available
Picnic area
Three waymarked paths through mixed woodland.

THE HERMITAGE (NTS)
nr Dunkeld
Off A9, 2 miles W of Dunkeld
Tel: (0796) 473233
Open: All reasonable times
There is a picturesque folly set above the wooded gorge of the River Braan. Nature trails lead to the waterfall and rapids.

PASS OF KILLIECRANKIE (NTS)
nr Pitlochry
Off A9, 3 miles N of Pitlochry
Tel: (0796) 473233
Open: Site daily; centre Apr – Oct, daily 1000 – 1700
Free, £ for centre
P: Available
Snack bar
Disabled facilities
A famous wooded gorge where in 1689 the Government troops were routed by Jacobite forces led by 'Bonnie Dundee'. The visitor centre features the battle, and natural history. The Pass is on the network of Garry – Tummel walks, which extend for 20 miles in the area. Toilet, baby-changing facilities.

KINNOULL HILL WOODLAND PARK
Perth
P: Available
Picnic areas
Disabled access and facilities at Jubilee Carpark
Toilets
Mixed woodland (brambles in the autumn) high above the Carse of

Gowrie. Signposted walks, including a children's nature walk, bridle way, cycling (in Deuchny Wood), orienteering.

RIVER LEVEN TOWPATH
Dumbarton
Tel: (0389) 58216
Wheelchair access at Howgate Lane, 1 mile N of Dumbarton
The towpath was used until the end of last century by horses who pulled flat-bottomed boats upriver to the loch. Follow their footsteps and walk along towpath from the River Leven to Loch Lomond.

Watersports

BCA WATERSPORT
Clachan Cottage Hotel, Lochearnhead
Tel: (05673) 367
Various charges
Boat hire, water-skiing, windsurfing, canoeing, sailing and mountain bikes for hire.

LOCHEARNHEAD WATER SPORTS CENTRE
Lochearnhead
On A85 to Crieff
Tel: (05673) 330
Open: Apr/May and Sep/Oct, Mon-Sat from 0930; Jun-Aug, daily
Various charges
Restaurant
A modern centre specialising in dinghy sailing, board sailing, kayaking and water-skiing (from ££ for 15 mins). Lessons are available. Hire a 3-seater Canadian canoe for family fun. Young teenagers enjoy jet-biking.

LOCHDOCHART WATERSPORTS
Lochdochart Estate, Crianlarich FK20 8QS
Tel: (08383) 315
Open: Easter – Oct 0800 – 2000
Various charges
Canadian canoe hire and instruction. Guided flat water trips to islands and ruined castle. Picnics can be arranged.

DUCK BAY
Loch Lomond nr Balloch
Off A82, 2 miles N of Balloch
Various charges
Picnic area
Toilets
Boat trips, watersports, play area.

LOCHEARN SAILING AND WATERSPORTS CENTRE
South Shore Road, St Fillans
Tel: (0764) 2292/85257
Open: Jun – Sep, daily 1000 – 1700
Various charges
Sailing, sailboarding canoeing, water-skiing, RYA approved courses. Junior residential courses (9 to 17-year-olds).

LOCH TAY BOATING CENTRE
Pier Road, Kenmore
Tel: (08873) 291
Open: Late Mar – Oct, 0900 – 1900
Various charges
Boat-launching facilities, water-skiing, canoes, mountain bikes.

LOCH LOMOND WATER-SKI CLUB
North Hall Cottage, Church Road, Luss G83
Tel: (043686) 632
Open: Easter – Sep, weekends and Glasgow Bank Holidays
From ££

Tuition at all levels, some small wet suits for over-7s.

Waterfalls

'POTS' OF GARTNESS
nr Killearn
A cauldron waterfall on the River Endrick which is most impressive in spring and autumn when the salmon are leaping and the water levels are high.

FALLS OF LENY
Callander
2 miles N of Callander on A84
Crashing waters between rocks in the narrow Pass of Leny.

BRACKLINN FALLS
Bracklinn Road, Callander
E end of Callander
P: Available
Wooded gorge with stepped falls.

ALVA GLEN
nr Alloa

Pleasant walk up steep-sided glen to the 70ft Craighorn Fall and the Big Fall, a hidden waterfall which pours into the Smuggler's Cave.

MILL GLEN
Tillicoultry
Off A91

Nature trail and walk to the upper part of glen where there are 8 waterfalls close together.

FALLS OF BRUAR
nr Blair Atholl
Off A9, 8 miles from Pitlochry
P: Available
Picnic area
Toilets

Signposted walk around a picturesque gorge to the falls. Take care on sections of the path running along steep cliffs.

RUMBLING BRIDGE
4 miles E of Dollar, off A823 at Rumbling Bridge
Open: All reasonable times
P: Available
Partial disabled access

A footpath from the north side (by hotel) gives good access on paths, walkways and bridges to viewpoints overlooking the spectacular gorges and falls.

Winter Sports

FIRPARK SKI CENTRE
Alva Academy, Firpark Annexe,
Tillicoultry
Tel: (0786) 816205
Open: All year
From £

Recreational skiing for those who are able to perform snowplough turns and control their speed. Lessons for beginners (over-9s), and experienced skiers. Membership fee.

PLACES TO EAT

Hotels and Restaurants

BAGHDAD RESTAURANT
16 – 18 Barnton Street, Stirling
Tel: (0786) 72137/64019
A wonderful Indian restaurant. Go on Wednesday evenings for the banquet where you eat all you can for a set price (children half price). There is also a children's menu available. Will heat up baby food. Birthday cakes can be provided if notified beforehand.

BAIGLIE INN
Aberargie, nr Perth
Tel: (073 885) 332
Main courses for children start at under £2. They can choose from the main bar menu or the children's menu. A high-chair is available.

BEIN INN
Glenfarg nr Perth
Tel: (05773) 216
Children can choose small portions off the main menu, or, if they prefer, they can have something off their own menu. Bar lunches and suppers start at under £5 for a main course, while a child's meal costs under £3 including a drink and a dessert.

BRIDGEND HOUSE HOTEL
Bridgend, Callander FK17 8AH
Tel: (0877) 30130
200yds from main street
Children are welcome and there is a garden for them to play in. Bar lunches (1200 – 1400) and bar suppers (1800 – 2100). Recommended in the Taste of Scotland guide.

CROFTBANK
30 Station Road, Kinross
Tel: (0577) 63819
Quite a formal setting for a special lunch or dinner with young teenagers.

FARLEYER HOUSE BISTRO
Aberfeldy PH15 2JE
Tel: (0887) 780332
Freshly prepared meals, home-made bread and ice-creams. Children can have small portions off the blackboard menu, while toddlers can have a boiled egg and toast soldiers. Special children's party meals can be arranged.

THE GRILL
South Street, Perth
No charge for food eaten by under-5s. Good size portions that you can share.

INVERALLAN LODGE HOTEL
116 Henderson Street, Bridge of Allan
Tel: (0786) 832791
Children can have small portions off the main menu or choose from the children's menu. A high-chair is available.

KILLIECRANKIE HOTEL
Killiecrankie PH16 5LG
Tel: (0796) 473220
Good bar meals from about £5. Children's menu available.

LITTLEJOHN'S
52 Port Street, Stirling
Tel: (0786) 63222
and
65 South Methven Street, Perth PH1 5NY
Tel: (0738) 39888

High-chairs. Children's menu, small portions or extra plates provided as required. Very busy at peak times. Lots of interesting memorabilia from the 1960s to keep children amused while they are waiting to eat.

LOCHEARNHEAD HOTEL
Lochearnhead FK19 8HP
On A84 at W end of Loch Earn
Tel: (056 73) 226
Open: Mar—Nov—bar meals 1100—2130
Children are made very welcome and can choose from a special menu. Recommended in the Taste of Scotland guide.

THE MUIRS INN
49 Muirs, Kinross
Tel: (0577) 62270
Bar lunches in the beer garden. High teas served from 1700—1800.

PACO'S RESTAURANT
16 St John's Place, Perth PH1 5SZ
Opposite City Hall
Tel: (0738) 22290
For £2.50 children have a choice of 5 main courses as well as an ice-cream and a drink. Baby-changing facilities

PIRNHALL INN
Bannockburn, nr Stirling
Tel: (0786) 811256/815373
Play area outside but close to a busy motorway roundabout.

THE SILVER TASSIE
Toby Restaurant, Causewayhead Road, Stirling
Very good with children.

TAJ MAHAL
39 King Street, Stirling
Disabled facilities

Children can have half-portions of mild dishes on the main menu. Very helpful and friendly staff.

Quick Meals and Snacks

ALTAMOUNT HOUSE HOTEL
Coupar Angus Road, Blairgowrie
Tel: (0250) 3512
Have tea by the lawn and the fun parlour.

AUCHTERARDER HOUSE
Auchterarder PH3 1DZ
Tel: (0764) 63646
Have a Victorian tea in the Winter Garden.

BALLINLUIG CAFÉ
Motorgrill, Ballinluig
Tel: (0796) 4782212
Inexpensive food in plentiful quantities.

BRAMBLES COFFEE SHOP
11 Princes Street, Perth PH2 8NG
Tel: (0738) 39091
Open 0745—1700
Delicious home-baking all day. Lunches and light meals (with small portions for children) from 1200 till 1445.

CAFÉ NOUVEAU
17 Barnton Street, Stirling
Friendly staff heat up baby food and are happy to provide extra plates for sharing a meal if a child's portion is too much. Lovely home-baking.

CASTLE TEAROOM
Stirling Castle, Stirling
Good selection of things for a snacky lunch—filled rolls, baked potatoes, home-baked tarts.

DEBENHAM'S
Thistle Centre, Stirling
High-chairs, children's menu. Will bring hot water so you can heat up baby food.

THE GRANARY COFFEE ROOM
Drummond Street, Comrie PH6 2DW
Tel: (0764) 6570838
Delicious home-baking and light meals.

MILL POND COFFEE SHOP
Burnside Apartments, 19 West Moulin Road, Pitlochry PH16 5EA
300 yds N of junct of A924 and Atholl Road
Tel: (0796) 2203
Open: Apr – Oct, 1000 – 1900
Recommended in the Taste of Scotland guide.

THE OLD GRANARY
Lower City Mills, West Mill Street, Perth
Tel: (0738) 30572
Phone to check opening hours. See
SCOTLAND AT WORK.

POWMILL COFFEE BAR
nr Kinross
Self-service coffee bar with really good food ranging from snacks and home-baking to soups, baked potatoes and salads.

SARAH'S
Thistle Centre, Stirling
High-chairs, children's menu or small portions.

TIMOTHY'S
24 St John Street, Perth PH1 5SP
Tel: (0738) 26641
Open: All day, Tue – Sat
Disabled access
Café-bistro serving Danish-style open sandwiches. Lunch menu available 1200 – 1430. Children's helpings.

TULLYBANNOCHER FARM FOOD BAR
Comrie PH6 2JY
Just outside village on A85
Tel: (0764) 70827
Open: Mar – Oct from 0930 – 1900
Tables on the lawn in good weather. Taste of Scotland recommended.

THE TEA ROOM
Brig o' Turk, nr Callander
Open: April – early Oct
A very convenient and inexpensive place to refuel hungry cyclists tackling the cycleway from Callander to Strathyre (*see* **BIKE HIRE & CYCLE ROUTES**). Excellent meals, snacks and home-baking.

THE AN CARRAIG COFFEE SHOP
Strathyre, nr Callander
Open: April – Oct
Traditional Scottish tea-room with tempting home-made gateaux. Also soup, toasties and baked potatoes.

THE LADE INN
Invertrossachs Road, Kilmahog, Callander
Tel: (0877) 30152
Varied selection of moderately priced food including a children's selection. Children can eat in the bar too. Garden area for playing. Large toilets for changing babies.

THE RIVERWAY RESTAURANT
Kildean, Stirling
Tel: (0786) 75734
Traditional high teas with lots of toast, scones and cakes to follow.

Ice-Creams

ORLANDI & SON
Park View, Alloa
Tel: (0259) 723759
Open: Thu – Tue, 0830 – 2130
Award-winning ice-cream to take away or eat on the premises. The flavours include liquorice and bubble-gum!

Fish and Chips

THE ALLAN WATER CAFÉ
15 Henderson Street, Bridge of Allan
Tel: (0786) 83360
Award-winning fish and chips and home-made ice-cream.

COMRIE FISH AND CHIPS
Main Street, Comrie
Great chips and ample portions of good hot food with added extras like onion rings and mushrooms in batter.

FISH AND CHIPS
Main Street, Dunkeld
Tasty food for a quick meal.

Fast Food Chains

BURGER KING
125 Port Street, Stirling

LITTLE CHEF
Balhaldie (South bound)
4 miles N of Dunblane
Tel: (0786) 822065
and
Balhaldie (North bound)
Tel: (0786) 822040
and
Killiecrankie
3 miles N of Pitlochry just off A9
Tel: (0796) 2169
and

Milton, Dumbarton
8 miles W of Glasgow on A82
Tel: (0389) 67520

McDONALD'S
52 – 54 Murray Place, Stirling
Tel: (0786) 51529
and
St James Retail Park, Glasgow Road, Dumbarton
Tel: (0389) 42500

DRIVE-THROUGH McDONALD'S
Dunkeld Road, Perth
Tel: (0738) 22722

OLIVER'S COFFEE SHOP AND BAKERY
29 Port Street, Stirling FK8 2EW
Tel: (0786) 70394

PANCAKE PLACE
22 Kind Edward Street, Perth
and
58 Thistle Centre, Stirling

PIZZALAND
Port Street, Stirling
High-chairs, children's menu and children's parties.

Bakeries

MacINTYRE'S
2 Main Street, Perth
Tel: (0738) 26962
Traditional Scottish baking, Danish pastries, muffins and scones, and the ever-popular iced buns sprinkled with coconut.

PROUDFOOT'S
55 Main Street, Perth
Tel: (0738) 23862
Mostly traditional baking, but children love the carrot cake as well.

PLACES TO STAY

Hostels

Facilities at all these hostels are Grade 1 and include family rooms, hot water, and heating in winter.

SYHA – ARDGARTEN
Arrochar G83 7AR
Tel: (03012) 362
Family rooms available outside July/August. Hill walking, pony-trekking, cycling and river and sea fishing in the area.

SYHA – CRIANLARICH
Crianlarich FK20 8QN
Tel: (08383) 260
Book in advance to be sure of a family room. Very close to bus and train stations. Good hill walking area.

SYHA – LOCH LOMOND
Rowardennan, by Drymen, Glasgow G63 0AR
Tel: (036087) 259
There is a beach in front of the hostel. Good area for canoeing and windsurfing. Fishing permits available. Busy during Glasgow holidays.

SYHA – PERTH
107 Glasgow Road, Perth PH2 0NS
Tel: (0738) 23658
Book in advance to be sure of a family room if your children are over 5. Families with babies and toddlers can stay in the cottage – sitting/dining-room, kitchenette, bathroom, 2 bedrooms with accommodation for 5.

SYHA – PITLOCHRY
Braeknowe, Knockard Road, Pitlochry PH16 5HJ
Tel: (0796) 472 308

Good area for cycling, walking and fishing. The hostel is a few minutes from the bus and railway station.

SYHA – STIRLING
St John Street, Stirling FK8 1DU
Tel: (0786) 73442
Close to bus and railway station. Pony-trekking, hill walking, cycle hire and fishing all available locally.

Caravan and Camping Sites

BLAIR CASTLE CARAVAN PARK
Blair Atholl PH18 5SR
Tel: (079681) 263
££
Large, attractive site with a play area and lots of space for ball games. The village was used for filming the TV series *Strathblair*.

CASHEL CARAVAN AND CAMPING SITE
3 miles NW of Balmaha on B837
Open: mid Apr – Sep
££
A Forestry Commission site on the shore of Loch Lomond. Play area and walks along the West Highland Way.

COBELAND CAMPSITE
Aberfoyle
Tel: (08772) 383
Off A81, 2 miles S of Aberfoyle turn off on to unclassified road
£££
Wooded Forestry Commission campsite by the River Forth with short walks along the riverbank and

slow-moving shallow water to play in. Bikes for hire.

ERIGMORE HOLIDAY PARK
Birnam, by Dunkeld PH8 9XX
Tel: (03502) 236
Open: mid Mar – Oct
From ££ – £££
An attractive site by the waterside.

KENMORE CARAVAN AND CAMPING PARK
Kenmore, Aberfeldy
Tel: (08873) 226
£
Attractive site with a good play area and games room.

KILVRECHT CARAVAN AND CAMPING SITE
Loch Rannoch
3.5 miles along the S side of Loch Rannoch
Tel: (08822) 335
£
Forestry Commission site near the loch side. Usually quiet enough for children to ride bikes near the tents and caravans. Child-length woodland walks and play area.

TROSSACHS HOLIDAY PARK
Aberfoyle FK8 3SA
Tel: (08772) 614
S of Aberfoyle on A81
£
An attractive site with games room, play area, bikes for hire. Cots may be hired. Satellite TV hookup for early in the season when the nights are long.

SCONE PALACE HOLIDAY CARAVANS
Scone Palace, by Perth PH2 6BD
Tel: (0738) 52308
££

Nice wooded site with good play areas.

Hotels

ATHOLL PALACE HOTEL
Pitlochry PH16 5LY
Tel: (0796) 472400
£££
Family rooms. Children sharing with parents stay free and meals are free for under-5s. Baby listening service. The well-equipped playroom has toys and games for toddlers, a pool table and table-tennis. There is an outdoor swimming pool, tennis courts, putting and nature trail in the grounds and mountain bikes may be hired.

COVENANTERS INN
Aberfoyle
Tel: (08772) 347
£££
Has 4 family rooms, a library with children's games and a pool table, and a baby listening service. Under-4s stay free. Woodlands around the hotel.

CRIEFF HYDRO
Crieff
Tel: (07640) 2401
£££
A holiday resort in its own right and excellent for family weekends. Plenty of entertainment in the hotel and its grounds including cinema, indoor and outdoor play areas, paddling pool, swimming pool, tennis courts, nature trail and riding (*see* **RIDING**). The restaurants cater for different styles of eating, children can be looked after by staff while you eat and there is a baby listening service.

LOCH RANNOCH HOTEL
Kinlochrannoch PH16 5PS
Tel: (08822) 201
£££
There is an indoor pool and games room. Dry ski slope, squash, pottery, cycle hire, playground, nature trail. Self-catering lodges or hotel rooms with reduced rates for children.

ROSSLEA HALL HOTEL
Rhu, nr Dumbarton G84 8NF
Tel: (0436) 820684
£££
Family rooms. Babysitting service available with registered child-minders.

TRAVELODGE
Milton, Dumbarton
Economy room with sleeping accommodation for up to 5. Own bathroom; tea-making facilities. Part of the Little Chef group and right by the A82, W of Glasgow.

FIFE, DUNDEE AND ANGUS

From Edinburgh it is worth travelling north to Fife just to see the wonderful road and rail bridges which span the River Forth. But once you are there you should take the time to investigate the area a little more. The East Neuk is very picturesque but until recently, west Fife was a major mining area and much of the countryside still bears the scars. The area is rapidly becoming more attractive, particularly with the development at North Queensferry of the world's largest sealife aquarium. A few miles further north is Dunfermline which now boasts a brand new national water-skiing centre, and a fine heritage centre scheduled to open later this year. The most attractive route to the East Neuk is via Falkland Palace and the adventure playground at Cupar Deer Farm.

St Andrews is the world home of golf but children will probably be more interested in the country parks, swimming pool, the Sealife Centre and the beaches. It is disappointing that a large number of the beaches on this coast do not reach EC standards on water quality, particularly as this area was once a traditional summer holiday venue. All the same, there are still some beautiful places to build sand-castles and go paddling, while older children can have some fun trying out the various watersports on offer at Anstruther, one of the villages near St Andrews.

The road and railway line continue northwards to Dundee on the other side of the River Tay. The bridges are less spectacular than those crossing the Forth but you can't stop a shiver running up your spine when you think of the tragic collapse of the original rail bridge one stormy night in 1879. Dundee was once famous for jam, jute and journalism. Now it is the watery home of the Royal Research Ship *Discovery* and the Frigate *Unicorn*, both of which can appeal to older children. The nautical theme continues at Camperdown Park where the great sea battle, Camperdown, has been translated into an adventure play area for under-10s.

Although the beaches between Dundee and Arbroath are popular with holidaymakers they don't reach EC standards on sewage pollution. Go instead to the lovely beaches a little further north at Montrose and Lunan Bay.

The Carnegie Centre in Dunfermline (see Sport and Leisure Centres) runs a shoppers' creche all year round which is extended at Christmas (maximum stay 2 hours), and there is an in-store creche at the Asda Superstore (Halbeath Road, Dunfermline) for 3 to 8-year-olds. Apparently there is a shoppers' creche in Dundee as well. If you can find it, please let me know—I've had no luck in tracking it down (see p. 15).

PLACES TO VISIT

Adventure Playgrounds

CAMPERDOWN COUNTRY PARK – *see* COUNTRY PARKS

Ancient Monuments

DUNFERMLINE ABBEY AND MONASTERY (HS)
Monastery Street, Dunfermline
Tel: (031) 244 3101 (HS, Edinburgh)
Open: All year, closed lunchtime,
Sunday morning services
£
P: Available

This is the burial place of Robert the Bruce, the famous 14th-century king who defeated the English at the Battle of Bannockburn. The words 'KING ROBERT THE BRUCE' are carved in giant stone letters round the top of the Abbey tower. Look out for a life-size model of his head which is on display. You can look down on two large flower beds shaped like dolphins from the southern side of the graveyard. The ruined monastery overlooks PITTENCRIEFF PARK (*see* PARKS AND PLAYGROUNDS).

Animals and Birds

SCOTTISH DEER CENTRE
Old Rankeilour Farm, Bow of Fife by Cupar KY15 4NQ
A91, 3 miles W of Cupar, 12 miles W of St Andrews
Tel: (033 781) 391
Open: May – Oct, daily 1000 – 1800;
Nov – Apr, daily 1000 – 1600
££
P: Free

Picnic area, restaurant – high-chairs and children's menu
Full disabled facilities
Toilets with baby-changing mat

The main attraction, for children at least, is the giant outdoor play area which is tough enough to keep children as old as 13 busy for at least an hour, often longer. There is also a wet weather play area in a barn at the exhibition centre though it is not really suitable for under-5s.

You can feed and stroke the deer – except during the rutting season when the stags get rather boisterous. Beyond the deer pens there is a treetop walkway which is fun for those with a head for heights. This leads round to the play area and a maze of wire fencing which small children like because it's not too claustrophobic. A word of warning – not many children have time to stop for the educational film, the fact-finding room or the ranger tours.

ST ANDREWS SEALIFE CENTRE
The Scores, St Andrews
Tel: (0334) 74786
Open: 7 days a week, most of the year
£££, free to Blue Peter Badge wearers
P: Available
Restaurant

Huge sea-water tanks house seals, sharks, sting-rays, conger eels, octopuses and other sea creatures. The fish often come right to the surface of the open-topped pools where they are disconcertingly close to your face. Children are encouraged to handle hermit crabs, snails

and anemones in the touch pools, and to feel the roughness of dried shark skin. Tickets are valid all day, so you can come and go as you please.

ELMWOOD COLLEGE FARM
nr Cupar
Tel: (0334) 52781
Free
Café
Toilets
This is a place for a springtime visit so you can see calves, piglets and lambs at close quarters. Pony rides.

ISLE OF MAY
off Anstruther
Open: Easter – Oct
£££
Access by boat from Crail and Anstruther

Contact: I. Gatherum (0333) 7248
R. Ritchie (0333) 310697
J. Raeper (0333) 310103
J. Smith (0333) 50484
A wonderful place for bird lovers. The 5-hour round trip includes 3 hours on the island, a very important seabird and wildlife reserve.

EDEN ESTUARY LOCAL NATURE RESERVE
nr St Andrews
Access near Guardbridge, from St Andrews, and at Kinshaldy
Tel: (0334) 73666
Free
P: Available
A small reserve of inter-tidal mud-flats and sand with walks and hides. There is a programme of ranger-led walks during the year. Watch out

for fighter planes flying in and out of Leuchars Airport, just across the estuary.

TENTSMUIR POINT NATIONAL NATURE RESERVE
nr St Andrews
A919, B945 from St Andrews or Tayport
Tel: (0334) 54038
Open: All year
Free
P: Small charge
Picnic areas and toilets at the carpark
No disabled access to the beach
The huge beach is featured in the Good Beach Guide for its clean sand and unpolluted water. It is a good place for kite flying and paddling but swimmers should watch out for strong offshore currents. There is a nature trail and lovely walks in the inland area of dunes and trees. Depending on your interests, it is a good area for birdwatching or for cycling away from traffic.

ST CYRUS NATURE RESERVE
nr Montrose
Turn left before river, 1 mile S of St Cyrus
Tel: (067485) 736
Open: Apr – Oct, Tue – Sun 0900 – 1700
Free
P: Available
Disabled facilities
The reserve has many interesting plants and birds. The visitor centre houses displays on local history, natural history and salmon fishing. There are children's games, a salt-water aquarium and an audio-visual display. No guide dogs allowed.

LOCH OF KINNORDY NATURE RESERVE (RSPB)
nr Kirriemuir

On B951, 1 mile W of Kirriemuir
Open: Daily (not Sat in Sep – Oct)
Free
P: Available
Freshwater marsh with large numbers of nesting water birds which you can see from the two observation hides.

CAMPERDOWN COUNTRY PARK – *see* COUNTRY PARKS

Beaches

There are numerous sandy and rocky beaches along the Fife and Angus coastline but it is very disappointing to find that many of them fail to meet the EC standards on cleanliness. According to information in the 1992 Good Beach Guide you should avoid ABERDOUR SILVERSANDS, PETTYCUR, KINGHORN, KIRKCALDY LINKTOWN, LEVEN WEST, LEVEN EAST, LOWER LARGO, UPPER LARGO, PITTENWEEM, TAYPORT, BROUGHTY FERRY, MONIFIETH, CARNOUSTIE and the beaches at ARBROATH. The beaches at ELIE and ST ANDREWS EAST passed their most recent inspections but failed in previous years.

For an area that could have a great deal to offer, the few beaches with reasonably clean sand and unpolluted water are listed below.

SHELL BAY, ELIE
Over a mile of sands along the edge of the Firth of Forth backed by an attractive village.

WEST SANDS, ST ANDREWS
P: Available
Picnic areas
Look out for horses being put through their paces on this long sandy beach. It is sometimes possible

to have donkey rides in the summer and it is a good place for paddling whatever the season. (Remember to take spare clothes!)

LUNAN BAY
nr Arbroath
P: Available
Large, unspoilt, sandy beach with safe bathing except at the river mouth.

MONTROSE BEACH
Montrose
P: Available
Access from the carpark at S end of town
Café and toilets at the carpark
Four miles of sandy beach between the North and South Esk rivers. Litter is removed regularly and at low tide there are 220yds of firm clean sand backed by 30ft-high dunes. Don't bathe near the river mouths because of currents. The further north you walk the quieter the beach becomes. There is a huge tidal basin inland from Montrose which is an important feeding ground for over-wintering birds.

TENTSMUIR POINT – *see* ANIMALS AND BIRDS
Other beaches which have passed inspection include DALGETY BAY, ABERDOUR HARBOUR, BURNTIS-LAND, LUNDIN LINKS, ANSTRUTHER and CRAIL.

Boats and Boat Trips

FRIGATE *UNICORN*
Victoria Dock, Dundee DD1 3JA
Close to Tay Road Bridge, city centre, station

Tel: (0382) 200900
Open: Apr–Oct, 1000–1700, Sat and rest of year 1000–1600
££
P: Free
Disabled facilities and access to gun deck
The *Unicorn*, a 46-gun wooden warship which was launched at Chatham in 1824, is the oldest British-built warship afloat and the third oldest worldwide. Although it never fired a shot in anger, it is fun to imagine being a sailor and living in the very cramped conditions.

ROYAL RESEARCH SHIP *DISCOVERY*
Discovery Quay, Craig Harbour, Dundee
Tel: (0382) 201175/25282
Open: Jun–early Sep, daily 1000–1700; Sep–end Oct, weekdays 1300–1700
££
P: Free
Disabled access to upper deck only
The *Discovery* was Captain Scott's famous Antarctic exploration vessel, built like a whaling ship so the hull could withstand the pressure of pack ice. How would you like to have to share a 10ft x 8ft cabin with 10 men? See, hear and smell what it was like on board. School groups welcome, particularly in winter. The new visitor centre opens this spring and will have displays on Polar exploration.

Bus Trips

OPEN-TOP BUS TRIPS
Departing from Church Street, St Andrews
Tel: (0334) 74238
Open: Jun–Sep
££

Sight-seeing tours round the town leave every hour. Passengers can get off at places of interest and continue the tour on a later bus.

Castles and Stately Homes

ST ANDREWS CASTLE
The Scores, St Andrews
Tel: (0334) 77196
Open: Summer, Mon – Sat 0930 – 1900, Sun 1400 – 1900 (closes 1600 in winter)
Visitor Centre: Mon – Sat 0930 – 1800, Sun 1400 – 1800
£

The castle started off as a fortress almost 800 years ago. It has a deep bottle-shaped dungeon carved out of the rock and a secret passage formed from a mine dug by soldiers trying to break into the castle. A counter-mine was dug by the defenders so they could retaliate. There is a special children's guide available describing the castle and nearby cathedral. The new visitor centre has life-like models of James II and John Knox.

FALKLAND PALACE AND GARDENS (NTS)
Falkland
A912, 11 miles N of Kirkcaldy
Tel: (0337 57) 397
Open: Apr – Oct, Mon – Sat 1000 – 1800, Sun 1400 – 1800
Palace gardens ££, gardens only £
Wheelchair ramp into gardens
Toilets

The guided tour is a bit too staid for most children, although they do enjoy being told of the toilet habits of the inhabitants. Tennis is still played on the Royal Tennis Court of 1539 – the oldest in Britain. The beautiful gardens include two giant draughtboards which are set in a suntrap where parents can relax while the children play. It also makes a good place for a picnic. Check for special events in the summer, e.g. archery displays, craft fairs.

KELLIE CASTLE (NTS)
nr Pittenweem
On B9171, 3 miles NNW of Pittenweem
Tel: (033 38) 271
Open: May – Sep, daily 1400 – 1800; Easter/Apr/Oct weekends only 1400 – 1800
Castle and gardens ££, gardens only £
Picnic area, tea-room

The castle dates mainly from the 16th and 17th centuries but the oldest part is more than 600 years old. Among the rooms on view are the old-fashioned kitchen and nursery. There is an adventure playground in the gardens.

EARLSHALL CASTLE AND GARDENS
nr Leuchars
1 mile E of Leuchars, 6 miles from St Andrews
Tel: (033483) 9205
Open: Easter/Sun in Apr 1400 – 1800; May – Sep, daily 1400 – 1800
££
P: Free
Tea-room, picnic facilities
Partial disabled access

A 16th-century Scottish castle with 5ft thick walls, battlements and gun loops. It is said that a ghost walks the stairs from time to time. The yew trees in the garden have been pruned into chessmen. There is also a secret garden and woodland walks.

BALGONIE CASTLE
by Markinch
2 miles E of Glenrothes on B921 off A911
Tel: (0592) 750119
Open: All year 1400 – 1700
£
P: Available
Disabled access
A 14th-century castle with a 2-acre wildlife garden to explore. There are craft studios where you can see carved leather goods and woven tapestries being made.

ABERDOUR CASTLE (HS)
Aberdour
A921, 5 miles east of Forth Bridge
Tel: (031) 244 3101 (HS, Edinburgh)
Open: Apr – Sep 0930 – 1900 (open 1400 Sun); Oct – Mar 0930 – 1600 (shut Thu pm/Fri)
£
P: Free
Partial disabled access
A 14th-century ruined castle overlooking the harbour at Aberdour. Small children like to hear their voices echo in the doocot and they enjoy running round the perimeter of the walled garden.

GLAMIS CASTLE
nr Forfar
A94, 5 miles SW of Forfar
Tel: (030 784) 242
Open: Easter – mid Oct, daily 1200 – 1730
£££
P: Available
Restaurant, picnic area
Disabled facilities
This castle is owned by the Earl of Strathmore and is famous as the childhood home of Queen Elizabeth, the Queen Mother, and the birthplace of Princess Margaret. The square tower has walls 15ft thick.

Go on a 50-minute tour of the castle, then explore the large gardens, nature trail and children's playground.

Caves

ST FILLAN'S CAVE
Cove Wynd, nr Harbour, Pittenweem
Tel: (0333) 311495
Open: All year, 1000 – 1300, 1430 – 1730
£
No disabled access
In the 12th century, Augustinian monks from the Isle of May established the Priory, the Great House and the Prior's Lodging above the cave. They cut through the rock from the garden to the holy cave-shrine below which was restored and rededicated in 1935.

MacDUFF'S CAVE
Elie
At far end of West Bay
Free
The cave is reputed to have been a refuge for MacDuff, Thane of Fife, who hid there while fleeing from MacBeth. *See also* CHAIN WALK (**WALKS**).

QUEEN MARGARET'S CAVE
Off Bridge Street Carpark, Dunfermline
Charge to be decided
St Margaret, who was once Queen of Scotland, used to pray in a cave which she used as a shrine. The cave has been boarded up for years but is due to be opened this year.

Country Parks

CAMBO COUNTRY PARK
Kingsbarns, nr St Andrews
1 mile S of Kingsbarns on A917
Tel: (0333) 50810

Open: Weekends from Easter, May – Sep daily, 1000 – 1800
££
P: Available
Cafeteria, restaurant, picnic area
Disabled access and limited disabled facilities
Mother and baby room

A good place for an outing with children of all ages. There are nature trails, a woodland walk, indoor and outdoor play areas. The unusual farm animals on display include iron-age pigs. The walks lead right down to the shore where there are rocky and sandy beaches to explore. Watch out for chickens jumping on to the picnic tables and grabbing your sandwiches!

CRAIGTOUN COUNTRY PARK
by St Andrews KY16 8NX
B939
Tel: (0334) 73666
Open: End Mar – early Oct, daily 1000 – 1730
Charge (grounds open free of charge outwith these hours)
£
P: Free
Full catering
Disabled facilities

A very popular park, known to regulars as CCP. Once you have paid the entry charge the facilities are free. These include a miniature railway, crazy golf, trampolines, boating, 2 adventure play areas (one for very young children), open-air theatre, flower garden, glasshouses, aviaries and animals. The visitor centre has displays and interactive games and makes a good refuge if it rains.

SILVERBURN ESTATE
nr Leven

Half a mile E of Leven, off A915
Tel: (0333) 27890 x 214/27568
Open: Farm: Apr – Sep, Mon – Fri 0830 – 1630 (Oct – Mar 1530), Sat and Sun 1400 – 1600
P: Available
Picnic areas
Disabled access
Toilets

The gardens are open from dawn to dusk all year round. Look out for the old flax mill and a display of old-fashioned farm implements. There are walks to use up excess energy – a sea shore trail, a tree trail and a nature trail – before visiting the craft centre. Under-10s love the play area and mini-farm where they can stroke pygmy goats, geese, saddleback pigs, hens, ducks and pigeons.

LOCHORE MEADOWS COUNTRY PARK
Lochgelly nr Dunfermline
Between Lochgelly and Ballingry on B920
Tel: (0592) 860086
Open: All times; centre: summer 0800 – 2000, winter 0900 – 1700
Charges for fishing and golf
P: Free
Cafeteria, picnic areas, barbecues for hire
Disabled facilities
Toilets

The park was reclaimed from coal-mining waste in the 1960s. Although some of the trees are still small it is very attractive. Most children make a bee-line for the beach and adventure playground which has a wide range of well-maintained equipment for toddlers upwards. You can have lessons in sailing, windsurfing, canoeing, golf and riding (*see* RIDING) from about 8. Youngsters might feel inspired to join the conservation group, 'The Midges', after an afternoon with the rangers hunting for fish and wriggly insect larvae in the loch.

TOWNHILL COUNTRY PARK
Townhill, nr Dunfermline KY12 0HT
Tel: (0383) 725596
Open: All year
P: Free
A small country park with lots of potential, especially since the introduction of a new water-skiing centre in 1992 (*see* WATERSPORTS). There is a good adventure playground with 2 wooden forts and a variety of free-standing equipment to suit 3 to 7-year-olds. It rarely seems to get busy, even in the height of summer. There is also a more traditional play area close by. Try out the trim trail before walking in the woods and look out for brambles, shaggy inkcaps and stinkhorns in the autumn. Ranger-led walks are arranged at weekends.

CAMPERDOWN COUNTRY PARK
Liff Road, Dundee DD2 4TF
Off A93, near junction with A972, 3m NW of city centre
Tel: (0382) 623555
Open: All year, daily
Free: £ for wildlife park
P: Free
Restaurant, barbecue and picnic areas
Full disabled facilities
Climb the rope-ladders and board 'old' sailing ships in the award-winning recreation of the Battle of Camperdown. Ships that have been holed by cannonballs list and sink in a sea of sand. A wonderful place for swash-buckling sailors (under the age of 10) to test their climbing skills. Toddlers have their own small ships

to climb on. Watch out, though, for sand being thrown or blown into children's eyes. A boating pond, bouncy castle and miniature cycle track add to the pleasure of a visit here while older children can go horse-riding (tel: 0382 632879) or play a game of tennis or putting.

The wildlife park has animals from Scotland's past and present including deer, wildcats, pine martens, European brown bear, lynx and wolves.

CLATTO COUNTRY PARK
Dalmahoy Drive, Dundee
Tel: (0382) 89076
Open: All year, 1000 – dusk
P: Available
Picnic, barbecue areas
No disabled access
The reservoir is sheltered by a belt of conifer and mixed woodland. It is particularly popular for windsurfing, canoeing, dinghy sailing (instruction available) and swimming. Rowing boats, windsurfing, canoeing and sailing equipment for hire. Children's play areas.

CROMBIE COUNTRY PARK
Monikie nr Dundee
On B961, 3.5 miles NE of Newbigging
Tel: (02416) 360
Open: All year, 1000 – dusk
P: Free
Picnic and barbecue areas
Disabled facilities and limited access
Victorian reservoir which looks like a natural loch. Try fishing or take a walk in the 250 acres of woodland. There are wildlife hides, trails, a visitor centre, playpark and conservation areas.

MONIKIE COUNTRY PARK
Newbigging nr Dundee
1 mile N of Newbigging, 10 miles N of Dundee
Tel: (082623) 202
Open: All year, 1000 – dusk
Tea-room in summer, picnic and bar-becue areas
Disabled facilities and access

Explore the parkland and mixed woodland around the loch on your own or on a ranger-led walk. Various watersports include rowing, sailing, canoeing, fishing and windsurfing. Equipment may be hired and instruction is available.

FORFAR COUNTRY PARK
Forfar
Tel: (0307) 64201

Have a go at canoeing, sailing or fishing. Or take a walk round the loch where you will see unusual trees like turkey oaks which have a 'mossy' cup holding the acorn, and lots of wintering and migrating birds. There are sports facilities at the LOCHSIDE LEISURE CENTRE – *see* **SPORTS AND LEISURE CENTRES** and a play-scheme in the summer holidays.

Fairgrounds

THE LINKS MARKET
Kirkcaldy

A large funfair is set up near the beach every summer with all the usual stomach-churning rides. Children love it but parents generally hate it!

For a less expensive outing to the fair go to BURNTISLAND EDWARDIAN FAIR (*see* **MUSEUMS**).

Fish

DEEP SEA WORLD
North Queensferry, Fife
Close to Forth Road Bridge
Tel: (0383) 411411
Open: All year, daily, 0900 – 1800
£££
P: Free (also accessible by bus and ferry)
Café
Disabled access and facilities
Mother and baby changing-room

Scheduled to open in March 1993, this is the biggest and newest aquarium in the world. Get a diver's-eye view of underwater life as you take a walk along the seabed in the acrylic viewing tunnels. Among the 5,000 sea creatures from the coastal waters of Scotland are huge sharks which glide within inches of your face, conger eels, tidal fish, lobsters and crabs. Children enjoy the wet and dry interactive displays which include a touch pool with rays and turbots. There is also an octopus exhibit, a sunlit coral display and an audio-visual theatre.

LOCH FITTY TROUT FARM
Kingseat by Dunfermline
On B912 NE of Dunfermline
Tel: (0383) 620666
Open: Mar – Dec, daily 1000 – dusk
P: Available
Restaurant

How about catching a trout for your tea? There are special deals on parent and child tickets (£££) which include up to 5 fish. Pre-schoolers enjoy the sandpit and swing and like to see the lambs in spring, but the highlight is feeding the ducks and trout.

Gardens

BOTANIC GARDENS
Canongate, St Andrews KY16 8RT
Tel: (0334) 53722
*Open: Daily Apr–Oct, 1000–1900
(1600 Apr/Oct); Nov–Mar, Mon–Fri
1000–1600*
£
Has 18 acres of trees, shrubs, rock
and peat gardens, an ornamental
lake and glasshouses with fishponds
and streams.

UNIVERSITY BOTANIC GARDEN
Riverside Drive, Dundee
Nr junction of A85 and Perth Road
Tel: (0382) 66939
P: Available
£
Disabled facilities
Toilets
Beautiful gardens. There are giant lily
pads and banana trees with red fruits
in the hothouses.

DAMSIDE GARDENS HERB CENTRE
by Johnshaven, Montrose DD10 0HY
Off A92 or A94
Tel: (0561) 61496
*Open: Apr–Sep, Tue–Sun 1030–1900;
weekends Oct–Dec*
£
P: Available
Café
Disabled access and facilities
Lots of lovely scented herbs planted
in traditional Celtic, Knot, Roman,
Monastic and Elizabethan patterns.

Graveyards and Gruesome Places

TAY BRIDGE
Open: All year
The first Tay Bridge was blown down

in a storm in 1879 with the loss of
a train and 75 lives. It had been in
use for less than two years. You can
see the remains of the bridge jutting
out of the river from the riverside or
from the trains crossing the new
railbridge.

Heritage Centres

DUNFERMLINE HERITAGE CENTRE
Maygate, Dunfermline
Cafeteria
*Details of opening hours and charges
still to be decided*
Due to open in autumn 1993
The Heritage Centre is near the
ABBEY (*see* ANCIENT MONUMENTS). Many
skeletons have been uncovered in
this area which was once a burial
ground, and an old road, dating back
hundreds of years, has been unearthed during the gutting of the building
which is to become the centre.

Indoor Fun

THE MERCAT SHOPPING CENTRE
High Street, Kirkcaldy
Tel: (0592) 267998
Open: During centre hours
Free
Tiny tots don't mind going shopping
here if they can get a ride on
the merry-go-round. It moves round
very slowly so toddlers can clamber
on and off in safety.

Monuments

ROBINSON CRUSOE
Lower Largo
Free

The story of Robinson Crusoe's and Man Friday's life on a desert island is based on the real-life adventures of Alexander Selkirk who was born in Lower Largo in 1676. He lived for more than 4 years on the island of Juan Fernandez, 400 miles off the coast of Chile.

Museums

SCOTTISH FISHERIES MUSEUM
Harbourhead, Anstruther KY10 3AB
Tel: (0333) 310628
Open: Apr – Oct, Mon – Sat 1000 – 1730, Sun 1100 – 1700; Nov – Mar, restricted hours
£
Tea-room
An interesting museum tracing the history of the fishing industry in Scotland. Attractions include a marine aquarium, reconstructed fisher-homes, and 2 old fishing boats in the harbour called *Fifie* and *Zulu*.

THE NORTH CARR LIGHTSHIP
The Harbour, Anstruther
Tel: (0333) 310589
Open: Easter – Sep, daily 1000 – 1700; weekends in Oct
£
You can go on board and look round the lightship which used to be stationed off Fife Ness, warning passing ships of the dangers of the Carr Rocks.

MUSEUM OF ST ANDREWS PRESERVATION TRUST
St Andrews
Open: Jul – Aug, Mon – Sat 1400 – 1700
Free
Old fishermen's houses have been converted into 19th-century grocers' and chemists' shops.

ST ANDREWS MUSEUM
Kilburn Park, Double Dykes Road, St Andrews
Tel: (0334) 77706
Open: Apr – Sep, daily 1100 – 1800; reduced hours Oct – Mar
Free
P: Street parking
Café
Disabled facilities
The museum tells the history of St Andrews over the past 700 years, complete with appropriate sounds and smells.

BRITISH GOLF MUSEUM
Bruce Embankment, St Andrews KY16 9AB
Tel: (0334) 78880
Open: May – Oct, daily 1000 – 1730; Nov – Apr, Tue – Sun 1000 – 1600 (1700 Mar – Apr)
££
The museum has displays covering 500 years of golfing history. Test your knowledge with an interactive video.

BURNTISLAND EDWARDIAN FAIR
Above Library, 102 High Street, Burntisland
Tel: (0592) 260732
Open: All year, Mon – Sat 1000 – 1300, 1400 – 1700
Free
P: Nearby
The museum has recreated the town's fair as it was in 1910 with all its sounds and smells. Look for differences between the rides, stalls and side-shows of then and modern fairs like the LINKS MARKET (*see* **FAIRGROUNDS**).

KIRKCALDY MUSEUM AND ART GALLERY

War Memorial Gardens, Bennochy Road, Kirkcaldy
Tel: (0592) 260732
Open: Mon – Sat 1100 – 1700, Sun 1400 – 1700
Free
P: Available

An interesting mixture of objects are on display, including a chair carved from parrot coal, a penny farthing bike, old toys and wedding clothes. Children particularly enjoy the handling sessions and 'please touch' areas. There are special events for children such as story-telling and painting which run in conjunction with exhibitions. Worksheets available.

CARNEGIE BIRTHPLACE MUSEUM

Moodie Street, Dunfermline
Tel: (0383) 724302
Open: Apr – Oct, Mon – Sat 1100 – 1700, Sun 1400 – 1700; Nov – Mar, daily 1400 – 1600
Free
P: Free
Disabled facilities

One of Dunfermline's claims to fame is that it is the birthplace of the world-famous philanthropist, Andrew Carnegie. His father was a weaver and the family lived in a tiny cottage which has been furnished as it would have been in his childhood. His adult life is chronicled in an adjacent building.

PITTENCRIEFF HOUSE MUSEUM

Pittencrieff Park, Dunfermline
Tel: (0383) 721814
Free

The museum houses displays of local history and old-fashioned clothes as well as a model of the 'Dunfermline Giant' who was 7ft tall.

DUNFERMLINE MUSEUM

Viewfield Terrace Carpark, Dunfermline
Open: 1100 – 1700
Free

Displays of natural history, linen weaving, and an old kitchen crammed full of equipment that Granny (or Great-Granny) might have used. Worksheets are available to stimulate interest.

BARRACK STREET MUSEUM

Dundee
Tel: (0382) 23141 x 65152
Open: All year, Mon – Sat 1000 – 1700
Free
Partial disabled access
Toilets

Dundee's museum of natural history. Large displays on wildlife of Tayside. Also the skeleton of the famous Tay Whale which was immortalised in a poem by McGonagall.

McMANUS GALLERIES

Albert Square, Dundee
Tel: (0382) 23141
Free

We probably walk over interesting archaeological remains every day but only ever find out about them when they are unearthed by farmers and builders. Some local finds are displayed in the museum along with items from the days when Dundee was a whaling port. There is also a fascinating selection of household objects including old food packets. The staff are very helpful and make learning about history fun.

BARRIE'S BIRTHPLACE (NTS)
9 Brechin Road, Kirriemuir
Tel: (0575) 72646
Open: Mar — Sep, Mon — Sat 1100 — 1730,
Sun 1400 — 1730
£
Tea, coffee available
Partial disabled access
J. M. Barrie was born in this cottage in 1860. The outside wash-house is said to have been his first theatre and contains a Peter Pan display. Educational visits welcomed.

ANGUS FOLK MUSEUM (NTS)
Glamis
Tel: (030 784) 288
Open: End Apr — Sep, 1100 — 1700, also Easter weekend
£
P: Available
A picturesque row of 19th-century cottages housing a fine folk collection including life-size models dressed in period costume. Good for school visits.

Parks and Playgrounds

KINBURN PARK
St Andrews
Open: All year
Free
A special feature of this park is the scented garden for the blind. There is a small aviary, putting and bowling greens, and tennis courts.

COCKSHAUGH PARK AND LADE BRAES WALK
St Andrews
A peaceful park for toddlers who enjoy the playground, feeding the ducks on the pond, and walking beside the burn.

CELLARDYKE PARK — *see* EAST NEUK OUTDOORS (SPORT AND LEISURE CENTRES)

BEVERIDGE PARK
Abbotshall Road, Kirkcaldy
Southern end of the town
Open: All year, facilities 1200 — 2000
P: Free
Picnic areas
Disabled facilities
Toilets
This park appeals to a lot of pre-schoolers. The large boating pond is home to hundreds of hungry ducks and geese which children love to feed. They also enjoy the modern play area and the small aviary in the formal gardens. Older children can play tennis, putting, crazy golf, and table-tennis in the summer.

DUNNIKIER PARK
Kirkcaldy
On the A910
Open: Facilities 1200 — 2000
Picnic area
A large park with woodland walks as well as a putting green, paddling pool, nature trail, crazy golf, play areas, gardens, trampolines, table-tennis and skateboard rinks.

RAVENSCRAIG PARK
Kirkcaldy
On the A955 just before Dysart
P: Available
Picnic areas
Has all the usual facilities like tennis, putting, nature trail, pitch and putt, play areas, trampolines, table-tennis and gardens. What makes Ravens-craig a bit different, though, is the walled-off seashore with lots of half-hidden gateways separating it from the park. Children can spend hours

scrambling over the rocky outcrops and looking in the rockpools. If you have time, visit Ravenscraig Castle (limited opening hours) which is close to the carpark.

BALBIRNIE PARK AND GLENROTHES RIDING CENTRE
Glenrothes
Tel: (0592) 742428
P: Available
Take an energetic walk through the woodlands or along 2 miles of public bridle paths (*see* GLENROTHES RIDING CENTRE — **RIDING**) before visiting the craft centre. Pottery, clothing, furniture, jewellery, leather work and stained glass are all on show (tel: 0592 756016).

LETHAM GLEN
Leven
Tel: (0333) 29231/27890
Open: Daily
Picnic area
Toilets
A small but popular park with a pets' corner, putting, nature trail, gardens, doocot, wishing well and deer enclosure. Special events in the summer include craft demonstrations and band concerts.

THE LINKS
Burntisland
Open: Facilities 1100 – 2100
Picnic areas
Disabled facilities
Toilets
Putting green, paddling pool, crazy golf, play areas, trampolines and a summer fairground add to the attraction of the nearby beach. Look for people water-skiing and speeding round the bay in motor-boats.

GLENROTHES
Glenrothes is a new town with lots of modern art. Many areas in the town have huge sculptures which children can play on, such as hippos, mushrooms, totem poles and giant hands.

PUBLIC PARK, DUNFERMLINE
nr railway station
P: Free
Toilets at the railway station
Both the modern playgrounds are well suited to under-5s. One also has a giant spider's web and see-saw swings for older children. The park is on a hill which makes it good for sledging. Crazy golf, trampolines, tennis and table-tennis in the summer.

PITTENCRIEFF PARK
Dunfermline
Tel: (0383) 721814
Open: Daily
Cafeteria, picnic areas
Limited disabled access
This large park, more commonly known as The Glen was given to the people of Dunfermline by the philanthropist, Andrew Carnegie (*see* **MUSEUMS**). There are formal flower gardens, woodland walks along the banks of a burn, a very small zoo, two new children's play areas (one especially suitable for toddlers) and a roadway system for under-9s to cycle round complete with working traffic lights (bikes may be hired). Check for special events such as kite flying and magic shows during the summer months.

VALLEYFIELD WOOD
Valleyfield nr Dunfermline
Between A985 and B9037
Open: All year
P: Free

Attractive woodland walks along the river, with a small adventure play area for young children near to the carpark.

Playschemes and Creches

CARNEGIE LEISURE CENTRE
Pilmuir Street, Dunfermline
Tel: (0383) 723211
£ per hour
People going shopping or using the facilities at the centre may leave babies and children up to 8 in the well-equipped creche.

Railways

LOCHTY RAILWAY
nr Crail
Off B940, Cupar to Crail, 7 miles W of Crail
Tel: (0334) 54815
Open: Mid Jun—early Sep, Sun 1345—1700
£
P: Free
Disabled access
This private railway is run by the volunteers of the Fife Railway Preservation Group who operate and maintain the railway and run a steam-hauled passenger train service between Lochty and Knightsward. You can see steam and diesel locomotives, passenger coaches and goods wagons.

KERR'S MINIATURE RAILWAY
West Links Park, Arbroath DD11 3BY
1.5 miles from Arbroath Station
Tel: (0241) 79249
Open: Apr—Sep, Sat & Sun 1400—1700; Jul—mid Aug daily 1400—1700
£
Disabled access

Steam and diesel trains operate for 400 yards alongside BR mainline. Features include tunnel, footbridge, platforms, turntable and loco shed. A miniature bus and fire engine give children's trips along the promenade.

CALEDONIAN RAILWAY
Brechin Station, Brechin
Tel: (0334) 55695
££—£££
Steam trains run from the classic Victorian station in Brechin on an 8-mile round trip to Wayside Station at Bridge of Dun. From there you can take a vintage 1950s' bus to the HOUSE OF DUN to see handloom weaving (*see* SCOTLAND AT WORK).

Riding

CHARLETON RIDING CENTRE
Colinsburgh nr Largoward
B941 from Largoward, turn right at far end of Colinsburgh
Tel: (0333 34) 231/535
£££
Trekking or hacking over the estate, riding lessons, indoor and outdoor arenas. The beach and picnic rides make a nice treat.

BARBARAFIELD RIDING CENTRE
Craigrothie by Cupar
Off A916
Tel: (033 482) 223
From £
Lessons and treks. There are ponies and horses to suit all ages and abilities.

WOODMILL FARM
Dunshalt by Auchtermuchty
Tel: (0337) 28414
Open: Weekends and school holidays

or by arrangement
From £
Shetland pony for children's rides.

KILCONQUHAR ESTATE RIDING STABLES

Kilconquhar by Elie KY9 1EZ
Tel: (033 334) 501 x 295
Open: Daily
££

All ages and standards catered for on Shetland ponies and other docile horses. Try hacking, trekking, beach rides, pony and trap rides or picnic rides. Lessons given. STRA approved.

STRAVITHIE RIDING STABLES

by St Andrews
4 miles S of St Andrews on B9131 just before Dunino
Tel: (033 488) 251
£

Riding for all ages and standards

GLENROTHES RIDING CENTRE

Balgeddie Farm, by Leslie, Glenrothes
Tel: (0592) 742428
££

Complete beginners welcome (age 6 or over).

LOCHORE MEADOWS RIDING CENTRE

Crosshill, Lochgelly nr Dunfermline KY5 8LY
Tel: (0592) 861596
££

The riding centre is only a few minutes walk from the play area at LOCH ORE MEADOWS (*see* COUNTRY PARKS) so non-horsey members of the family can have fun too. STRA approved.

CAMPERDOWN COUNTRY PARK — *see* COUNTRY PARKS

GLENMARKIE FARM RIDING CENTRE

Glenisla PH11 8QB
Tel: (057 582) 341
££ for an hour's trekking

STRA approved. Novices welcome. There are child seats so very small children can have 30 minutes on a lead rein.

Science and Technology

MILLS OBSERVATORY

Balgay Hill, Dundee
N side of city
Tel: (0382) 67138
Open: Apr – Sep, Mon – Fri 1000 – 1700; Oct – Mar, Mon – Fri 1500 – 2200, Sat 1400 – 1700
Free
P: Available
Partial disabled access

Britain's only full-time public observatory with an astronomer in residence. Book ahead and see the stars from the comfort of the small planetarium. There are displays on astronomy and space exploration and you can look at the stars through the telescope if the sky is not too cloudy. Audio-visual programme.

Scotland at Work – Past and Present

SHAW'S SWEET FACTORY

Fulton Road, Wester Gourdie, Dundee
W end of Kingsway by NCR factory
Tel: (0382) 610369
Open: Mar – Dec, Thu 1330 – 1630; mid Jun – mid Aug, Mon, Tue, Thu, Fri 1330 – 1630
Free

P: Available
Disabled access
It must be every child's dream to work in a sweet factory, and a visit to one is the next best thing. The machinery in this 1940s' sweet factory has been restored to its original condition. Old-fashioned sweets are made using traditional methods and recipes which date back as far as 1879. Watch the sweet-maker demonstrate and explain the different processes and then taste the finished product. Look round a mini-museum of sweet-making.

BARRY MILL (NTS)
Barry
On A930, 2 miles NW of Carnoustie
Tel: (0241) 56761
Open: May—mid Oct, daily 1100—1300, 1400—1700
£
P: Available
Picnic area
A newly restored 18th-century meal mill producing animal feed for a nearby pig farm. The guided tour by a miller is fascinating for school parties and children over 9. There are waymarked walks along the lade burn.

HOUSE OF DUN (NTS)
nr Montrose
On A935, 3 miles W of Montrose
Open: House—May-mid Oct, daily 1100—1730; gardens—daily, all year from 1000—sunset
££ for house; grounds and garden free
Restaurant
See damask linen weaving being done on an old Jacquard loom. This was once a major industry in the Angus area. *See* CALEDONIAN RAILWAY—**RAILWAYS**.

Sport and Leisure Centres

EAST SANDS LEISURE CENTRE
East Sands Beach, St Andrews
Tel: (0334) 76506
Open: Mon—Fri 0900—2200, Sat—Sun 0900—1700
£
P: Available
Restaurant
Disabled access and facilities
The main swimming pool has a 50m water slide, but there is a toddler pool for the less adventurous. Swimming lessons are available. In addition to the pool there are table-tennis tables, squash and racquet ball courts, and snooker and pool tables.

CUPAR SPORTS CENTRE AND SWIMMING POOL
Duffas Park, Cupar
Tel: (0334) 54793
Open: Mon—Fri 0900—2200, Sat—Sun 0900—1700
£
The swimming pool has children's fun sessions, toddler sessions and lessons. Other facilities include 5-a-side football, basketball, table-tennis, trampolines, volleyball, unihoc, archery, tennis, netball, hockey, cricket and karate. Creche.

EAST NEUK OUTDOORS
Anstruther
Tel: (0333) 311929
Open: 1000—1700
Various charges
Activity holidays are very popular. Learn new skills like abseiling, archery, boardsailing, canoeing, climbing and cycling. Those less keen on sport will still enjoy the coastal walks, bird-watching and historic tours. These

may be combined in special mixed activity groups designed for children (££ for a half-day). You can also drop in for a round of putting, a bounce on the trampolines and bouncy castle, or a session at the playgroup (2 to 5-year-olds). Bike hire from £ per half-day.

SPORT FOR CHILDREN
Fife Sport Institute, Viewfield Road, Glenrothes
Tel: (0592) 771700
Open: Centre 0700 – 2300, swimming pool 0700 – 2100
Games morning (Sat 1000 – 1200, over-7s) with football, unihoc, short tennis, trampolining, archery, shooting and swimming. The Tumble Club is a movement class for the under-5s. Older children can do recreational gym (over-5s). There is a swimming pool and a dry ski slope (lessons for children aged 6 upwards). And if the children are still bouncing when they've finished indoors, there is an outdoor play area too.

THE FRASER TEN-PIN BOWLING CENTRE
Kingdom Shopping Centre, Central Way, Glenrothes
Tel: (0592) 752433
Open: Daily, 1100 – late evening
From ££
Snack bar
Disabled facilities and access
Has 10 bowling lanes and lighter balls for young children.

CRYSTALS ARENA
Viewfield, Glenrothes
Tel: (0592) 773774
Open: Daily
££
Ice-skating, ice hockey and curling

rink. Lessons, family sessions.

KIRKCALDY ICE RINK
Rosslyn Street, Kirkcaldy
Tel: (0592) 52151
Open: Sep – Apr, daily from 1000
££
Ice-skating, ice hockey, curling. Lessons.

CARNEGIE LEISURE CENTRE
Pilmuir Street, Dunfermline
Tel: (0383) 723211
Open: Daily
Cafeteria
Disabled access and facilities
Swimming pool with fun sessions, toddler pool, trainer pool, lessons for 4-year-olds and above. Mini-movers (18 months or more), judo, football, table-tennis, karate, gymnastics, badminton, climbing wall. Swim parties, football parties and soft playroom parties are very popular with children (and with parents who don't have to tidy up afterwards). Creche.

ROLLERBOWL
Primrose Lane, Rosyth nr Dunfermline
Tel: (0383) 418811
Restaurant, ice-cream parlour
Has 32 ten-pin bowling lanes, some with bumpers to help young children – though it's still a bit hard for under-5s. Indoor and outdoor tennis, snooker, children's play area with bouncy castle and ball pond.

KNOCKHILL RACING CIRCUIT
by Dunfnline KY12 9TF
On A82. of Dunfermline
Tel: (038 723337
From ££; under-12s free
P: Available
Weekend meets vary from motor racing to supertrucks a vintage car rallies. Children from years old

can try karting on a 500m track (£££) — phone (0383) 620748 for details. Very small children can be amused in the play park between races.

GX SUPERBOWL
Milton of Craigie, Kingsway East, Dundee
Tel: (0382) 461202
Open: Daily, 1000 – 2400
££ per game
Café
Fully computerised and automated 10-pin bowling. Under-10s can find it a bit frustrating unless the bumpers are in place (these can be booked in advance).

MEGABOWL
Stacks Leisure Park, Lochee, Dundee
Tel: (0382) 400414
Open: 1000 – 2400
From £
A 10-pin bowling centre which also has something a bit different — the 'Zap Zone', where over-8s can run round in a dark, smoke-filled room 'firing' at each other with laser guns.

OLYMPIA SWIMMING AND LEISURE CENTRE, LEVENMOUTH SWIMMING POOL AND SPORTS CENTRE — *see* SWIMMING

Swimming

LEVENMOUTH SWIMMING POOL AND SPORTS CENTRE
Leven
Tel: (0333) 429866
Open: Daily, swimming: 0800 – 2200 (Sat-/Sun 2100); other facilities from 0900
£
Cafeteria
A free-form pool with all sorts of watery attractions including geysers, fountains, a whirlpool, jets and cannons, 75m flume and a wave machine. More serious swimming takes place in the 25m training pool. Sports include 5-a-side football, badminton, table-tennis, archery and fencing. Creche.

KIRKCALDY SWIMMING POOL
The Esplanade, Kirkcaldy
Tel: (0592) 265366
Open: Daily from 0800
Swimming and canoeing lessons.

COWDENBEATH LEISURE CENTRE
Pit Road, Cowdenbeath KY4 9NN
Tel: (0383) 514520
Open: Daily from 0900
Toddler pool, 25m pool with water chute sessions. Lessons. The family changing-rooms are great for dressing wet babies and toddlers.

OLYMPIA SWIMMING AND LEISURE CENTRE
Earl Grey Place, Dundee
Tel: (0382) 203888
Open: Mon – Fri 0900 – 2100, Sat – Sun 0900 – 1600
££
Restaurant
Flumes, a wave machine, rapid river, water slides and diving pool combine to make this a great pool and a lot less crowded than the leisure pool in Perth. The climbing wall can be quite a challenge for older children.

FORFAR SWIMMING POOL
The Vennel, Forfar
Tel: (0307) 62995
Disabled access and facilities including pool hoist
Forfar is 100 miles further north than

Moscow but the pool is kept at Mediterranean temperatures.

MONTROSE SWIMMING POOL
The Mall, Montrose
Tel: (0674) 72026
Disabled access and facilities including pool hoist
A 25m pool with springboards and diving platform, family sessions and inflatable chute.

CUPAR SPORTS CENTRE, EAST SANDS LEISURE CENTRE, CARNEGIE LEISURE CENTRE – *see*
SPORT AND LEISURE CENTRES

Theatres and Cinemas

ADAM SMITH THEATRE
Bennochy Road, Kirkcaldy
Tel: (0592) 260498
Open: All year
Restaurant
Shows throughout the year include a Christmas pantomime, and plays like *The Wizard of Oz* and Roald Dahl's *George's Marvellous Medicine* are performed during the summer holidays and at other times of the year. A Saturday morning children's club runs from 1045 to 1230 with films, live theatre and entertainment.

Toys

CHILDHOOD DREAMS
6 Elphinstone Street, Kincardine
Tel: (0259) 31356
Adults and children alike will be entranced by the doll's-houses, miniature shops, furniture and fittings on display.

Walks

SERPENTINE WALK
Largo
While you are in Lower Largo looking at the monument of ROBINSON CRUSOE it's worth following the serpentine walk between Lower and Upper Largo. Start this short woodland walk by the Upper Largo Hotel. The path is about 2 miles long and leads down to a sandy beach.

REDMYRE
nr Auchtermuchty
Tel: (0383) 830240
Unmarked road off A91 headings towards Newburgh
Attractive walks through the forest.

LOMOND HILLS
nr Falkland
P: Available
Picnic area
Toilets
Walk up East or West Lomond from the carpark on the unclassified road between Leslie and Falkland. Look out for information boards describing how the hills were formed from volcanic plugs. Gliders from Scotlandwell fly quite close to the hills in good weather. Falkland looks like a toy town from the summit of East Lomond.

CHAIN WALK
Elie
It is possible to make your way along the rocky headland between Shell Bay and Elie by means of chains fixed to the rock. This is an exciting traverse for older children who also enjoy visiting MACDUFF'S CAVE (*see* CAVES). You can return the same way or continue the circuit along the

shore and back along the clifftop.

ST ANDREWS TO BOARHILLS
St Andrews
Catch bus to Boarhills and walk back to
St Andrews
This is a long walk along unspoilt coastline and seacliffs – good for bird-watching.

Watersports

ELIE WATER SPORTS
The Harbour, Elie
Off A917
Tel: (0333) 310366/330962
Open: Weekends in May/Sep; daily Jun –
Aug from 1000
Children can have lessons in windsurfing (££ per hour for hire and instruction), canoeing, and sailing. Equipment, including pedaloes (over-9s), may be hired and junior wet suits and buoyancy aids are provided. There are jet bikes for older children, while youngsters can frolic in the waves with a fun board (£).

SCOTTISH WATER-SKI CENTRE
Town Loch, Townhill, Dunfermline, KY12 0HT
Tel: (0383) 620123
Open: All year
Beginner's lessons £££
Disabled facilities
A brand-new centre where children and families can learn to water-ski with professional equipment. Small wet suits are available. It's an expensive hobby but you have the choice of single ski tows, as well as day or week-long courses. The adventure playground at TOWNHILL COUNTRY PARK is only a short walk away.

EAST NEUK OUTDOORS – *see*
SPORTS AND LEISURE CENTRES

PLACES TO EAT

Hotels and Restaurants

THE BUT 'N' BEN
Auchmithie by Arbroath DD11 5SO
Tel: (0241) 77223
Open: 1200 – 1430, high tea 1600 – 1730
Disabled access and facilities
A small restaurant (near LUNAN BAY – *see* **BEACHES**) serving good home-made soup and fresh baking. Being a seaside village, many of the dishes are made with local fish, though there are vegetarian choices too. Children's helpings and old-fashioned high teas.

CLOISTERS
1 Canmore Street, Dunfermline
Tel: (0383) 722501
Excellent high teas.

COLLIESTON INN
Collieston by Arbroath
Tel: (0241) 89232
Simple, traditional food like stovies.

CRAW'S NEST HOTEL
Anstruther KY10 3DS
On A917 coast road S of St Andrews
Tel: (0333) 310691
Lunches 1215 – 1350
Good local produce, especially fish. Children welcome. French spoken. £10 for 3-course lunch in restaurant (half-price for children). Bar lunch from £3.95 (reductions for children). Features in Taste of Scotland guide.

FISHERMAN'S INN
57 High Street, Arbroath
Tel: (0241) 70776
Good lunches.

GARFUNKLES
Commercial Street, Dundee
Fast food, quick service, fun atmosphere.

THE GOURDIE CROFT
Beefeater Restaurants, Kingsway West, Dundee
Tel: (0382) 561115
Children enjoy the outdoor play area while parents relax in the nearby beer garden. Meals and snacks are available in the no-smoking area of the bar, or children can choose from the Mr Man menu in the dining-room. Nappy-changing facilities.

GULISTAN TANDOORI
Queen Street Hall, Broughty Ferry, by Dundee
Tel: (0382) 738844
Tasty Indian food to take away or eat on the premises.

HALFWAY HOUSE
Kingseat, near Dunfermline
Tel: (0383) 731661
This hotel and restaurant has good food with a children's menu or small portions off the standard menu. Colouring books available and lollipops for those who eat all their food.

IL PESCATORE
41 Main Street, Limekilns, nr Dunfermline
Tel: (0383) 872999
Good pizza and pasta dishes in small portions if required. The waiters go out of their way to make children feel special. Those with birthdays get sparklers in their ice-creams. Main

courses from £3.50 with reductions for children. High-chairs available.

KHAN'S
33 Carnegie Drive, Dunfermline
Tel: (0383) 739478
Open: 1200–1500, 1730–2400
A pleasant Indian restaurant where very friendly waiters make children welcome. A special menu of mild dishes is available with main courses from £2.95.

LITTLEJOHNS
75 Market Street, St Andrews
Tel: (0334) 75444
Open: 1200–2300, daily
This isn't just a burger, steak and pizza house: look for interesting Mexican dishes which are great for vegetarians. Main courses start at £5 (or £2.45 for a child's meal of main course, ice-cream and a drink). The food is not the only attraction though, as children are entranced by the huge display of memorabilia from the '40s and '50s which hang from the ceiling and cover the walls. There aren't many restaurants which come complete with traffic lights and model trains running round a track 10 feet up the walls.

THE MANDARIN PALACE
118 High Street, Arbroath
Tel: (0241) 74240

THE MELDRUMS
56 Main Street, Ceres, nr St Andrews
Tel: (033 482) 286
Recommended by local people who enjoy Sunday lunch in the bar or in the restaurant. Special children's menu with main dishes at £1.95. Baby diner seat available.

THE OLD BREWHOUSE
3 High Street, Arbroath
Tel: (0241) 79945
Very popular with local people for tea or supper.

PINEWOODS HOTEL
Tayport Road, St Michaels, nr Leuchars
Tel: (0334) 838262
A pleasant hotel for high teas, bar lunches and bar suppers. High-chairs and a children's menu are available. Parties can be arranged in the special children's function suite where clowns entertain the young guests.

QUEENSFERRY LODGE HOTEL
North Queensferry
Tel: (0383) 410000
The food is good, especially the self-service salad bar where children can pick and choose. High-chairs available. Main courses from under £4 with reductions for children. Good views over the River Forth and the Forth Road Bridge. Small but exciting exhibition and shop at the entrance to amuse under-8s.

RAFFLES RESTAURANT
18 Perth Road, Dundee
Tel: (0382) 201139
Restaurant with Italian leanings, favoured by students.

RESCOBIE HOTEL AND RESTAURANT
Valley Drive, Leslie, Glenrothes KY6 3BQ
8 miles from M90, just off A911 in the village of Leslie
Tel: (0592) 742143
Lunch 1200–1400 (Sun 1230–1430)
A country-house hotel recommended in the Taste of Scotland guide. Children are very welcome and there are reductions for their

meals if they choose small portions off the menu. Less adventurous eaters can have sausages, scrambled eggs and so on. French and German are both spoken. High-chair available. Main courses from over £3.

ST ANDREWS GOLF HOTEL
40 The Scores, St Andrews KY16 9AS
Tel: (0334) 72611
Lunches 1200 – 1430
Children are welcome in this hotel which has the additional appeal of being close to the beach. Italian and some French spoken. Bar lunch main course from under £3, restaurant lunch main course from £5 with appropriate reductions for children. Features in Taste of Scotland guide.

SULTAN TURKISH RESTAURANT
127 Castle Street, Forfar
Tel: (0307) 67941
Excellent food which children enjoy as it is not too hot or spicy.

WOODLANDS HOTEL
13 Panmure Terrace, Barnhill, Monifieth nr Dundee DD5 2QN
Tel: (0382) 480033
A country-house hotel in 4 acres of mature gardens. Lovely food.

ZIGGY'S
6 Murray Place, St Andrews
Tel: (0334) 73686
Open: Daily 1200 – 1430, 1700 – 2030
Old records decorate the walls of the restaurant, while the food includes steaks, burgers, fish and baked potatoes. Main courses start under £3 while a child's meal, including ice-cream and a drink, costs £2.50.

Quick Meals and Snacks

BRECHIN BOOKS
20 – 22 St David Street, Brechin
Tel: (035 62) 5272
A bookshop with a good coffee shop serving delicious home-baking.

THE BUTTERCHURN
Cocklaw Mains Farm, Kelty
E of Dunfermline
Tel: (0383) 830169
Open: Daily 1000 – 1730
Good farm food. Outdoor play area has pets' corner with calves, lambs, piglets, goats, rabbits and Highland cows. Willing to warm bottles for human babies and serve booze to their parents!

CAFÉ CONTINENTAL
6 Hill Place, Kirkcaldy
Tel: (0592) 641811
Open: Daily 1200 – 2200
Café with tasty fast food; children's portions available. Restless children can colour their placemats, do quizzes and, at weekends, there is a lego table.

THE COTTAGE TEA-ROOM
28 Largo Road, Lundin Links
Tel: (0333) 320648
Open: Daily 1000 – 1700 (2230 Thu – Sun)
Local people go here for the good home-baking. There is a children's menu. Main courses from £3.40 with appropriate reductions.

THE HAYLOFT
Back Wynd, Falkland
Tel: (0337) 57590
Flagging children revive after a snack from the small but mouth-watering menu. Parents recommend the

delicious scones with jam and fresh cream.

KIND KYTTOCH'S KITCHEN
Cross Wynd, Falkland KY7 7BE
Off the main street in village
Tel: (0337) 57477
Open: Feb–Dec

Delicious home-baking and light meals. Winner of the Tea Council 1991 Award of Excellence and featured in the Taste of Scotland guide.

MARCANTONIO'S
Carnegie Drive, Dunfermline
Opposite the fire station

Children rave about the food sold here, including ecologically friendly edible chip cones.

Pubs

BETTY NICOL'S
297 High Street, Kirkcaldy
Tel: (0592) 642083

A welcoming pub with a family room equipped with games like dominoes and bagatelle. Bar lunches are served between 1230–1430 with main courses starting at just over £2 (reductions for children's portions).

THE GRANGE INN
Grange Road, St Andrews
Tel: (0334) 72670

The relaxed atmosphere has proved a perfect refuge from the elements for a number of families. Main course dishes from under £5, children's portions are half-price. Baby diner seat available.

HOFFMAN'S
435 High Street, Kirkcaldy
Tel: (0592) 204584
Open for lunches: Mon–Sat 1200–1400, Sun 1230–1430

Award-winning pub food with main courses starting at under £4. Children's portions are half-price. A baby diner chair is available.

PITSCOTTIE INN
New House, Pitscottie
Tel: (033 482) 244

Children's/Granny portions are available for a number of the dishes on the bar lunch menu. Main courses from £3.25 with reductions for small portions. Parents can ask for a side plate and share their meal with toddlers for no extra charge. There are three high-chairs and a baby diner seat available. The toilet for the disabled can be used for nappy changing.

THE UNICORN INN
15 Excise Street, Kincardine
Tel: (0259) 30704
Open: 1200–1400

Very good pub lunches with main courses from £5 (half portions for children or choose from children's menu). The owners have a young family, so children are well entertained and catered for.

Ice-Creams

BRUCEFIELD CAFÉ
76 Hospital Hill, Dunfermline
Tel: (0383) 722763
Open: Mon–Sat 0900–2100, Sun 1000–2100

Award-winning ice-creams in over 10 flavours.

DIVITO'S
59 Main Street, Crossgates, by Dunfermline
E of the Halbeath roundabout, junction 3 on M90

Tel: (0383) 510872
Open: Daily 0900–2130
Prize-winning ice-cream in 12 flavours.

JANETTA'S ICES
31 South Street, St Andrews
Tel: (0334) 73285
Open: 7 days
The finishing touch to a day out in St Andrews is an ice-cream from Janetta's. They have a wonderful selection of home-made award-winning ice-creams and sorbets in 24 flavours including Irn Bru! Ice-cream gateaux can be ordered for birthdays and special occasions.

VISOCCHI'S ICE-CREAM
37 High Street, Kirriemuir
Tel: (0575) 72115
and
40 Gray Street, Broughty Ferry, nr Dundee
Delicious ice-cream, espresso and cappuccino coffee.

Bakeries

GOODFELLOW & STEVENS
Broughty Ferry, nr Dundee
Branches at Arbroath, Monifieth, Barnhill, Dundee and Carnoustie.

WALLACE'S
Stobswell Baker, 78 Dura Street, Dundee
Tel: (0382) 462124
Good pies.

Fish and Chips

COMRIE FISH AND CHIPS
Comrie
Excellent chips.

PEPPO'S
53 Ladybridge Street, Arbroath
Tel: (0241) 72373

Award-winning fish and chips. Very good fresh fish.

VALENTE'S
73 Overton Road, Kirkcaldy
Tel: (0592) 51991
Voted the second best fish and chip shop in Scotland.

WYSE'S FISH AND CHIP SHOP
Pittenweem
Good, light batter and excellent fish.

Fast Food Chains

BURGER KING
163 High Street, Kirkcaldy
Tel: (0592) 267962
and
117 High Street, Dunfermline
Tel: (0383) 728692

LITTLE CHEF
Kingsway, Dundee
On A972, 1 mile N of the city
Tel: (0382) 623413
and
Brechin
4 miles W of Brechin on A94
Tel: (03563) 236

McDONALD'S
207/217 High Street, Kirkcaldy
Tel: (0592) 201035
and
106 High Street, Dunfermline
Tel: (0383) 621074
and
21/25 Reform Street, Dundee DD1 1RH
Tel: (0382) 200821

DRIVE-THROUGH
McDONALD'S
Longtown Road, Kingsway, Dundee DD4 8JB
Tel: (0382) 500577

OLIVERS COFFEE SHOP AND BAKERY
151 High Street, Kirkcaldy
Tel: (0592) 206317
and
133 High Street, Dunfermline KY12 7DR
Tel: (0383) 726378

THE PANCAKE PLACE
28 Kirkwynd, Kirkcaldy
Tel: (0592) 264982
Open: Mon – Sat 0930 – 1700
and
Kingsgate Centre, Dunfermline
Open: Daily 0930 – 1700 (shorter hours

on Sun)
and
22 Reform Street, Dundee
Tel: (0382) 23008

THE PIZZA GALLERY
39 Bell Street, St Andrews
Tel: (0334) 76268
Open: Daily
and
8/12 High Street, Dunfermline
Tel: (0383) 620370

PIZZA HUT
2/4 Nethergate, Dundee
Tel: (0382) 200320

PLACES TO STAY

Campsites

SHELL BAY CARAVAN SITE
Shell Bay, Elie KY9 1HB
Tel: (0333) 330283
££
An open campsite right by the beach (*see* **BEACHES**). There are good walks through the sand dunes to the village of Elie or a more adventurous route via the CHAIN WALK (*see* **WALKS**). There is a play area, laundry, games room and restaurant on site.

TAYPORT CARAVAN PARK
Tayport
Follow signs from B945
Tel: (0382) 552334
£££
A top-grade site for tents, caravans and camper vans with lovely views over the Tay. It even has a heated outdoor swimming pool. Games room, laundry and drying facilities. The recreation ground is only a few hundred yards away.

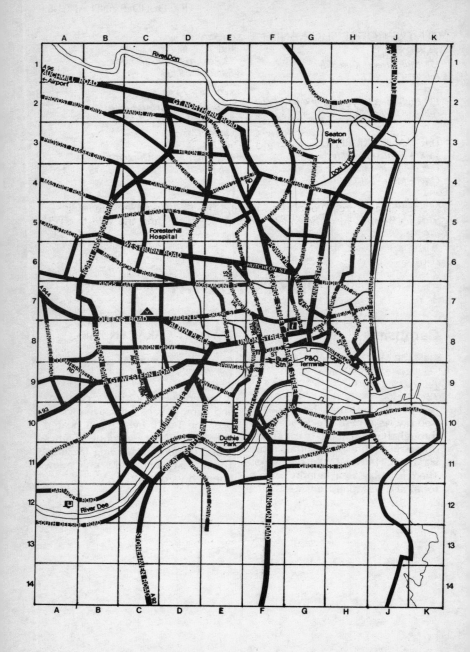

ABERDEEN AND THE NORTH-EAST

This is an area of great contrasts, with the towering Grampian mountains to the south and west, the Moray Firth to the north, and the wild North Sea to the east.

The main road and rail routes follow the coast round from Dundee and up to Aberdeen. The railway then heads north-west across country towards Inverness and the heart of the Highlands, while three main roads fan out from Aberdeen – one following a similar route to the railway, one heading to the fertile farmland of the north, and the last going west along Royal Deeside to Balmoral where the Queen and royal family spend part of every summer.

Aberdeen is a prosperous city thanks to North Sea oil. It has excellent museums and art galleries, beautiful parks and well-maintained playgrounds. There is a shoppers' creche at the Bonaccord Centre, plus an in-store creche at Fraser's department store (65 Union Street). Mother and baby facilities can be found at Debenham's (155 Union Street), Mothercare (122 Union Street) and at the airport.

In addition to the big city attractions, wonderful beaches stretch for miles and miles along the coast or nestle in quiet coves. There are dramatic ruins perched on clifftops and fairytale castles with wooded grounds which are ideal for walking, cycling or orienteering. The country parks have lots to offer, but the most famous attraction is undoubtedly Storybook Glen.

As well as typical summer activities like riding, walking and cycling, you can go cross-country or downhill skiing on artificial trails and slopes. Get in some practice before the winter comes so you can try the real thing at Cairnwell, Tomintoul or the Lecht which is specially geared to family skiing and even has a creche for very young children.

PLACES TO VISIT

Ancient Monuments

CULSH EARTH HOUSE (HS)
by Culsh Farmhouse nr Tarland
On the B9119, 2 miles E of Tarland
Tel: (031) 244 3101 (HS, Edinburgh)
Open: Apr – Sep, Mon – Sat 0930 – 1900,
Sun 1400 – 1900; Oct – Mar until 1600
Free
No disabled access
A well-preserved earth house built more than 2000 years ago, during the Iron Age, with roofing slabs intact over a large chamber and entrance. Take a torch to see the interior.

Animals and Birds

LEYHEAD SHEEP DAIRY
Lumphanan AB31 4QH
A980
Tel: (03398) 83256
Open: Easter – Jun, weekends and bank holidays 1500 – 1730; Jul – Sep, Thu – Sun and bank holidays 1500 – 1730
£
Disabled access
This is the first sheep dairy in the north-east. Go on a guided tour of the milking parlour at 1515 and watch ewes with names like 'Borage', 'Vanilla' and 'Elderberry' being milked. You can also see cheese being made.

FOWLSHEUGH NATURE RESERVE (RSPB)
Crawton nr Stonehaven
Off A92, 3 miles S of Stonehaven
Tel: (031) 557 3136 (RSPB, Edinburgh)
Open: All year, though best during spring and summer
Free (donation)
P: Available
'Seabird city' is one of the biggest seabird colonies in Scotland with over 100,000 nesting birds. It is best in the spring and summer when the nesting birds can be seen from the clifftops. Take care near the edge. Exhibition centre. No public toilets.

MUIR OF DINNET NATURE RESERVE
Midway between Aboyne and Ballater on A97, 1 mile N of junct with A93
Tel: (03398) 81667/81669
Open: Mid May – Sep, Thu – Mon 1000 – 1800
Free
P: Available
Disabled facilities
Visitor centre, nature trails and walk to the spectacular Burn o' Vat.

THE MEARNS HEAVY HORSE CENTRE AND FARM MUSEUM
Durie Mains Farm, Luthermuir
Off B974 to Fettercairn, S of Laurencekirk
Tel: (067484) 447
Open: May – Oct, daily 1000 – 1600
£
Clydesdale horses, mares and foals. Also harness room, blacksmith shop.

THE NORTH-EAST FALCONRY VISITOR CENTRE
Broadland, Cairnie, Huntly AB54 4UU
3 miles NW of Huntly on road linking A920 to A96
Tel: (0224) 212112
Open: Daily, 1000 – 1800
££
P: Available
Café and picnic area

Get really close to falcons, owls and eagles. There are regular flying demonstrations where children can volunteer to help. It is a good outing for teenagers as well as much younger children, who like the Highland cattle and red deer.

SANDS OF FORVIE NATIONAL NATURE RESERVE
Little Collieston Croft, Collieston
Tel: (035887) 330
Open: Centre May–Sep, daily 1000–1700, Oct–Apr Sat–Sun
Free
The dunes on this part of the coast are an important feeding ground for waders, eider duck, and other fowl.

LOCH OF STRATHBEG NATURE RESERVE (RSPB)
Crimond nr Fraserburgh
6 miles S of Fraserburgh. Thistle signposted from Crimond on A952
Tel: (0346) 32017
Free (donation)
Open: Daily, dawn–dusk
About 40,000 geese, ducks and swans spend the winter here. The observation room has binoculars for viewing the birds as well as displays and interactive games. Lochside board walk and bird-watching hides. No public toilets.

HONEYNEUK BIRD PARK
Bruntyards, Longmanhill, nr Macduff
Signposted off A947 and A98
Tel: (02616) 262
Open: May–Oct, Tue–Sun 1200–1800
£
P: Available
Tea-room, picnic area
Over 100 species of birds and animals including poultry, pigeons, birds of prey and pigs. School parties

and groups may use the classroom facilities. Children's play area.

CLOVERLEAF FIBRE STUD
Mill of Kinnairdy, Bridge of Marnoch nr Aberchirder
Off A97 beside Kinnairdy Castle, 10 miles S of Banff
Tel: (0466) 780879
Open: Guided tours at 1100, 1300 and 1500 all year
£
Although nowadays a lot of knitwear is made from by-products of the oil or coal industry (such as acrylics and polyesters), some jumpers and cardigans are still made from real sheep's wool. You might be surprised to see how many animals apart from sheep are reared for their fleeces – among them llamas, guanacos, alpacas, cashmere, angora and cashgora goats and reindeer.

MAUD MART
Maud
Sales held on Tue 1030, Wed 1000
12 miles W of Peterhead
Free
One of Britain's largest livestock marts with sheep and cattle auctions.

Arts and Crafts

ART GALLERY – CHILDREN'S WORKSHOP
Art Gallery, Schoolhill, Aberdeen
Tel: (0224) 646333
Open: Mon–Sat 1000–1645, Sun 1400–1645
Free
Coffee shop
Disabled access
Art and dance workshops in the school holidays. Also term-time pro-

gramme with quizzes and other activities to stimulate interest.

Beaches

The north-east has many lovely sandy beaches. Most of them have passed the minimum EC standards on sewage pollution but, according to the 1992 Good Beach Guide, you should avoid ST CYRUS, BANFF LINKS and LOSSIEMOUTH EAST as they have high levels of contamination.

The coast between Fraserburgh and Inverness is sometimes called the Banffshire Riviera. Long sweeping beaches contrast with small sheltered coves and bays nestling under towering cliffs. Some of the best beaches are described here but others that are definitely worth a visit include (from east to west) ROSEHEARTY, CULLEN, CUMMINGSTON and EAST BEACH at Hopeman.

ABERDEEN BEACH
Aberdeen
P: Available
Over 2 miles of golden sand are sandwiched between the 'silver city' and the grey North Sea.

BALMEDIE BEACH
nr Aberdeen
N of Aberdeen, off A92
Has 10 miles of sand and dunes with lots of walks and a visitor centre. *See* BALMEDIE COUNTRY PARK—
COUNTRY PARKS.

CRUDEN BAY BEACH
Cruden Bay nr Peterhead
8 miles S of Peterhead
Over 2 miles of soft sand on a crescent-shaped beach.

CULLYKHAN BAY
nr Pennan
Signposted off B9031
P: Available
Footpaths lead from the carpark to sandy bay, a bronze-age fort and a deep cliffside gash leading to a sea tunnel called Hell's Lum.

FRASERBURGH BEACH
Fraserburgh
P: Available
Café
A 3-mile stretch of dune-backed sand which has won awards for cleanliness. Play equipment, paddling pool. Toilets.

PETERHEAD BEACH
off South Road, Peterhead
P: Available
Café
A sandy beach sheltered by harbour breakwaters. Safe bathing and ideal for watersports.

BOYNDIE BEACH
Banff
Restaurant nearby
Toilets
Long sandy beach with play equipment.

THE LEIN
Kingston on Spey nr Elgin
B9015
Scottish Wildlife Trust Reserve with a vast shingle beach and play area.

SILVERSANDS
Lossiemouth
The sand and shingle beach stretches for 8 miles to either side of Lossiemouth. Take your buckets and spades to Silversands, which lies to the west of the town, but don't go to East Sands as the water quality

there is not up to EC standards (1992 Good Beach Guide).

CULBIN SANDS

nr Forres
Access from Cloddymoss (parking); Wellhill (parking and picnic area)
Picnic areas
The beach was named after the village of Culbin which was engulfed by sand during a storm in 1694. From the carparks there are lovely walks through the forest to the beach.

Bike Hire and Cycle Routes

A. J. STEWART

The Square, Tarland
Tel: (03398) 81231
£ per day
Cycle hire (no mountain bikes).

125 MAIN STREET

Buckie
Tel: (0542) 33070
££ per day
Cycle hire, including children's bikes and child seats.

MINI-CHEERS

5 Fife Street, Dufftown AB55 4AL
Tel: (0340) 20559/20906
££
Mountain bike hire. Special family rates on request.

BRIDGE OF BROWN TEAROOM

Grantown Road, Tomintoul AB37 9HR
Tel: (08074) 335
£££
Mountain bike hire for older children and adults.

BRAEMAR NORDIC SKI HIRE —

see WINTER SPORTS

Boats and Boat Trips

FRASERBURGH LIFEBOAT SHED

Fraserburgh Harbour, Fraserburgh
Open: Jun – Sep, Mon – Sat 1400 – 1600
Current lifeboat *City of Edinburgh* is on view.

PETERHEAD LIFEBOAT SHED

Lodge Walk, The Harbour, Peterhead
Open: Mid Jun – Sep, Mon – Fri 0930 – 1200, 1330 – 1600, Sat 0930 – 1200
Look round a working lifeboat.

Castles and Stately Homes

SLAINS CASTLE

Cruden Bay
Footpath from Main Street carpark
Open: All reasonable times
Free
P: Available
No disabled access
Some parts of this extensive clifftop ruin are about 400 years old. It was the inspiration for the vampire's castle in Bram Stoker's *Dracula*. Take great care on the cliffs.

FYVIE CASTLE (NTS)

Fyvie
25 miles NW of Aberdeen on B9005
Tel: (06516) 266
Open: Castle Apr/May/Sep 1400 – 1800, Jun – Aug 1100 – 1800; grounds all year
££
P: Available
Tea-room, picnic area
A 13th-century castle with a good collection of armour and weapons. Woodland and lochside walks in the castle grounds.

DUNNOTAR CASTLE

nr Stonehaven
Off A92, S of Stonehaven
Tel: (0569) 62173

*Open: Apr – Oct, Mon – Sat 0900 – 1800,
Sun 1400 – 1700; Nov – Mar 0900 – dusk,
not weekends
£
P: Available
Disabled access*
An impressive ruined fortress on a
rocky cliff 160ft above the sea. A
stronghold of the Earls Marischal of
Scotland from the 14th century.

FASQUE
*Fettercairn
On B974, 1 mile N of Fettercairn
Tel: (05614) 202
Open: May – Sep, Sat – Thu 1330 – 1730
£*
The house was built for the Gladstone family 170 years ago, and was
lived in by William Gladstone, Prime
Minister under Queen Victoria. It
is a good example of a Victorian
'upstairs-downstairs' household with
grand state rooms, library and bedrooms contrasting with the kitchen,
sculleries, washroom, knives hall,
bakery and buttery full of strange,
old-fashioned domestic implements.

CRATHES CASTLE AND GARDENS (NTS)
*nr Banchory
Off A93, 3.5 miles E of Banchory
Tel: (033 044) 525
Open: Castle and visitor centre Apr –
Oct, daily 1100 – 1800; gardens all year
Castle and gardens – £££; grounds, visi-
tor centre, exhibitions and trails – £
P: Available
Restaurant, snack bar
Disabled facilities
Toilets, mother's room*
A fine castle with a ghost. Nature
trails and woodland walks including
one designed for wheelchair-users
(wheelchairs available on request).

Wayfaring trails for those with maps
and compasses and a desire to nego-
tiate rougher ground. Visitor centre
with exhibition rooms, field study
centre and ranger service offering
guided walks in summer. Young
Naturalists club. Small adventure
playground for under-8s.

DRUM CASTLE (NTS)
*by Peterculter, Aberdeen
Off A93, 10 miles W of Aberdeen
Tel: (03308) 204
Open: Apr – Sep, daily 1400 – 1800, and
Oct week; grounds open all year
Castle – ££
P: Available
Tea-room, picnic area
Disabled facilities and partial access*
The house stands in pleasant
grounds with lawns, rare trees and
shrubs. Visitors may climb the 700-
year-old keep and explore the rest
of the castle. There are woodland
walks through the Forest of Drum
which has been a Site of Special
Scientific Interest for 10 years. Other
activities include the farmland trail,
wayfaring course, an arboretum for
tree spotters and a small adventure
play area for under-8s.

BALMORAL CASTLE
*Crathie by Ballater
8 miles W of Ballater on A93
Tel: (03397) 42334
Open: May – Jul, Mon – Sat 1000 – 1700
(except when royal family in residence)
£
P: Metered carpark
Refreshments*
The castle has been the royal family's
holiday retreat since 1856. There
are country walks, gardens and an
exhibition in the ballroom. For pony-
trekking on the estate, *see* RIDING.

LEITH HALL (NTS)

nr Huntly
B9002, 7 miles S of Huntly
Tel: (04643) 216
Open: House end Apr – Sep, daily 1400 –
1800; Garden all year 0930 – sunset
Castle – ££; Grounds – donation
P: Available
Picnic area, tea-room
Disabled facilities

The mansion house is at the centre of a 286-acre estate. The grounds contain varied farm and woodlands. There are two ponds, a bird observation hide and three countryside walks, one leading to a hilltop viewpoint. Unique 18th-century stables, Soay sheep, ice-house.

CASTLE FRASER (NTS)

Sauchen nr Kemnay
16 miles W of Aberdeen off A944
Tel: (03303) 463
Open: Castle May – Sep, 1400 – 1800
(Jul – Aug 1100 – 1800); gardens
0930 – dusk
Castle – ££; Grounds – donation
Tea-room, picnic area

A spectacular castle with a Laird's Lug – a secret hiding place where the laird could listen in to conversations. Work off some energy in the 26 acres of parkland, walled garden and adventure playground.

CRAIGIEVAR CASTLE (NTS)

nr Alford
Off A980 Alford – Lumphanan road
Open: Grounds all year, 0930 – sunset;
Castle May – Sep 1400 – 1800
Castle – ££; Grounds – free
Picnic area
No disabled access to castle

A 17th-century tower house with a secret staircase. Woodland walks and a countryside trail.

KILDRUMMY CASTLE AND GARDENS (HS)

nr Alford
A97, off A944, 10 miles W of Alford
Tel: (09755) 71264
Open: Grounds Apr – Oct, daily 1000 –
1700
£
P: Available
Disabled facilities and access to garden

Quite a lot remains of this 13th-century castle. There are shrub and alpine gardens as well as water gardens, a play area, video room and a woodland walk.

HUNTLY CASTLE (HS)

Huntly, A96
Tel: (0466) 3191
£

The ruins, which date back 300 to 400 years, are in a beautiful wooded riverside setting close to COOPER PARK (*see* PARKS AND PLAYGROUNDS).

BRODIE CASTLE (NTS)

Brodie nr Forres
3 miles W of Forres, to the N of A96 to
Inverness
Tel: (03094) 371
Open: Grounds open all year, daily
0930 – sunset
Castle – ££; Grounds – donation
Picnic area, tea-room
Disabled facilities and assisted access

The castle is a bit too staid for children but they enjoy walks through the grounds and round the 4-acre pond. It is especially attractive in spring when the daffodils are in flower. There is a play area.

Caves

SUNNYSIDE BAY

Between Cullen and Sandend
Free

At the west end of this sandy beach is Charlie the Hermit's Cave, where a Frenchman lived before WWII. There are lots of other signposted walks along the coast and inland to Fordyce.

COVESEA CAVES
nr Lossiemouth
3 miles W of Lossiemouth
Free
One of the caves is reputed to be connected by an underground passage to Gordonstoun House. The perfect setting for an Enid Blyton story?

Chairlifts

GLENSHEE CHAIRLIFT
Off A93, S of Braemar
Open: All year 0900 – 1630
££
P: Available
Restaurant
Take a trip to the summit of Cairnwell (3039ft) and watch the hang-gliders. *See* **WINTER SPORTS**.

Country Parks

BRIMMOND AND ELRICK COUNTRY PARK
nr Aberdeen
Off A96/A944
Open: All year
Picnic area
Follow the marked walks across rolling hillside and moorland and find the 'Robber's Cave'. Go on a ranger-led walk during the summer.

HADDO COUNTRY PARK (NTS)
Tarves
nr Methlick on B9170

Tel: (06515) 440
Open: All year 0930 – dusk; centre 1100 – 1800 during summer
House – ££; Gardens – donation
P: Available
Picnic area
Disabled facilities
There's plenty to do in the 180 acres of parkland which include woodland walks, nature trails, a lake and ponds with ducks, bird hides, a small adventure playground, pony and trap rides as well as the Discovery Room and Haddo House itself. Ranger service.

HAUGHTON COUNTRY PARK
nr Alford
25 miles W of Aberdeen on A944, half a mile N of Alford
Tel: (09755) 62453/62107
Open: All year; centre: Easter – Sep weekend 0830 – 1630
P: Available
Picnic areas
Disabled facilities
Lots of parkland with riverside walks, putting, a walled garden and a playground. There is a children's wayfaring course and a ranger service.

BALMEDIE COUNTRY PARK
nr Aberdeen
8 miles N of Aberdeen
Tel: (0358) 42396
Open: All year; centre – Easter – Sep 1000 – 1630
Picnic and barbecue areas
Award-winning wheelchair access
Coastal park with sandy beach and dunes. *See* **BEACHES**.

ADEN COUNTRY PARK
Mintlaw AB4 8LD
On A950 between Old Deer and Mintlaw, 30 miles N of Aberdeen
Tel: (0771) 22857
Open: Park – all year; centre – May – Sep 1100 – 1700, Apr/Oct weekends

Free entry to the park, £ for Heritage Centre
Restaurant, picnic areas
Disabled facilities and partial access

A quarter of Scotland's arable land lies in the north-east so it is not surprising to find many farming museums in the area. The award-winning heritage centre has exhibitions on old farming methods and implements as well as domestic scenes. Imagine making oatcakes on a griddle over an open fire like people would have done 100 years ago instead of popping down to the shops! There are woodland walks, a nature trail and an adventure playground as well as fishing on the River Ugie. The rangers organise special events like the popular Easter Eggstravaganza. There is a camping and caravan site in the park with a separate campsite for youth groups (see PLACES TO STAY).

GLENLIVET ESTATE

Forest Office, Main Street, Tomintoul AB37 9EX
Tel: (08074) 283
P: Available
Picnic areas

Waymarked trails suitable for walking, cycling or riding. Ranger service with guided walks and Land Rover tours.

MILLBUIES COUNTRY PARK

nr Elgin
5 miles S of Elgin and W of A941 to Rothes
Tel: (034386) 234
Picnic area
Assisted disabled access

A peaceful beauty spot with nature trails, a wayfaring course and fishing.

Fairgrounds

RAMBOLAND

Codona's Amusement Park, Beach Promenade, Aberdeen
Tel: (0224) 595910/595909
Open: Easter and summer holidays from 1300, weekends in May/Sep
Free for adults, ££ for children

A large and permanent fairground with all the usual head-spinning rides and money-spinning stalls. As a compromise (for under-10s), try Ramboland – an adventure playground within the fair with a ball pool, slides, rope-ladders and so on.

BANCHORY FAIR

Dee Street Carpark, Banchory
Open: Apr – Sep
From £

Roundabout, mini-dodgems, side stalls for youngsters.

Farms

DOONIES FARM

Old Cove Road, off Greyhope Road, Nigg, Aberdeen
Tel: (0224) 276276
Open: All year, daylight – dusk
Free

A small model farm and rare breed centre featuring Clydesdales, cattle, sheep, pigs and Shetland ponies.

BELWADE FARM

Dess, Aboyne
Tel: (03398) 87186
Open: Wed 1400 – 1700, Sat – Sun 1100 – 1600
Free

International League for the Protection of Horses is a charity for the rest and rehabilitation of horses from all over Scotland. Go on a free guided tour of the centre and see 20 to 30 horses and ponies.

DARNAWAY FARM VISITOR CENTRE

nr Forres
On A96, 3 miles W of Forres
Tel: (03094) 469
Open: Jun – mid Sep, daily 1000 – 1700
£
P: Free
Picnic areas and tea-room
Disabled facilities
Toilets

Where does milk come from? If your answer is 'Cartons and bottles in the supermarket' then it is time you came to watch cows being milked. Find out even more about farming from the exhibition and the audio-visual show. Then go and meet the other farm animals, follow the nature trail and woodland walks, and have fun in the small adventure play area.

Festivals

ABERDEEN INTERNATIONAL YOUTH FESTIVAL

August is festival time in Aberdeen. An extravaganza of dance and musical entertainment at different venues throughout the city. Details from the Tourist Information Centre.

KALEIDOSCOPE

In June 1993, a new international children's festival is to be staged with a variety of shows for kids. This is to be an annual event.

Fish

ABERDEEN FISHMARKET

Off Market Street, Aberdeen
Tel: (0224) 897744

Open: Best between 0700 – 0800 Mon – Fri
Free

If you are an early riser, make a visit to the fishmarket before breakfast. How many kinds of fish can you recognise? Aberdeen is one of Britain's major fishing ports and hundreds of tons of fish are landed daily.

FRASERBURGH HARBOUR AND FISHMARKET

Fraserburgh
Open: Mon – Sat from 0730
Free

Watch the catches being landed and sold – almost 500,000 boxes are sold each year.

MACDUFF HARBOUR AND FISHMARKET

Macduff
Open: Fishmarket Mon – Fri from 0800
Free

About 10,000 boxes of fish are sold each week.

PETERHEAD HARBOUR AND FISHMARKET

Peterhead
Open: Mon – Fri from 0730, Sat from 0800
Free

Up to 14,000 boxes of fish are sold each day. Catches including whiting, herring, haddock, sole, cod and mackerel.

LOSSIEMOUTH FISHMARKET

West Harbour, Lossiemouth
Open: Mon – Fri from 0800 depending on tides and catches
Assisted disabled access

An outing for early risers. See the trawlers in the harbour, try and identify the shellfish and white fish that are for sale, then go home for breakfast.

Gardens

JOHNSTON GARDENS
Viewfield Road, Aberdeen
A small garden with stream, cascades, waterfowl and alpines. Fun for toddlers.

CRUICKSHANK GARDENS
Botany Dept, University of Aberdeen, Old Aberdeen
Tel: (0224) 272000
Lots of flowers, ponds and undulating ground which is great for games of hide and seek.

CANDACRAIG WALLED GARDEN
Strathdon AB36 8XT
W of Roughpark on A944
Tel: (09756) 51 226
Open: End Apr—mid Oct 1000—1700 daily
Picnic area, coffee shop
Disabled facilities
Victorian walled gardens and various themed gardens devoted to roses, bog plants, wild flowers, old-fashioned cottage flowers and a secret garden. Formal in design but casual in approach.

PITMEDDEN GARDEN AND FARMING MUSEUM (NTS)
Pitmedden
Outskirts of village on A920, 14 miles N of Aberdeen
Tel: (065 13) 2352
Open: End Apr—Sep, daily 1000—1800
££
P: Available
Picnic area, tea-room
Disabled facilities

The 17th-century formal garden has been recreated with elaborate floral designs, pavilions, fountains and sundials. There are also woodland and farmland walks, a herb garden and a visitor centre. The museum contains a wide selection of agricultural and domestic implements.

CRAIGHEADS GARDEN
Whitehills nr Banff
Look out for this cottage garden with its colourful displays of ornamental windmills, birdboxes and life-size figures—very appealing to under-10s.

Museums

PROVOST ROSS'S HOUSE (NTS)
Shiprow, Aberdeen
Tel: (0224) 585788
Open: All year, Mon—Sat 1000—1700; centre: May—Sep, Mon—Sat 1000—1600
Free
P: Available
Disabled access
Situated in one of Aberdeen's oldest buildings (1593), the museum uses models, paintings and audio-visual displays to tell the story of local shipbuilding, the fishing industry, and North Sea oil and gas developments. Phone for details of special exhibitions between Oct—Mar.

ANTHROPOLOGICAL MUSEUM
Marischal College, Broad St., Aberdeen
Tel: (0224) 273131
Open: Mon—Fri 1000—1700, Sun 1400—1700
Free
Museum of the Year winner with all sorts of gruesome artefacts including shrunken heads, bound Chinese feet, an Egyptian mummy, gilded

buddhas and remains of Scotland's prehistoric inhabitants. A great place for a rainy day outing.

JONAH'S JOURNEY

120 Rosemount Place, Aberdeen
Tel: (0224) 647614
Open: All year, Mon–Fri 1000–1600 (not Tue Oct–Mar), Sat/Sun by arrangement
£
P: Available
Coffee shop

An activity-based learning centre showing life in biblical times. Children can dress up in period costume and try grinding grain, spinning and weaving. Go inside a nomad tent or an Israelite house. See what it was like to write on papyrus, wax or clay. There are workshops, games, quizzes and activity sheets. This award-winning heritage museum is mainly geared to Sunday schools and educational visits.

NORTHFIELD FARM MUSEUM

nr New Pitsligo
From A98 follow signs to New Aberdour or B9031 to New Pitsligo
Tel: (07717) 504
Open: May–Sep, daily 1330–1730
£
P: Available
Disabled facilities

A large collection of farm equipment including working tractors, implements, stationary engines, old motor bikes and household bric-à-brac from the 1870s. Other attractions include the reconstructed smiddy, an aviary and llamas.

GRAMPIAN TRANSPORT MUSEUM

Alford AB33 8AD
25 miles W of Aberdeen on A944
Tel: (09755) 62292
Open: Apr–Sep, daily 1030–1700, Oct week
£
P: Free

There are lots of things to see and do. Hop on board a double-decker bus to watch videos on motor sport and transport history. Test your skills on the driving simulator. Look round the extensive collection of historic road vehicles and clamber aboard the snowplough and snowmobile. You can listen to a 1920s' dance organ, play in the adventure playground, or look at the railway exhibition and narrow gauge railway, and road safety exhibition. Phone for details of major events throughout the year.

REMAINS TO BE SEEN

nr Ellon
From Ellon, B9005 to Methlick until QuilQuox sign on right
Tel: (03587) 229
Open: Apr–Oct, daily 1000–1900; Nov–Mar 1100–1600
Free
P: Available
Tea, coffee

An exhibition of period clothes and accessories, lace, jewellery and porcelain. Good for older children interested in clothing, fashion and design.

MORAY MOTOR MUSEUM

Bridge Street, Bishopsmill, Elgin
A941 from Elgin centre bypass, 800yds on right
Tel: (0343) 544933/54713
Open: Easter–Oct 1100–1700
£
P: Available
Assisted disabled access and facilities

Collection of over 40 veteran, vintage and classic cars and motorcycles housed in an old converted mill building.

THE VILLAGE STORE
The Square, Aberlour
In centre of village on main street
Tel: (0340) 871243
Open: Thu – Sat, Mon – Tue 1000 – 1800,
Sun 1300 – 1700; restricted hours Nov –
Feb
Free
P: Available
Step back in time and see an old general store complete with all the original fittings, records and stock dating from the 1920s.

TOMINTOUL MUSEUM
The Square, Tomintoul
Tel: (0309) 73701
Open: Apr – Oct
Free
A reconstructed farmhouse kitchen and village smiddy. Displays on local environment and skiing.

FOCHABERS FOLK MUSEUM
Fochabers
A96 between Aberdeen and Inverness
Open: Daily 0930 – 1300, 1400 – 1730
£
Reconstructed village shop, a large collection of horse-drawn carts, and domestic artefacts going back 200 years.

LADYCROFT FARM MUSEUM

Elchies, Archiestown nr Elgin
Off B9102
Tel: (03406) 274
Open: All year, daily from 1000 – dusk
£

Collection of old agricultural implements and equipment from the time when farming was done with horses, not tractors. Life-size models of men and horses.

ELGIN MUSEUM

High Street, Elgin
Tel: (0343) 543675
Open: Apr – Sep, Tue – Fri 1000 – 1700, Sat 1100 – 1600
£
Disabled facilities

An award-winning museum housing a world-famous collection of old red sandstone, Permian and Triassic fossils. Other displays on local history from prehistoric times as well as animals and birds found in the area.

PITMEDDEN GARDEN AND MUSEUM OF FARMING LIFE –

see GARDENS

Novelties

GARDENSTOWN

Spectacular seashore village built on the side of the cliff in a series of narrow terraces. Some of the houses have doorways on to the main road at 3 different levels. Some parts of the village can only be reached on foot.

CRIMOND KIRK

Crimond
Between Fraserburgh and Peterhead
An hour in Crimond is longer than an hour anywhere else. Or is it? The church clock shows 61 minutes to the hour because the clockmaker mistakenly put six marks into the last five minutes.

Parks and Playgrounds

HAZELHEAD PARK

Groats Road, Hazelhead Avenue, Aberdeen
Tel: (0224) 276276
Open: All year, daily from 0800; sport facilities – May – Sep from 1000
P: Free
Restaurant and small kiosk
Disabled access

This is the largest park in Aberdeen. There are walks, a woodland assault course and a wayfaring course through the extensive woodland. Plenty of open grass and flowers galore in the rose, heather and azalea gardens. The maze has over a mile of paths – a long walk if your toddler falls asleep somewhere near the middle and you have to carry him or her out again! Other attractions include trampolines, swingball, table-tennis and an adventure playground suitable for toddlers and young children. The small zoo has lambs, rabbits and pot-bellied pigs and a wonderful walk-in aviary full of exotically coloured birds. For riding in the park, *see* HAYFIELD EQUESTRIAN CENTRE (RIDING).

DUTHIE PARK AND WINTER GARDENS

Polmuir Road/Riverside Drive, Aberdeen
Tel: (0224) 583155
Open: All year, including public holidays, 1000 – dusk; sport facilities – May – Sep
P: Free

Self-service restaurant
Disabled access
The park has a children's play area, two boating ponds, tennis, putting, table-tennis, swingball, trampolines, and pony and trap rides. Climb the 'rose mountain' and smell the perfume of over 100,000 roses. The Winter Gardens feature exotic plants, terrapins, fish and a giant plastic frog which small children love to watch as it bursts up from the depths of the pool at regular intervals. The Japanese garden has a little stream and lots of wee bridges and stepping-stones. Part of the restaurant may be booked for children's parties. The park is also the start of the Deeside walkway and cycle path to Peterculter.

SEATON PARK
Don Street, Aberdeen
Also accessible from the Chanonry
Tel: (0224) 276276
Open: All year
Picnic area
A mixture of formal gardens and woodland by the River Don. Come in the spring to see the spectacular banks of daffodils. There is a small adventure playground.

WESTBURN PARK
Westburn Road, Aberdeen
Tel: (0224) 276276
Open: All year
Restaurant, picnic area
Disabled access and facilities
Children's cycle track with mini road signs and roundabouts – good for toddlers on trikes and still fun for energetic 8-year-olds. Play areas, paddling pool, table-tennis and tennis. One playground is especially for

disabled children and there is a trim track for the disabled too.

VICTORIA PARK
Westburn Road, Aberdeen
Garden and maze for the disabled
Aberdeen's oldest park has large grass areas, a maze and a conservatory for cool days. The spectacular fountain incorporates tiny cymbals which tinkle as the water cascades over them, and the fragrant garden has strongly scented flowers and braille nameplates.

QUEEN'S LINKS ADVENTURE PLAYGROUND
Beach Esplanade, Aberdeen
Tel: (0224) 276276
Playground on the theme of a fishing village with a paddling pool, crazy golf and tennis.

COOPER PARK
Huntly
Try table-tennis, trampolining, tennis and cross-country skiing during the summer! The small ski trail has artificial snow tracks so you can practice all year round.

LOCH SOY
Seafield Street, Portsoy
Open: Facilities available during summer months
Picnic area
Hire a paddle-boat for a trip round the loch; practice your putting skills; or monkey about in the adventure playground.

BLACKPOTS HARBOUR
nr Whitehills
E of Whitehills Harbour, 2 miles W of Banff
Picnic area
A picturesque harbour with large

landscaped seashore park. Extensive children's playground, playing fields.

SILVERSANDS LEISURE PARK
Lossiemouth
Go-karts and children's motorcycles can be hired 500 yds W of the park.

Picnic Sites

Fettercairn: DRUMTOCHTY CASTLE
Ballater: CAMBUS O'MAY FOOTBRIDGE
Turriff: INVERKEITHNY VIEWPOINT
Cullen: THE LINKS
Dufftown: OLD STATION
Glenlivet: BRIDGE OF LIVET
Kingston on Spey: BIRD WATCH CORNER
Rothes: DOONIE WALK
Nr Tomintoul: GLENFIDDICH DISTILLERY VISITOR CENTRE

Playschemes and Creches

BON-ACCORD LEISURE CENTRE CRECHE
Bon-Accord Shopping Centre, George Street, Aberdeen
Tel: (0224) 626260
Open: daily 0900 – 1700
££ per hour, maximum stay 2 hours
Shoppers' creche for 2½ to 7-year-olds.

Railways

ALFORD VALLEY RAILWAY
Murray Park, Alford
Tel: (09755) 62326
Open: Weekends Apr/May/Sep 1100 – 1700, daily Jun/Jul/Aug 1100 – 1700
£
P: Available
Disabled facilities
The narrow gauge railway runs from Alford Station and Museum to Haughton Country Park then on to Murray Park. Terminus near Alford Transport Museum.

MINI-RAILWAY
The Beach, Fraserburgh
Open: Daily (depending on weather), Jul – Aug
£
Mini-railway adjacent to beach.

DISTILLERY COTTAGE CRAFT SHOP
28 Bridge Street, New Byth, nr Turriff AB53 7XB
Tel: (08883) 729
£
Children can ride on the miniature railway or work off some energy in the adventure play area. The museum (free) has miniature steam locomotives, wind-up gramophones, magic lanterns and other items from the 1800s.

Riding

HAYFIELD EQUESTRIAN CENTRE
Hazelhead Park, Aberdeen AB1 8BB
Tel: (0224) 315703
Open: All year, Tue – Sun
£££
Riding for the disabled
STRA approved. Miles of traffic-free riding round Hazelhead Park. Hacking and instruction, indoor school. Half-hour 'walkies' for very little children and 'paddock hacks' for inexperienced riders.

CRAIG GOWAN RIDING CENTRE
Main Street, Fettercairn
Tel: (056 14) 498
From ££

Hourly, half-day and day rides, indoor tuition, holiday courses and fun weeks – all on your own horse if you like. Minimum age 2. STRA approved.

NORTH GELLAN STABLES ACTIVITY HOLIDAYS
Coull, Tarland AB34 4YR
Tel: (03398) 81245
From ££
Riding for over-5s. Forest and mountain trails, holiday courses. STRA approved.

LONACH FARM HORSE RIDING AND PONY-TREKKING CENTRE
Strathdon AB3 8YB
Tel: (09756) 51275
Open: All year, daily
£££
STRA approved. Riding for over-5s. Forest and hill tracks. Half day and full day.

LAW RIDING CENTRE
Kennethmont, Insch AB52 6YT
Tel: (04643) 550/548/218
££
Disabled facilities
STRA approved. Safe, supervised riding on 200-acre farm for toddlers upwards. Specially geared to unaccompanied residential children. Also wildlife pond, mountain bike trails, indoor sports.

TOMINTOUL TREKKING AND TRAIL RIDING CENTRE
Tomintoul AB37 9ET
Tel: (08074) 210
£££
STRA approved. Hourly, half-day or full day treks. Trail rides for experienced riders or 15 minutes on a lead rein for small children.

KNOCKANDHU RIDING SCHOOL
Craigellachie AB38 9RP
Tel: (05426) 302
£
Hacking, cross-country jumps, indoor and outdoor schools. Children over 4 welcome.

REDMOSS RIDING CENTRE
Drybridge, Buckie AB56 2JD
Tel: (0542) 33140
£
Families welcome. Toddlers can ride Shetland ponies on a lead rein. Lessons, hacking, trekking.

Science and Technology

SATROSPHERE
19 Justice Mill Lane, off Union Street, Aberdeen
Tel: (0224) 213232
Open: All year, Mon, Wed – Sat 1000 – 1700 (1600 in term-time), Sun 1330 – 1700 (open Tue in holidays)
£
P: Municipal carpark
Snack bar
Disabled access
You don't have to be a genius to learn about science in this exciting, hands-on science and technology centre. There are 70 to 100 experiments exploring sound, light, energy and the environment. Be prepared for a long visit even with pre-school children as they love to make giant bubbles, generate electricity and balance balls on jets of air. Phone for details of special events every 2 or 3 months.

PLANETARIUM
Aberdeen College of Further Education, School of Science and Techology,

Gallowgate, Aberdeen
Tel: (0224) 640366
Shows: Tue–Fri 1400, 1600, Wed–Thu 1330, 1700, 1900 (no 1900 show during early Jul–early Aug)
Free
Disabled access
Discover which is the brightest star, why there are seasons, what black holes are, and how to find the Pole Star. See stars and planets moving across the night sky whatever the weather or the time of day, and all from the comfort of a chair in the star theatre. Morning shows (Tue, Wed, Thu) for school groups.

Scotland at Work – Past and Present

FINZEAN BUCKET MILL
Forest of Birse
Off B976 W of Banchory
Tel: (033045) 633/372
Open: Easter–Sep, Tue–Sun 1100–1700
£
P: Available
A working 19th-century wood-turning mill where you can see buckets being turned. Guided tours at 1430 and 1530 (and 1100 in Jul–Aug). Bee observation hive. The mill has won a conservation award.

BAXTERS VISITOR CENTRE
nr Fochabers
1 mile W of Fochabers on A96
Tel: (0343) 820393
Free
P: Free
Restaurant (see PLACES TO EAT)
Disabled facilities but no wheelchairs on factory tour
Interesting guided factory tours where you can watch huge batches of soup being made. Audio-visual

show, museum. There are Highland cattle and woodland walks in the landscaped grounds.

LOSSIE SEAFOODS
Couldbank Road, Lossiemouth
Tel: (034381) 3005
Open: Weekday afternoons by prior arrangement
Factory tours – see fish processing, smoking and curing.

MILL OF TOWIE
Drummuir, Keith
Tel: (054 281) 274
Open: Easter and May–Oct 1030–1630
£
Picnic area
Disabled facilities
In days before supermarkets and Quaker Porridge Oats everyone came to the mill with their sacks of oats. Nowadays the miller is kept busy giving tours of this restored 19th-century oatmeal mill. An interesting visit for over-9s. Younger children can have fun in the play area by the River Isla.

OLD MILLS
Old Mills Road, Elgin
Tel: (0343) 540698
Open: May–Sep, Tue–Sun 1000–1730
£
Picnic area, coffee bar
Assisted disabled access
There has been a water-mill here for almost 800 years. The current mill has been restored to full working order and you can see and hear the machinery in action. Wheat, barley and oats are grown nearby so you can see what cereals look like before milling. The visitor centre has old farm implements on display as well as a resident craftsman making wooden toys.

TOMINTOUL PEAT MOSS
2 miles N of Tomintoul
P: Available
Visitor trail to a peat bank where you can see peat being dug for household fuel, the whisky industry and, controversially, for use in horticulture.

Sport and Leisure Centres

BEACH LEISURE CENTRE – *see*
SWIMMING

ABERDEEN SKATING RINK
Stoneywood Road, Aberdeen
Tel: (0224) 724454
Open: Fri 1700 – 2200, Sat 1000 – 2200
£££
Small, friendly skating rink with skate hire.

ABERDEEN SUPERBOWL
197 George Street, Aberdeen
Tel: (0224) 643001
Open: Daily from 1000
Café
From £
Disabled access
Choose lighter balls or bump 'n' bowl for children aged 5 or more. Keep a crowd of children happy with an hour-long bowling party and save your nerves and your carpets into the bargain.

STONEHAVEN LEISURE CENTRE
Queen Elizabeth Park, Stonehaven
Tel: (0569) 63162
£
Has a 25m indoor pool and a games hall with basketball, netball, volleyball, 5-a-side football, gymnastics.

ABOYNE ACADEMY AND DEESIDE COMMUNITY CENTRE
Aboyne
Tel: (03398) 82222
£
Swimming pool, games hall, squash.

BALMEDIE LEISURE CENTRE
Eigie Road, Balmedie AB23 8YS
Tel: (0358) 43725
Open: Mon – Fri
£
Children can learn Highland, tap, ballet or disco dancing, badminton (over-8s), karate (over-9s), gymnastics (over-5s) and football (over-6s). Pre-schoolers can flex their muscles in the kindergym sessions. Rooms may be hired for parties but no special equipment is provided.

WESTDYKE LEISURE CENTRE
4 Westdyke Avenue, Westhill
Tel: (0224) 743098
Open: Daily
£
Gymnastics (over-8s), football coaching (over-9s), badminton (over-10s), kindergym for pre-schoolers. Highland dancing, junior rugby and bowling lessons are all on offer. The hall may be leased for football or sports parties.

HIGHLANDER ADVENTURES
Glenavon Hotel, Tomintoul
Tel: (08073) 250
From ££
Instruction in hill walking, rock and ice climbing, abseiling, canoeing etc.

BURGHEAD FUN TRACK – *see*
PARKS AND PLAYGROUNDS (SILVER SANDS LEISURE PARK)

Swimming

BEACH LEISURE CENTRE
Beach Promenade, Aberdeen
Tel: (0224) 647647/276276
Open: Daily 0830 – 2230
££
P: Free
Cafeteria
Pleasure pool with waves, currents, water cannon, flumes, toddler pool, hot tub and family changing-rooms. Sports arena with badminton, short tennis, table-tennis and trampolines. Creche. Playground.

OPEN-AIR POOL, STONEHAVEN
Open: Jul – Aug
£
Heated outdoor pool. Wide range of children's amusements nearby including paddling pool, adventure unit, swings etc.

ALFORD
Tel: (09755) 62922
Open: After school hours and in holidays
£
Special sessions for parents and toddlers, and families. There are polystyrene rafts, balls and rings to play with. Changing-rooms have a playpen and changing-mats. Lessons for over-5s.

HUNTLY POOL
Tel: (0466) 792397
£
The main 25m pool has a slide at the deep end. nearby is a 'paddling pool' which is kept very warm for young children and babies. The pool may be hired for parties. Lessons for all ages (3 years old minimum).

INVERURIE POOL
Tel: (0467) 20654
Open: Daily 0800 – 1800
£
Special sessions for parents and toddlers with balls, floating mats etc. Lessons are available for over-5s. Swimming parties can be arranged. The changing-rooms have a playpen and changing-tables.

STONEHAVEN LEISURE CENTRE and ABOYNE ACADEMY – *see*
SPORT AND LEISURE CENTRES

Theme Parks

STORYBOOK GLEN
Maryculter, Aberdeen AB1 0AT
B9077 5 miles W of Aberdeen
Tel: (0224) 732941
Open: Mar – Oct, daily 1000 – 1800
££
P: Free
Restaurant
Once upon a time there was a park in a lovely wooded glen where you could meet more than 100 fairy-tale and nursery-rhyme characters. The models lack charm but children under 8 love it all. See Postman Pat, Humpty Dumpty, Snow White, Cinderella with her coach and horses, and lots more. Climb-on toys, play areas and a small animal farm.

Toys

THE CRAFT AND DOLL'S-HOUSE SHOP
Petersfield, Kemnay
On B993, 2 miles from Kemnay, 3 miles from Inverurie
Tel: (0467) 42332

Open: Thu – Tue 1000 – 1700
Disabled access
A wide selection of doll's-houses, shops and miniature. Also has a craft section.

Walks

COUNTESSWELLS FOREST
Countesswells Road, Aberdeen
Picnic area
Disabled facilities and paths
Forest walk and horse trails.

OLD DEESIDE LINE RAILWAY
Aberdeen
Walk or cycle from DUTHIE PARK (*see* PARKS AND PLAYGROUNDS) to Peterculter. Other access points at Auchinyell Road, Cults, Bieldside and Milltimber.

BRAELOINE VISITOR CENTRE
Glen Tanar, Aboyne
Off B976
Tel: (03398) 86072
Open: Apr – Sep, daily 1000 – 1700
Picnic area
Exhibition on local wildlife, walks, nature trail, ranger service and guided walks.

SHOOTING GREENS
Blackhall Forest by Banchory
1.5 miles N of B976, on unclassified Feughside – Potarch road
P: Available
Picnic area
Forest walks. Toilets.

MORRONE BIRCHWOOD
Chapel Brae, Braemar
P: Available
The finest example of upland birchwood in Britain. Also has a network of footpaths.

DRUMTOCHTY GLEN
Auchenblae nr Laurencekirk
Off B975
P: Available
Picnic area
Walk through mixed woodland and wetland. Toilets.

LINN O' DEE
Iverey by Braemar
6 miles W of Braemar
P: Available
Local beauty spot with narrow chasm on the River Dee. The nearby Linn of Quoich is also very attractive.

TYREBAGGER WOOD
Dyce, Aberdeen
Off A96 and B979 near airport
Tel: (0224) 790432
P: Available
Forest walks and a wayfaring course (information pack available). One trail passes the 'Robber's Cave' which is said to have been used by brigands in the 17th century.

BENNACHIE HILL WALKS AND WEST GORDON WAY
Donview by Monymusk
A96 from Aberdeen, left off B9002 beyond Ardoyne
Tel: (04645) 611
Picnic and barbecue areas
Path for disabled
Toilets
A series of long and short walks including an ascent of Bennachie. Play area.

RANDOLPH'S LEAP
Logie nr Forres
7 miles S of Forres by A940 then B9007 towards Carrbridge
No disabled access
The river Findhorn winds through a deep gorge.

EARTH PILLARS
Fochabers
At Aultdearg, 1 mile S of Fochabers off
Ordiquish to Boat o' Brig road
P: Available
Earth pillars formed by erosion.

SPEY VIADUCT
Garmouth nr Elgin
A footpath from Garmouth to Spey Bay over a viaduct which once crossed the River Spey.

Watersports

SUBSEA WATERSPORTS
631 George Street, Aberdeen
Tel: (0224) 638588
From £££
Windsurfing lessons. Equipment hire available.

Winter Sports

KAIMHILL DRY SKI SLOPE
Garthdee Road, Bridge of Dee, Aberdeen
Tel: (0224) 311781
Open: Mon–Fri 1200–1330, 1800–1930, Sat 1300–1645, holidays 1200–1630
££
Price includes equipment hire.

ALFORD DRY SKI SLOPE
Greystone Road AB33 8JE
Tel: (09755) 62380/63024
£££
Coffee lounge
Public sessions, classes, equipment and tows included in price. Toilets.

BRAEMAR NORDIC SKI CENTRE
15 Mar Road, Braemar
Tel: (03397) 41242
Open: All year from 0830
££ per day

Cross-country ski hire and instruction (for over-5s). Also mountain bikes for hire in a variety of sizes (£££). Safety helmet, tool kit and padlock supplied.

HIGHLAND ACTIVITY HOLIDAYS
Northeim, Church Street, Dufftown AB55 4AR
Tel: (0340) 20892
From ££
Cross-country skiing for beginners aged 8 and above.

GLENMULLIACH NORDIC SKI CENTRE
Tomintoul AB37 9ES
Tel: (08074) 356
From ££
Has over 10 miles of prepared trails. Instruction and ski hire available.

GLENSHEE SKI CENTRE
Cairnwell by Braemar AB35 5XU
Tel: (03397) 41320
From £££
P: Free
Café and restaurant
Winter skiing on Cairnwell (3039ft). The chairlift also operates in summer for walkers and tourists (*see* CHAIR-LIFTS). Equipment hire and ski school for over-8s. Ski creche.

LECHT SKI CENTRE
Strathdon AB36 8YP
By A939 Strathdon/Tomintoul road
Tel: (09756) 51440/51412
P: Available
££££
Café
Winter skiing for beginners and families with fun weekends. Ski school and hire of equipment including snow boards, sledges and baby skis.

An artificial ski slope with moguls can be used in summer or when there is not enough real snow in winter. The creche for 2 to 8-year-olds is staffed by qualified nannies.

COOPER PARK — *see* **PARKS AND PLAYGROUNDS**

PLACES TO EAT

Hotels and Restaurants

BAXTER'S VISITOR CENTRE
Fochabers
Tel: (0343) 820393
Restaurant mainly serves Baxter's own fine foods. Delicious pancakes (*see* SCOTLAND AT WORK).

BOULTENSTONE HOTEL
Strathdon
Tel: (09756) 51254
Good, cheap food with small portions available.

BUGLES RESTAURANT BAR
14 West High Street, Inverurie
Tel: (0467) 22433
A café/restaurant which serves breakfast too. The trendy food includes lots of garlicky things and baked potato skins as well as cappuccino and espresso coffee. Highchairs, children's menu.

CAFÉ SOCIETY
9 Queen's Road, Aberdeen
Tel: (0224) 208494
A trendy restaurant popular with local business people as well as parents with young children in tow. There are high-chairs and a small verandah to sit out on in warm weather. Meals include burgers, vegetarian pasta dishes and baked potatoes.

CARMINE'S PIZZA AND PASTA
32 Union Terrace, Aberdeen
Tel: (0224) 624145
A small restaurant serving fixed-price lunches. Book ahead as it is popular.

CHARLIE'S AMERICAN BAR AND RESTAURANT
Bon-Accord Terrace, Aberdeen
Tel: (0224) 213337
Open: Daily
Good American food which most children love. But don't come with a pushchair or pram as the restaurant is up a couple of flights of stairs.

CHINA GARDEN
156 High Street, Elgin
Tel: (0343) 545000
Children are made very welcome and really enjoy the tasty Chinese food.

CRAIGENDARROCH HOUSE AND COUNTRY CLUB
Ballater AB35 5XA
Tel: (03397) 55858
A luxury country house with indoor swimming pool. Wonderful high teas.

THE CREEL INN
Catterline, nr Stonehaven
On the coast, S of Aberdeen
Tel: (056 95) 254
Reasonably priced seafood.

FERRY HILL HOUSE HOTEL
Bon Accord Street, Aberdeen AB1 2UA
A Georgian house in its own grounds, 5 minutes from the city centre.

GARMOUTH HOTEL
South Road, Garmouth, Fochabers IV32 7LU
Tel: (0343) 87 226
Good high teas.

THE GHILLIE'S LAIR
Beefeater Restaurant & Pub, Great Southern Road, Aberdeen
By the Bridge of Dee
Tel: (0224) 249924
Children's menu until 1930. Small play area.

KINTORE ARMS
Inverurie
Tel: (0467) 20304
The Cherubs restaurant is 'family friendly' but not particularly good for small children.

LAICHMORAY HOTEL
Maisondieu Road, Elgin IV30 1QR
Tel: (0343) 540045
Good high teas.

MANSEFIELD HOUSE HOTEL
2 Mayne Road, Elgin IV30 1NY
Tel: (0343) 540883
Good high teas with generous helpings. Children under-5 eat free.

MILL OF MUNDURNO
Murcar, Bridge of Don, Aberdeen
Tel: (0224) 821217
Reasonably priced meals for the whole family. Lego table and other toys to keep children happy.

NORWOOD HALL HOTEL
Garthdee Road, Aberdeen AB1 9NX
2 miles from the city centre
Tel: (0224) 868951
Friendly staff make eating out with young children easy. You can sit outside in the summer. Emphasis is on pub food – stovies, pies and so on. High-chairs available.

OLYMPIC CHINESE RESTAURANT
137 Rosemount Place, Aberdeen
Tel: (0224) 646449
Good food, children's menu.

RADAR'S EATING HOUSE
9 Belmont Street, Aberdeen
Tel: (0224) 648000
Open: Daily, 1100 – 2400
Children's menu, free second-helpings of spaghetti. Remember to leave room for an ice-cream. Will warm bottles and baby food.

Quick Meals and Snacks

BON APPETIT FOOD COURT
Bon-Accord Centre,
George Street,
Aberdeen
Tel: (0224) 625829
Open: Centre shopping hours
Variety of kiosks selling pasta, ice-cream, salads, jacket potatoes, sandwiches, burgers and patisserie. Children's portions.

BRIDGE OF BROWN TEA-ROOM
The Croft, Bridge of Brown, Tomintoul
Tel: (080 74) 335
Good home-baking in the midst of the wild and spectacular scenery of the Cairngorm mountains.

BRODIE COUNTRYFARE
Brodie, Moray
Tel: (03094) 339
A restaurant and coffee bar.

CAFÉ CONTINENTAL
The Promenade, Aberdeen
Tel: (0224) 588396
A good place for a snack or a full meal after an afternoon on the beach.

HIGHLAND BAKED POTATO
11 Harrow Inn Close, Elgin
Tel: (0343) 552448
Wide selection of fillings for baked potatoes and sandwiches which are made up on request.

INVERSNECKY CAFÉ
7–8 Esplanade, Aberdeen
Tel: (0224) 595631
Tasty fast food. Children's menu. Fish tank inside, the beach outside.

MITCHELL'S DAIRY
Market Place, Inverurie
Tel: (0467) 21389
A family café which also caters for the mart so you get real country lunches with home-made soup, meat, two veg and potatoes, pudding and custard. High-chairs available.

MUFFIN AND CRUMPET BISTRO
Main Street, Udny Station Village AB41 0QJ
Tel: (06513) 2210
Off A92, 4m along Culter Cullen Village road
Children are especially welcome — there is a special menu and provision for them. As the name suggests, muffins and crumpets are used in many of the dishes. Featured in the Taste of Scotland guide.

TASTIE BITE
32 High Street, Inverurie
Tel: (0467) 24018
A fast food carryout with baked potatoes, burgers and great chips.

Fish and Chips

ASHVALE FISH RESTAURANT AND TAKEAWAY
46 Great Western Road, Aberdeen
Tel: (0224) 586981
The best fish and chips in Britain. Children's menu, high-chairs.

FISH 'N' THINGS
8 Scotstoun Road, Bridge of Don, Aberdeen
Tel: (0224) 820263
Large portions to take away.

Bakeries

DONALD'S BAKERY
Portsoy

J. G. ROSS
Market Place, Inverurie
Tel: (0467) 23425
A bakery and restaurant with a 'sit-outerie' at the back. Good chips and gravy. There are other branches in Aberdeen and Old Meldrum.

STRATHBOGIE BAKERY
Golden Square, Huntly
Tel: (0466) 792769
Make up a picnic with some of the excellent bread, baking and sweetmeats you can buy here.

Pubs

BROADSTRAIK INN
Elrick, by Westhill
Tel: (0224) 743217
An olde worlde pub where you can throw horseshoes in the garden. Barbecues in summer. Children allowed to stay till 1900.

COACH AND HORSE COUNTRY INN
Balmedie, nr Bridge of Don, Aberdeen
Tel: (0358) 43249
Reasonably priced bar food.

WATERWHEEL INN
North Deeside Road, Bieldside,
Aberdeen
Tel: (0224) 861659
Great pub lunches.

Fast Food Chains

BURGER KING
221 Union Street, Aberdeen
Tel: (0224) 596008
and
48 Upper Kirkgate, Aberdeen
Between St Nicholas Centre and Bon-
Accord Centre
Tel: (0224) 625378

LITTLE CHEF
Foveran, nr Aberdeen
Tel: (0358) 689743
On A92, 6 miles N of Aberdeen
Disabled facilities
Convenient fast food for travellers. They have a children's menu, high-chairs, baby changing facilities and free baby food.

McDONALD'S
117 Union Street, Aberdeen
Tel: (0224) 212960

OLIVERS COFFEE SHOP AND BAKERY
Unit 10, Trinity Centre, Aberdeen
Tel: (0224) 572769
and
259 High Street, Elgin IV30 1DW
Tel: (0343) 546844

THE PANCAKE PLACE
402 Union Street, Aberdeen
Tel: (0224) 646047

THE PIZZA GALLERY
152 High Street, Elgin
Tel: (0343) 542835

PIZZA HUT
7 Union Street, Aberdeen
Tel: (0224) 573363

PIZZALAND
31 Union Street, Aberdeen
Tel: (0224) 571177
and
261 Union Street, Aberdeen
Tel: (0224) 575737

PLACES TO STAY

Hostels

SYHA – ABERDEEN
The King George VI Memorial Hostel,
8 Queens Road, Aberdeen
Tel: (0224) 646988
Book in advance to be sure of a family room.

Caravan and Camping Sites

ADEN COUNTRY PARK CARAVAN SITE
Mintlaw, Banffshire
Tel: (02612) 2521
Turn S off A950
Open: May – Sep
£
All the faciliites of the country park are close by. (*See* COUNTRY PARKS.)

HAUGHTON HOUSE COUNTRY PARK
Montgarrie Road, Alford AB3 8NA
Tel: (0336) 2107
Open: Apr – Sep
££
Tent and caravan park set in beautiful surroundings. (*See* COUNTRY PARKS.)

SILVER SANDS LEISURE PARK
Covesea, West Beach, Lossiemouth IV31 6SP
Tel: (0343 81) 3262
From ££
Caravan site by the sea (*see* BEACHES). Watch out for the attraction of the video arcade.

STATION CARAVAN PARK
West Beach, Harbour Street, Hopeman, by Elgin IV30 2RU
Tel: (0343 83) 0880
Open: Apr – mid Oct
From £
Play area popular with young children. Attractive surroundings.

Bed and Breakfast

MRS EVELYN COOK
Lime Meldrum, Tarves
£
A beautiful farmhouse on a working farm. Mrs Cook is great with kids and very flexible and understanding. The farm is next door to HADDO COUNTRY PARK (*see* COUNTRY PARKS).

Hotels

PITTODRIE HOUSE HOTEL
Chapel of Gairioch, nr Pitcaple AB51 9HS
Tel: (0467) 681444
Off A96, near Inverurie
£££
An expensive country house with a 3-acre walled garden, surrounded by fields and open countryside and lovely views of Bennachie. A place for well-behaved children though staff are very helpful. A listening service means parents can eat dinner without continually checking that children are asleep. Featured in the Taste of Scotland guide.

RAEMOIR HOUSE HOTEL
Banchory, nr Aberdeen AB3 4ED
Tel: (033 02) 4884
£££
Family rooms or self-catering apartments. Expensive but reductions possible. Vast grounds to explore; toys and board games.

THE HEART OF THE HIGHLANDS

This area, which stretches from Inverness and Nairn in the north, along Loch Ness and across to Aviemore and Speyside, has much to offer families. Whether you want to go skiing or monster-spotting, good road and rail links to Aberdeen and Perth make it easy to get here for an action-packed break in the midst of the Highlands.

Aviemore is the cosmopolitan heart of the area and attracts large numbers of tourists but there is beautiful countryside all around just asking to be explored. Families with small children can stroll through the beautiful woodlands around Loch Morlich or potter on the sandy shore. There are tractor and trailer rides close by on the Rothiemurchus estate; wolves still stalk the Highlands (at the Wildlife Park) and there are reindeer to feed at Glenmore. A ride on the steam train makes a good outing for Thomas the Tank Engine fans and in winter there is usually plenty of snow for sledging or skiing. Even toddlers can be fitted with skis, and competent cross-country skiers with babies can tow them along in a special cosy sledge called a pulk. There is talk of building an artificial snow field in the area to make up for the vagaries of the weather and this would let older children experience the thrill of downhill skiing even in the mildest of winters.

Landmark in Carrbridge has an adventure playground and other attractions which are very popular in the summer with pre-school and primary children alike. Try canoeing, windsurfing or sailing in the summer at Loch Morlich or Loch Insh, or further north at Nairn near Inverness. And, of course, this is monster country so keep a look out for strange creatures in Loch Ness. If Nessie doesn't oblige with an appearance, you can still find out all about her at one of the Nessie exhibitions instead.

There is a small in-store creche at the Co-op Superstore at Inches, Inverness, while mother and baby rooms are provided in the East Gate Shopping Centre in Inverness, and at the public toilets in Aviemore (near the Bank of Scotland).

PLACES TO VISIT

Adventure Playgrounds

LANDMARK HERITAGE AND ADVENTURE PARK
Carrbridge PH23 3AJ
On A9 N of Aviemore, half a mile from Carrbridge Station
Tel: (047984) 613
Open: Apr – Oct, daily 0930 – 1800 (2000 in Jul/Aug)
£££
P: Free
Restaurant, snack bar and picnic area
Full disabled facilities

In spite of all the other activities going on at Landmark, the adventure playground is the main attraction as far as 5 to 10-year-olds are concerned. They can test their nerves on the net walkways that lead to the giant slide or head into darkness in the 50ft-long tube slide. There is a less daunting play area for toddlers as well as a balancing trail and woodland maze. If you can get away from the playground, there is more fun to be had on the tree-top trail or up the 65ft forest viewing tower. Have a look at the steam-powered sawmill, complete with Clydesdale horse, and, if you have time, go to the 3-screen audio-visual show on the history of the Highlands.

Animals and Birds

LOCH GARTEN NATURE RESERVE (RSPB)
nr Aviemore
Off B970, 8 miles NE of Aviemore
Tel: (0479) 83694
Open: Daily mid Apr – Aug 1000 – 2000
£
P: Free
Picnic area
Partial disabled access

Ospreys were extinct in Scotland for many years but returned here to breed in 1959. Their tree-top eyrie may be viewed through fixed binoculars from the observation hut. There is also a closed-circuit TV fitted on the osprey nest so you can see live and recorded pictures. Book a place on a guided walk to look for dragonflies, butterflies and wildflowers in the old Caledonian Pine forest.

CAIRNGORM REINDEER CENTRE
Reindeer House, Loch Morlich nr Aviemore
E of Coylumbridge
Tel: (047 986) 228
Open: All year, daily (subject to weather) 1100 departure
££
P: Available
Disabled visitors welcome, but prior notice would be helpful

Visitors may accompany the guide to see the reindeer in their natural surroundings. Children can pat the deer and help to feed them. The visitor centre has videos and displays of antlers.

INSH MARSH RESERVE (RSPB)
nr Kingussie
B970, 1.5 miles from Kingussie
Tel: (0540) 661518
Free (donation)
P: Available off B970

There are trails and hides to explore as well as guided walks with titles like 'Missing Passengers and Other Puzzles' which appeal to children. Phone for details.

HIGHLAND WILDLIFE PARK
Kincraig, Kingussie PH21 1NL
Turn off A9 to the B9152, entrance signposted
Tel: (054 04) 270
Open: Mid Mar – early Nov, daily 1000 – 1700, 1800 in Jul/Aug
£££ (for car and passengers)
P: Free
Café
Disabled toilets and ramps
See wolves and other animals which once ran wild in Scotland. Make sure that toddlers have been to the toilet before driving through the reserve amongst herds of red deer, bison and Highland cattle. Grouse, eagles, wolves, wildcats, bears and other animals can be seen in a separate, walk-round area.

LOCH NESS MONSTER VIDEO SHOW
Kiltmaker Building, 4 – 9 Huntly Street, Inverness
2 mins walk from Tourist Office
Open: Mid May – Sep, Mon – Sat 0900 – 2100; Oct – mid May, Mon – Sat 0900 – 1700
You can't come to Loch Ness without looking for the monster. The exhibition and 30-minute film show some of the search methods that have been used on the 23-mile long, 700ft-deep loch. There is also a section on the art of kiltmaking.

THE OFFICIAL LOCH NESS MONSTER EXHIBITION CENTRE
Drumnadrochit Hotel, Drumnadrochit IV3 6TU
On A82, 14 miles SW of Inverness
Tel: (045 62) 573

Open: Daily, except Christmas and New Year
£££
P: Free
Restaurant
Disabled facilities
See a life-size Nessie in the outdoor lochan and a baby monster hatching from a giant egg. Exhibition of the various methods and equipment used to search for the monster, plus pictures of what was found.

Bike Hire and Cycle Routes

BADENOCH MOUNTAIN BIKES
Sonnhaide, East Terrace, Kingussie
By the clock tower
Tel: (0540) 661266
Open: Daily 0900 – 1700
£££ for a full-day hire
Child-size bikes and child seats available on 18 and 21-speed bikes, with safety helmets and toolkits.

LOCH INSH WATERSPORTS CENTRE – *see* WATERSPORTS

Castles and Stately Homes

URQUHART CASTLE (HS)
nr Drumnadrochit
On A82 by Loch Ness
Tel: (04562) 551
Open: Mon – Sat 0900 – 1900, Sun 1400 – 1900
£
P: Available
The rocky ruins overlook Loch Ness so it is a fine place to break a long car journey and do some monster-hunting. It can be very busy in the height of summer.

FORT GEORGE (HS)

by Ardersier
11 miles N of Inverness
Tel: (031) 244 3101 (HS, Edinburgh)
Open: Apr−Sep Mon−Sat 0930−1900,
Sun 1400−1900; Oct−Mar closes at
1600
££

The fortress was built after the Jacobite Rising and has lots of cannons and life-size models of soldiers.

CAWDOR CASTLE

Cawdor nr Nairn
On B9090, off A96, between Inverness and Nairn
Tel: (066 77) 615
Open: May−early Oct, daily 1000−1730
£££
P: Available
Snack bar, restaurant, picnic area

The castle is owned by the Earl of Cawdor and has a drawbridge, a dungeon and the original kitchens. There are 4 nature trails, swings, mini-golf, a putting green and ducks to feed in the grounds.

KILRAVOCK CASTLE

Croy nr Inverness
12 miles E of Inverness, off B9091
Tel: (066 78) 258

Open: May−Oct, Wed 1000−1700
£
P: Free
Tea shop (see PLACES TO EAT)

Walk round the tree garden and the nature trails by the river. Museum and guided tours of castle.

Chairlifts

CAIRNGORM CHAIRLIFT

nr Aviemore
Tel: (0479) 861261
Open: 0900−1600
£££ return
Snack bar at the top of the lift

Scotland's longest chairlift takes you to 3600ft. From there it is an easy walk, in fair weather, to Cairngorm summit at 4084ft. Look out for reindeer and other wildlife.

Estates

ROTHIEMURCHUS ESTATE VISITOR CENTRE

nr Aviemore
1 mile from Aviemore
Tel: (0479) 810858
Open: All year, 0900−1700

Free entry – various charges for tours and activities
P: Available
Disabled facilities

Lovely walks through ancient pine woods around the loch, with wonderful echoes from the castle on the island. Pre-schoolers are quite content to spend a few hours pottering by the water's edge. If this is too tame, go on a tractor and trailer ride round the farm to see Highland cattle and feed 200,000 trout at the fish farm. A superb family day out for over-7s. School groups can learn about the environment and ecology.

Farms

SHEEP DAIRY – *see* SCOTLAND AT WORK

Fish

AIGAS DAM FISH LIFT
Beauly nr Inverness
Open: Jun – Oct, Mon – Fri at 1500
Migrating salmon are lifted into a viewing chamber on their way to completing their journey to spawning waters.

Forest Parks

GLENMORE FOREST PARK
nr Aviemore
7 miles E of Aviemore off B9152
Tel: (05404) 223/(047986) 271
Open: All year
Free access – charge for some activities
P: Available
Picnic areas, café
Partial disabled access
Over 5000 acres of coniferous woodland and mountainside on the north-west slopes of the Cairngorms, with Loch Morlich at its centre. If you are lucky you might see red deer, reindeer, wildcat or golden eagles. Try canoeing, windsurfing, sailing or fishing on the loch, or take a hike round the forest trails, hill walks, and wayfaring trail.

Graveyards and Gruesome Places

CULLODEN MOOR BATTLEFIELD (NTS)
nr Inverness
B9006, 5 miles E of Inverness
Tel: (0463) 790607
Open: Site open all year; centre: Apr – Oct 0930 – 1730
£
P: Available
Restaurant
Disabled access

On 16 April 1746 Bonnie Prince Charlie was defeated in a battle which lasted 40 minutes: the Prince's army lost 1200 men, and the King's army 310. Walk round the battlefield and see the communal Graves of the Clans, the Well of the Dead, and the huge Cumberland Stone where the victorious Duke of Cumberland is said to have stood to view the battle. The visitor centre has an excellent audio-visual show.

Museums

HIGHLAND FOLK MUSEUM
Duke Street, Kingussie PH21 1JG
Tel: (0540) 661307
Open: Apr – Oct, Mon – Sat 1000 – 1800,

Sun 1400–1800; Nov–Mar, Mon–Fri 1000–1500
£
P: Available
Picnic garden
Disabled facilities
Toilets

Would you be able to fit a dress with an 18-inch waist? Could you bake bannocks on a hot stone? Visit a black house from Lewis complete with byre, kitchen and boxbed, a clack mill, barn, dairy and stables and find out what life was like for crofters in the past. During the summer (Jun–Sep, Mon–Sat) there are demonstrations of baking, lacemaking, spinning etc.

INVERNESS MUSEUM
Castle Wynd, Inverness
Tel: (0463) 237114
Open: Mon–Sat 0900–1700
Free
P: Parking nearby
Cafeteria
Partial disabled access

Examples of local wildlife are on display. It is sometimes possible to see a taxidermist at work. Special activities are laid on for children and school visits–phone for details.

Novelties

PARALLEL ROADS
Glen Roy
Unclassified road off A86, 18 miles NE of Fort William
Free
Disabled access

These 'parallel roads' are actually hillside terraces marking the levels of lochs which were dammed by glaciers during the Ice Age.

Parks and Playgrounds

BELLFIELD PARK
Inverness
B862

New all-weather tennis courts, putting green, paddling pool, play area and ornamental gardens.

BUGHT PARK
Inverness
Tel: (0463) 236795/235533

Small boats for hire on the boating pond, 10 minute rides on a $7\frac{1}{4}"$ gauge railway, trampolines and crazy golf. Go-karts, small electric trikes and large quad bikes can be hired. Inverness Bears BMX track in Paddock Field is open to visitors– training sessions are available though parents must supervise very young children.

Picnic Sites

FESHIE BRIDGE
nr Aviemore
B970 from Aviemore, R at Inverdruie to Feshie Bridge
P: Available

Forestry Commission picnic site with woodland walk. Toilets.

STRATHMASHIE
Inverness
A86 Newtonmore-Spean Bridge, 4 miles past Laggan Bridge
P: Available

Forestry Commission picnic site with viewpoint and forest walk. Toilets.

DOG FALLS
Glen Affric
A831 to Cannich then unclassified road up glen
P: Available

Forestry Commission picnic site. Toilets.

Railways

STRATHSPEY RAILWAY
Dalfaber Road, Aviemore
B970 then Dalfaber Road; on foot—underpass at Bank of Scotland
Tel: (0479) 810725
Open: Daily Jun—Sep; check for other opening times
£££
P: Available
Disabled access
Take the steam train from Aviemore to Boat of Garten, then a vintage omnibus to see the ospreys at LOCH GARTEN (*see* ANIMALS AND BIRDS). The railway is part of the former main line between Perth and Inverness which closed in 1965. It was re-opened in 1978 by the Strathspey Railway Company which also runs Santa trains at Christmas and New Year. A great day out for Thomas the Tank Engine fans!

Riding

HAFLINGER TREKKING CENTRE
Newtonmore
Tel: (0540) 673527
££
Trekking for families (including toddlers) through mountain and moorland.

BRAESIDE TREKKING AND RIDING CENTRE
Ardendrain, Kintarlity, Beauly
Tel: (0463) 74525
Open: Daily 0900—1800
££
Moorland treks for all levels. Children aged 4 or above welcome for special treks. Paddock rides for toddlers.

Scotland at Work—Past and Present

CULLODEN POTTERY
Old Smiddy, Gollanfield nr Inverness IV1 2QT
Midway between Nairn and Inverness on A96
Tel: (0667) 62340
Open: Daily, 0930—1730
Free
Restaurant, picnic area
Disabled access
Watch the pottery demonstrations—it looks easy until you have a go on the wheel yourself. There is a safe play area for children with swings, log cabin and slide next to the pottery.

SHEEP DAIRY AND VISITOR CENTRE
Nairnside Farm, Cawdor
2 miles off A96, on Cawdor road (B9090), 1 mile W of Cawdor Castle
Tel: (06677) 621
Open: Apr—Oct, daily 1000—1700, milking at 1500
Picnic area, tea-room
The craft of making ewe's milk cheese almost died out in the 17th century. This farm has a flock of over 100 Friesland ewes which are milked every afternoon. The milk is made into cheese, yoghurt and yoghurt ice-cream which you can taste. Walk round the farm and see rare breeds and unusual cattle in the farm park. Young children like to stroke the lambs, calves, piglets and rabbits, run around in the playground and go on the ponies.

Schools and playgroups welcome by prior arrangement.

LANDMARK — *see* ADVENTURE PLAYGROUNDS

Sport and Leisure Centres

AVIEMORE CENTRE
Aviemore
Off A9, 32 miles S of Inverness
Tel: (0479) 810624
Open: All year, daily from 1000
Various charges
Restaurants
Disabled facilities
Bored teenagers might enjoy a visit to the centre if they have had enough of all the healthy, wholesome activities in the area. There is a cinema, an ice-rink, swimming, karting, a disco and an artificial ski slope.

ROLLERBOWL
Culduthel Road, Inverness
Tel: (0463) 235100
Open: Daily from 1200
££ – £££
Café
Ten-pin bowling with bumper lanes for children.

INVERNESS ICE CENTRE
Bught Park, Inverness
Tel: (0463) 235711
Open: Daily in Jul/Aug, weekends only Sep – Jun
££
Coffee shop
Even very young children can try skating as the small slip-on skates fit over their shoes.

NAIRN LEISURE PARK
The Links, Nairn
Tel: (0667) 53061

Open: Daily, all year from 0800 – 2100
£ for swimming, small charge for each piece of apparatus
The park is right by the beach and provides entertainment for all the family. There's a toddlers' playground and paddling pool as well as room indoors for them to play in bad weather. The adventure play trails, fort, outdoor sports and board games are great for older children, while parents can enjoy a walk through the woods or jog round the trim trail. The 25m swimming pool provides parent and toddler sessions, fun hours and lessons, and can be booked for birthday parties.

SUMMER ACTIVITIES CENTRE
Swimming Pool Building, Marine Road, Nairn
Tel: (0667) 55523
Open: Mon – Fri, morning and afternoon
Sports, talent contests, board games, music and dance workshops for 8 to 17-year-olds.

Swimming

INVERNESS SWIMMING POOL
Inverness
Tel: (0463) 233799
Open: Daily 0930
Cafeteria
A 25m pool and separate toddlers' pool with Loch Ness Monster slide and fountain.

NAIRN LEISURE PARK — *see* SPORT AND LEISURE CENTRES

Theatres and Cinemas

WALTZING WATERS
Balavil Brae, Newtonmore
Tel: (05403) 752

Open: Shows daily Easter—Jan every hour from 0900—1700, 2030
£££
P: Available
Coffee shop
Disabled access
Elaborate water, lighting and music show. Thousands of dazzling patterns of moving water synchronised with music. Children's play area.

Walks

LEITERFEARN
nr Fort Augustus
Off A82
P: Available
Walk along the old railway line by Loch Oich.

Watersports

LOCH INSH WATERSPORTS CENTRE
Insh Hall, Kincraig
B970, 7.5 miles from Kingussie
Tel: (05404) 272
Watersports: May—Sep; winter sports: Dec—Apr
Various charges, e.g. £ per half-day bike hire
Restaurant
Hire canoes, rowing boats, sailing dinghies, surfboards, bicycles and fishing gear. Children's classes and canoeing expeditions are available. Get in some practice on the artificial ski slope before going on the snow at Cairngorm.

NAIRN WATERSPORTS
Lochloy Holiday Park, East Beach, Nairn
Tel: (0667) 55416
From ££

Surfing or surf-canoeing is thrilling when the waves are high. You can hire equipment including buoyancy aids and wet suits. Instruction is available, though they say it is all easier than it looks!

GLENMORE FOREST PARK — *see* **FOREST PARKS**

Winter Sports

CAIRNGORM (*see* CHAIRLIFTS)
nr Aviemore
Tel: (0479) 861261
Tows from £
Downhill skiing. Equipment for children, including the very young, for hire.

CARRBRIDGE SKI SCHOOL
Carrbridge
Tel: (047984) 246
Beginners welcome. Instruction, lift passes and ski hire. Also bike hire and shop.

SLOCHD NORDIC SKI SCHOOL AND MOUNTAIN BIKE HIRE
Carrbridge
Just outside village
Tel: (047984) 666
££ ski hire per day
Try cross-country skiing on quiet tracks through splendid countryside, and get away from the crowds on the downhill slopes. Skis for over-4s. Families with babies or toddlers can hire a 'pulk', a special enclosed sledge with a windscreen, that you harness on and pull while skiing. Mountain bikes for 7 to 8-year-olds and children's seats for toddlers.

PLACES TO EAT

Hotels and Restaurants

THE BEEFEATER
Millburn Road, Inverness
Good quality children's menu.

LE BISTRO
Main Street, Aviemore
An expensive restaurant but the Italian food is wonderful. Children are made very welcome and have a good choice of dishes.

GIRVAN'S
East Gate, Inverness
There is a £3 minimum charge at lunchtime.

GOLF VIEW HOTEL
Seabank Road, Nairn
Tel: (0667) 52301
An easy-going place to have lunch with children. Good Christmas and New Year programmes are also organised.

HAUGHDALE HOTEL
Ness Bank, Inverness
Tel: (0463) 233065
Good for high teas.

THE ISLANDS
Toby Restaurant, Island Bank Road, Inverness
Tel: (0463) 231833
Open: Daily for lunches and dinner
Under-7s can choose their meal from the Shoe People menu – they get 3 courses for under £2 plus a comic, balloon, pencil etc. Half-portions from the carvery or off the main menu are also available. High-chairs.

KILRAVOCK CASTLE (*see* CASTLES)
Croy, nr Nairn
Tel: (06678) 213
Good high teas – a traditional Scottish meal with a cooked main course followed by scones and jam and a plentiful supply of cakes.

LITTLEJOHNS
Grampian Road, Aviemore
Tel: (0479) 811633
The walls and ceiling are decorated with 1960s' memorabilia guaranteed to keep youngsters amused while they are waiting to be served. Good food with Mexican influences.

THE NEW REGENT
Academy Street, Inverness
Tel: (0463) 711049
A good Chinese restaurant where children are really welcome.

PIERRE VICTOIRE
75 Castle Street, Inverness
Tel: (0463) 225662
Amazingly good value lunches. Part of the Edinburgh group of restaurants.

REDCLIFFE HOTEL
1 Gordon Terrace, Inverness
Tel: (0463) 232767
Good for high teas.

Quick Meals and Snacks

BRODIE COUNTRY FAYRE
nr Inverness
On A96
Wide variety of food from snacks to full meals. Plenty of space for

pushchairs. High-chairs available. Luscious ice-creams.

CLEICUM'S
Shopping Centre, Inverness
Plenty of room in the restaurant for pushchairs. Good food to revive toddlers after riding the escalators.

CULLODEN POTTERY AND RESTAURANT
Gollanfield, nr Inverness
Tel: (0667) 62749
Open: Daily
Disabled access
Coffee shop selling home-baking, wholefoods and vegetarian meals. High-chairs, children's portions and a play area by the POTTERY – *see* **SCOTLAND AT WORK.**

LOCH INSH WATERSPORTS CENTRE – *see* **WATERSPORTS**
A wide range of home-baking and good coffee. The portions are large and can be divided up for children to share. Barbecue meals during the summer.

CHEST, HEART AND STROKE ASSOCIATION COFFEE SHOP
Mealmarket Close, Inverness
Tel: (0463) 713433

Pubs

THE OLD BRIDGE INN
Aviemore
Nr old railway station
A very small pub with lovely food like curried parsnip soup. The children's menu has spicy chicken wings and other adventurous dishes, as well as the more conventional spaghetti bolognaise.

Fish and Chips

SMIFFY'S FISH AND CHIPS
Unit 2/3, Main Street, Aviemore Shopping Centre
Tasty fish and good chips.

Fast Food Chains

McDONALD'S
12 – 22 High Street, Inverness
Tel: (0463) 237499
Open: Daily

OLIVER'S
1 – 7 High Street, Inverness
Tel: (0463) 232664

PANCAKE PLACE
25 – 27 Church Street, Inverness
Tel: (0463) 226156
Open: Daily 0900 – 1800 (2100 in summer)

PLACES TO STAY

Hostels

SYHA – AVIEMORE
Aviemore PH22 1PR
Tel: (0479) 810345
Book in advance to be sure of getting a family room. Bikes can be hired at the hostel and winter sports courses are run from here too.

SYHA – CANNICH
Beauly IV4 7LT
Tel: (04565) 244
Has 2 family units for those with under-5s. Each one has a sitting/dining/kitchen area, 2 bedrooms with 2 double-tier bunks, and shared toilet and shower facilities.

SYHA – INVERNESS
Glenmoriston IV3 6YD
Tel: (0320) 51274
Book in advance to be sure of a family room.

SYHA – KINGUSSIE
Viewmount, Kingussie PH21 1JS
Tel: (0540) 661506
Family rooms are available but book in advance as they are popular.

Caravan and Camping Sites

FAICHEM PARK
Ardgarry Farm, Faichem, Invergarry
Tel: (08093) 226
From £
A small attractive site for tents and caravans.

FORT AUGUSTUS CARAVAN AND CAMPING PARK
Market Hill, Fort Augustus PH32 4DH
On A82
Tel: (0320) 6360
Open: Apr – mid Oct
From £
Sheltered site with a play area.

GLENMORE FOREST CAMPING AND CARAVAN SITE
nr Aviemore
Tel: (0479) 861271
Open: mid Dec – mid Nov
£ – ££
One of the Forestry Commission's top-grade sites. An attractive site a short walk from Loch Morlich. The loch has a sandy beach, woodland walks and good watersport facilities.

Bed and Breakfast

AVONDRUIE GUEST HOUSE
Inverdruie, Aviemore
Tel: (0479 810) 267
Open: All year
££
A very friendly bed and breakfast. Although dinner is not available, there is unlimited tea, coffee and juice. Plenty of toys and games for children.

Hotels

THE BOAT HOTEL
Boat of Garten nr Aviemore PH24 3BH
Tel: (047 983) 258
Open: All year
£££

Family rooms. Sporting activities can be arranged for energetic families.

CALEDONIA HOTEL
Inverness
£££
Babysitting and baby listening service, cots, high-chairs, booster seats. Children's activities. Swimming pool, sports facilities, playroom.

COYLUMBRIDGE HOTEL
Coylumbridge, by Aviemore PH22 1QN
Tel: (0479) 810661
£££
Families rave about the facilities here. It is a resort in itself which is ideal if the weather is inclement. Has 2 indoor pools, a games room, tennis courts, children's indoor adventure play area, supervised film shows in the evening, painting competitions and much, much more.

FOUR SEASONS HOTEL
Aviemore Centre PH22 1PF
Tel: (0479) 810681
Open: All year
£££
Family rooms. Children made welcome (under-5s free) and no request seems too much bother for the staff. Baby listening service, leisure facilities.

KINGSMILL HOTEL
Culcabock Road, Inverness IV2 3LP
Tel: (0463) 237166
Open: All year
£££
Leisure complex with a swimming pool, pitch and putt in the gardens.

ARGYLL AND THE ISLES

If you really want a peaceful holiday, the far west of Scotland is a good place to choose. From Mull and Oban in the north to the Mull of Kintyre in the south, you will find typical picture-postcard scenery such as towering mountains, great sea lochs, remote islands and beautiful beaches.

This is an area for outdoor activities – quiet or strenuous walks depending on your mood and fitness, riding, pottering on beaches or messing about with boats. The nearest you get to big visitor attractions are the reconstructed 19th-century jail at Inveraray and Oban's Sealife Centre.

There are regular scheduled services to most Inner Hebrides but you need some determination to get to Islay, Jura, Tiree, Coll and Colonsay as they can only be reached by a long slow car journey followed by at least a couple of hours on a ferry. Bute and the Cowall peninsula are easier to reach as the ferries leave from the Clyde coast at Wemyss Bay and Gourock. 'A Child's Guide to Bute', available from the Tourist Information Centre in Rothesay, gives a potted history of the island along with unusual things to look out for and pages to colour in on rainy days.

The Isle of Mull is less than an hour from Oban and attracts large numbers of visitors primarily because of the nearby tiny island of Iona which has strong Christian connections.

PLACES TO VISIT

Animals and Birds

OBAN SEALIFE CENTRE
Barcaldine, Oban PA37 1SE
On A828, 10 miles N of Oban
Tel: (063 172) 386
Open: Feb–Nov, 1000–1800 (1900 in summer holidays); weekends only Dec–Jan
£££ (free to Blue Peter Badge wearers)
P: Free
Restaurant, picnic area
Disabled facilities
Baby changing facilities
A wide ranging display of native marine life, from conger eels, sting-rays, cuttlefish and sharks to abandoned seal pups which are hand-reared and then returned to the wild. Children can follow a quiz trail, and are encouraged to touch hermit crabs and sea anemones in the touch pools. There is also a forest play area and a beach by the side of the loch. Cameras may be borrowed free of charge. Day and holiday passes are available. Educational packs and project material available for groups. Birthday parties can be arranged.

SHEEP AND WOOL CENTRE
Drimsynie Estate, Lochgoilhead
B839 at the head of Lochgoil, 6 miles off the A815
Tel: (03013) 247/344
Open: End Mar–Oct, daily 0900–1700.
Shows at 1100 (not Sat/Sun), 1300, 1500
£
Refreshments available
The centre's 19 breeds of sheep are in the limelight when they are paraded on stage. Their act does not include a song and dance routine but you can see sheep-shearing and sheepdog demonstrations. There is a 25m indoor swimming pool on the site and a pony-trekking centre.

ANGORA RABBIT FARM
Bremenvoir, Ardtun, Bunessan, Isle of Mull
Tel: (06817) 429
Free (donations)
Picnic area
Angora rabbits are quiet animals who don't mind being handled. Their soft hair is used for wool. They live indoors so even on wet days you can watch them being clipped and groomed. A nature trail which takes you round the other farm animals.

ARGYLL WILDLIFE PARK
Dalchenna, Inveraray
On A83, 2 miles S of Inveraray
Tel: (0499) 2264/2284
Open: All year 0930–1800/dusk
££
Tea-room, picnic area
A 60-acre site, with a collection of wildfowl and a large owl collection. The Scottish mammals on display include wildcats, badgers, foxes, red deer and fallow deer, wild goats and pine-martens. There are also oddities like white wallabies and Moufflon. Go on a nature walk and picnic by the pebble beach.

ISLE OF MULL LAND ROVER WILDLIFE EXPEDITIONS
Ulva House Hotel, Tobermory, Isle of Mull
Tel: (0688) 2044
£££

HUMUNGEOUS TROUTUS

Drive round the island stopping for short walks at a number of different locations in search of seals, otters, butterflies and other wildlife.

OLD BYRE HERITAGE CENTRE
Dervaig, Isle of Mull
Tel: (06884) 229
Open: Easter – Oct 1030 – 1830

P: Available
Tea-room
Museum with displays of local birds, flowers and animals. Audio-visual show every 30 mins.

Beaches

You will find some of the cleanest and most attractive beaches in Britain in this area with its sea lochs, towering mountains and fantastic sunsets over the islands. Virtually all the beaches here are good ones and if you are at the bucket and spade stage or enjoy collecting shells, a holiday on the west coast is just perfect (as long as it doesn't rain).

Boats and Boat Trips

SEALIFE CRUISES
Dervaig, Isle of Mull
Tel: (06884) 223
££££
Great educational trip on a modern, fast 40ft trawler yacht in search of whales. Inter-island wildlife trips.

LOCH ETIVE CRUISES
Etive View, Taynuilt
Tel: (08662) 430
Open: Daily, departures 1030, 1400
From ££
See seals on the rocks, red deer on the crags and Ben Starav's golden eagles.

KINGFISHER CRUISES
Hillview, Ardfern Lochgilphead
Ardfern Yacht Centre
Tel: (08525) 662
Open: Departures at 1015, 1400, occasional evenings
From ££
Various cruises to view seals and sea

birds on Loch Craignish, visit Jura and other nearby islands, or go through CORRYVRECKAN (*see* **NOVELTIES**).

LADY ROWENA, STEAM LAUNCH
BR Station Pier, Lochawe Village
A85
Tel: (08382) 440/449
Open: End May – Sep, daily sailings 1030 – 1600
From ££
Tea-room on the pier
Disabled access
A restored Edwardian launch with genuine steam engine and peat-fired boiler. Sit back on the cushioned seating and enjoy a trip to places of interest on Lochawe. Also ferry to Kilchurn Castle.

JOHNSTON BOATS
12 Lismore Crescent, Oban
Tel: (0631) 63138
Departs 1000 and 1400 from Esplanade
££
Trips on the MV *Maid of the Firth*. Spend 90 minutes ashore on Mull and visit Torosay Castle and gardens (*see* **RAILWAYS**).

Caves

FINGAL'S CAVE
Staffa, off Mull
Regular boat trips from Fionnphort, Mull and Iona
From £££
The small, uninhabited island of Staffa is famous for its strange rock formations and remarkable caves, the best known of which is Fingal's Cave, immortalised by Mendelssohn in his celebrated *Hebrides* overture.

Boat trips land at the jetty in good weather.

DAVAAR ISLAND
nr Campbeltown
At the entrance to Campbeltown Loch
Open: Low tide
Free

The island is linked to the mainland by a bank of shingle which may be crossed at low tide. Don't misjudge the tide or you will be caught in a real 'tourist trap'. There is a large cave on the island with a painting of the Crucifixion on the wall.

ST KIARAN'S CAVE
Kildalloig nr Campbeltown
Open: Low tide
Free

This cave is reputed to be the cell of St Kiaran, a contemporary of St Columba.

KEIL CAVE
Garvald nr Campbeltown
Free

A large cave in a red sandstone cliff where prehistoric cave-dwellers once lived.

ST COLUMBA'S CAVE
nr Ardrishaig
1 mile N of Ellary off B8024, 10 mile SW of Ardrishaig
Open: All times
Free
No disabled access

Traditionally associated with St Columba's arrival in Scotland, the cave contains a rock-shelf with an altar, above which are carved crosses. The cave was occupied in the Middle Stone Age. In front of it are traces of houses and the ruins of a chapel (possibly 13th-century). There is another cave nearby.

Farms

HOMESTON FARM
Southend, Campbeltown
5 miles S of Campbeltown, signposted off the B842
Tel: (0586) 52437
Open: Easter – Oct, daily 1030 – 1800
£
Tea-room

Farm park with a Clydesdale mare, a goat, deer and cattle. Children get a free bucket of food for feeding the animals and they may bottle-feed lambs in season. Pets' corner with rabbits and guinea pigs. The restored stable and bothy lets you see how the ploughman lived right in beside his horses. Watch sheep-shearing in Jul/Aug. The child-sized versions of four-wheeled farm bikes are a special attraction. They are fitted with speed restrictors and are used on a special supervised track. The first ride is free but there is a small charge for subsequent rides. The play area with swings and a sandpit is within view of the farmhouse kitchen so parents can have a coffee and still keep an eye on their children. Ceilidh and barbecue evenings are held every Thursday in Jul/Aug from 2000 (no alcohol).

OBAN RARE BREEDS FARM PARK
Oban
2 miles from Oban up Glencruitten Road, past golf course
Tel: (063177) 608/604
Open: Easter – Sep, daily 1000 – dusk
££
Tea-room, picnic area

The 30-acre park is part of a working farm with sheep, cattle, pigs and poultry. There are rare breeds of animals which are seldom seen on modern farms. The pets' corner has rabbits, goats, fawns and lambs. Woodland walk. School tours and birthday parties are catered for.

HOLY LOCH FARM PARK
nr Dunoon
At junct of A815 and B836, 1 mile from Sandbank
Tel: (0369) 6429
Open: Apr—Oct 1030—1800
££
P: Available
Tea-room and picnic areas
A small working farm with lots of animals including sheep, poultry, cattle, pigs, goats and a Clydesdale horse. Children can feed the sheep and goats and bottle-feed the lambs in the pets' corner. Birthday parties can be catered for, and school and pre-school groups are welcome.

Fish

GLENARAY FISH FARM
Inveraray
2 miles along Oban road
Tel: (0499) 2233
Open: Apr—Oct, daily 1000—1800
Picnic area and tea-room
Watch the trout, feed them and then catch them! There are 10 fish ponds where children may feed the trout and 2 fishing lakes. Rods for hire. Children's play area and a pets' corner.

HIGHLAND SALMON VISITOR CENTRE
Kilninver, by Oban PA34 4QS
On A816, 7 miles S of Oban
Tel: (085 26) 202
££
Restaurant

The life story of the 'King of the Fish'—how they hatch in Highland burns and rivers and then migrate to the feeding grounds of the Arctic before returning to the very same burn or river to spawn. Find out about traditional ways of catching salmon and see the biggest salmon ever caught with a rod. Finish the visit by walking out on pontoons to the fish farm in the loch where you can see live salmon.

Gardens

CRARAE GARDEN
nr Inveraray
10 miles S of Inveraray on A83
Tel: (0546) 86614/86607
Open: Summer 0900—1800, winter daylight hours
£
A superb natural gorge with a series of waterfalls. There are walks through the lovely gardens too where you can see a collection of mature trees and exotic shrubs.

YOUNGER BOTANIC GARDEN
Benmore nr Dunoon
A815, 7 miles NNW of Dunoon
Tel: (0369) 6261
Open: Mid Mar—Oct, daily 1000—1800
£
P: Available
Tea-room
Disabled facilities
Extensive woodland gardens featuring conifers, rhododendrons, azaleas and a magnificent avenue of Sierra redwoods. A path, starting from the gardens, leads past Loch Eck to Puck's Glen.

ARDENCRAIG GARDENS
Rothesay, Isle of Bute
Open: May – Sep, Mon – Fri 0900 – 16.30,
Sat – Sun 1300 – 1630
Free
Tea-room
The ornamental pond in the formal gardens is stocked with lots of interesting fish while the aviary has many exotic birds. All very appealing to toddlers.

HOUSE OF TRESHNISH
nr Tobermory, Isle of Mull
On B8073, 14 miles from Tobermory
Open: Apr – Oct
£
P: Available
The gardens are on a hillside near Calgary which gave its name to Calgary, Alberta, through the Canadian city's founder, Colonel J. F. MacLeod. There are extensive footpaths through rare and beautiful shrubs, with magnificent views over Calgary Bay.

JURA HOUSE WALLED GARDEN AND GROUNDS
Isle of Jura
Tel: (049 682) 315
Open: All year round, Mon – Sat 0900 – 1700
£
P: Available
Interesting woodland and cliff walks.

Graveyards and Gruesome Places

INVERARAY JAIL
Inveraray PA32 8TX
A83 Glasgow/Campbeltown
Tel: (0499) 2381
Open: Daily, Apr – Oct 0930 – 1800;
Nov – Mar 1000 – 1700
££

Disabled access to ground floor only
A reconstructed 19th-century prison with costumed 'prisoners' and 'warders' to answer your questions. Take a seat on the public benches beside life-like figures attending an 1820s' trial. Let yourself be locked in the cage-like exercise yard. Try to sleep in a prisoner's hammock or do some prison labour making herring nets or turning a crank machine. There are exhibitions of blood-curdling medieval tortures and punishments. Winner of a Scottish Tourism Oscar and Scottish Museum of the Year.

AUCHRINDRAIN OLD HIGHLAND TOWNSHIP
Inveraray
On A83, 5.5 miles SW of Inveraray
Tel: (049 95) 235
Open: Apr/May/Sep 1100 – 1600 (not Sat), Jun/Jul/Aug 1000 – 1700
££
P: Available
Refreshments, picnic areas
Partial disabled access
An old West Highland township has been restored to reflect different periods of life in the Highlands. Look round the visitor centre and thatched cottages and try to imagine what it would have been like to live without washing machines, hoovers, TVs and computers. There was only one sink in the whole village – indoor toilets and bathrooms did not exist then.

Museums

COMBINED OPERATIONS MUSEUM
Cherry Park, Inveraray Castle, Inveraray
Tel: (0499) 2203

Open: Mid May—end Sep Mon—Thu, Sat 1000—1800, Sun 1300—1800
P: Available
£
Disabled facilities

The museum shows the work of the Combined Training Centre which was based here during World War II. Thousands of men and women learned assault landing techniques for use in commando raids in North Africa, Dieppe and D-Day landings in Normandy. You can see the battle plans, old newspapers of the day and models of warships and landing-craft.

A WORLD IN MINIATURE
North Pier, Oban
Tel: (0631) 66300
Open: Easter—mid Oct, Mon—Sat 1000—1730, Sun 1200—1730
£
Disabled access

Doll's-house enthusiasts—both young and old—will be entranced by the miniature rooms, tiny pieces of furniture and dioramas which have been made by over 250 different artists.

IONA HERITAGE CENTRE
The Manse, Isle of Iona
Tel: (06817) 364

Displays show the life of the islanders over the last 200 years. Activities for children.

Novelties

CORRYVRECKAN WHIRLPOOL
Between the islands of Jura and Scarba
No disabled access

This treacherous tide-race covers an extensive area and is very dangerous for small craft. It is most impressive about 1 hour after low tide and may be seen from the north end of Jura or from Craignish Point. The noise can be heard from a considerable distance.

THE BELL TOWER
All Saints' Episcopal Church, Inveraray
Open: May—Sep, Mon—Sat 1000—1030, 1400—1700; Sun 1400—1700
£
No disabled access to tower

Climb the tower to see Scotland's finest bells, the second heaviest ring of 10 in the world. Ringers and bells can sometimes be watched in action. At other times recordings of the bells can be heard.

Railways

MULL AND WEST HIGHLAND NARROW GAUGE RAILWAY CO LTD
Craignure (Old Pier) Station, Isle of Mull
Off A849 or ferry from Oban and short walk from pier
Tel: (06802) 494
Open: Easter, end Apr—mid Oct
£ return fare; ££ entry to castle and gardens
P: Free
Tea-room at Torosay Castle
Limited disabled facilities

Take a 20-minute journey on a 10.25″ gauge steam and diesel railway to Torosay Castle and the gardens, which include a Japanese garden. The scheduled service coincides with the main sailings from Oban (JOHNSTONE BOATS—*see* **BOATS AND BOAT TRIPS**).

Riding

DALCHENNA RIDING CENTRE
Dalchenna, Inveraray PA32 8XT
Tel: (0499) 2194
££
Miles of rides on the Argyll Estates. Rides and treks can be for 1 hour, half-day or full-day. Children under 8 must be accompanied. RDA and Ponies of UK approved.

CASTLE RIDING CENTRE
Brenfield Farm, Ardrishaig nr Lochgilp-head
5 miles S of Lochgilphead on A83
Tel: (0546) 603274
From ££
Lessons, picnics, hacks, trail riding, swimming with horses. Hourly, daily or weekly rates. BHS, ABRS, STRA, Pony UK, RDA approved.

BALLIVICAR PONY TREKKING
Ballivicar Farm, nr Port Ellen PA42 7AW
4 miles from Port Ellen
Tel: (0496) 2251
££
Pony-trekking, hourly or longer by arrangement. All standards.

ROTHESAY RIDING CENTRE
Canada Hill, Rothesay, Isle of Bute
Tel: (0700) 504971
From £
STRA, POB, RDA approved. Pony-trekking, lessons. Weekly riding holidays for families or unaccompanied children.

LETTERSHUNA RIDING CENTRE
Lettershuna, Appin PA38 4BN
Midway between Oban and Fort William on A828
Tel: (063 173) 227
£££
Riding, trekking for all ages and abilities. BHS, STRA approved. Also LINNHE MARINE – *see* **WATERSPORTS**.

KILLIECHRONAN TREKKING
Killiechronan, Aros, Isle of Mull
Tel: (0680300) 403
Open: Easter – Oct
£
Children aged 5 and upwards can go for morning or afternoon treks on one of the 8 Highland ponies.

LOCHAWESIDE PONIES
c/o 42 Dalavich nr Taynuilt
On W shore of Loch Awe
Tel: (08664) 262
£££
Trekking for all the family on Highland ponies through pine forests or along the shore of Loch Awe.

ACHNALARIG FARM AND STABLE
Glencruitten, Oban PA34 4QA
Tel: (0631) 62745
Open: Mar – Oct
££ per hour
STRA approved. Unaccompanied children welcome.

COILESSAN ACTIVITY AND TREKKING CENTRE
Ardgartan by Arrochar G83 7AR
5 miles S of Arrochar off the A83
Tel: (03012) 523
Open: Mar – Oct, daily 0930 – 1630
Various charges
BHS approved. Activities available on a daily or weekly basis. Pony-trekking and trail riding, sea angling, loch fishing, archery, canoeing, abseiling.

SHEEP AND WOOL CENTRE –
see **ANIMALS AND BIRDS**

Science and Technology

CRUACHAN POWER STATION
Ben Cruachan nr Oban
On A85, 15 miles E of Oban
Tel: (08662) 673
Open: End Mar—Oct, daily 0900—1630
££
P: Available
Picnic area
Partial disabled access
Go almost a mile into a hollow mountain on an electric coach to the underground power station. Find out how the water from the reservoir 364m above is used to generate electricity. Many plants thrive in the artificial light deep underground.

Scotland at Work—Past and Present

OBAN GLASS STUDIO
Heritage Wharf, Railway Pier, Oban
Tel: (0631) 63386
Open: All year, Mon—Fri 0900—1700
Free
P: Available
Watch as blobs of red-hot molten glass are blown and shaped into ornaments, vases and paperweights.

SCOTTISH PRIDE CREAMERY
Townhead, Rothesay PA20 0LF
Tel: (0770) 503186
Open: Apr—Oct, Mon—Fri 1100—1500 (not much cheese-making on Wed); Nov—Mar, Thu/Fri 1100—1500
Watch Scottish cheddar being made from the special viewing gallery.

INVERAWE SMOKERY AND FISHERIES
Taynuilt
11 miles E of Oban on A85
Tel: (08662) 446
Open: All year, daily 0900—1700, Apr—Oct 0900—1800
Free entry to smokery; small charge to see trout in lochs; £££ for father and son fishing permits
Light refreshments
Disabled facilities
Toilets
A detailed exhibition of how fish is smoked in the old traditional smokery. Fish for trout in the 3 lochs. There are good walks in the area as well as a children's play area.

SGRIOB-RUADH FARM
Tobermory, Isle of Mull
Tel: (0688) 2235
Free
The only dairy farm on Mull. See cheese being made and then taste some.

Sport and Leisure Centres

DRIMSYNIE LEISURE COMPLEX
Lochgoilhead
Adjacent to Sheep and Wool Centre
Tel: (03013) 247/444
Various charges
Restaurant
A 25m swimming pool, pony-trekking, golf, ice-skating.

PORTINSHERRICH FARM
Portinsherrich, Lochaweside PA33 1BW
Tel: (08664) 202
Various charges
Grass-skiing, windsurfing, boating, fishing etc. All sorts of farming activities. Residential holidays.

Swimming

QUEEN'S HALL AND DUNOON SWIMMING POOL
Argyll Street, Dunoon PA23 7HH

Tel: (0369) 2800
£
Mother and baby changing facilities
Swimming pool. Other sports facilities on offer include table-tennis, pool, badminton and short tennis. The bouncy castle, football hall or swimming pool can be booked for a hassle-free birthday party.

Other indoor swimming pools with mother and baby changing facilities can be found at CAMPBELTOWN, OBAN and ISLAY, and at DRUM SYNIE HOTEL — see **SPORT AND LEISURE CENTRES**.

ROTHESAY LEISURE POOL
High Street, Rothesay, Isle of Bute
Tel: (0700) 504300
£
Mother and baby changing facilities
Has a 25m swimming pool.

Walks

ARGYLL FOREST PARK
W and NW from Loch Long to Loch Fyne
Access from A815, B839, B828 and A8
P: Available
Partial disabled access
Three forests — Argarten, Glenbrauter and Benmore — cover 60,000 acres. There are scores of forest walks of various lengths to choose from.

CARSAIG ARCHES
Isle of Mull
S of Pennycross, on shore W of Carsaig
Tel: (0688) 2182
Open: All times
No disabled access
A 3-mile walk from Carsaig leads to these remarkable tunnels which can only be reached at low tide. On the way is the Nun's Cave which has curious carvings. It is said that nuns driven out of Iona at the time of the Reformation sheltered here.

GLEN NANT FOREST TRAIL
2 miles S of Taynuilt on B845
Tel: (0631) 66155
P: Available
Trail through native deciduous woodland.

CRINAN CANAL
nr Lochgilphead
Crinan to Ardrishaig
Tel: (0546) 3210
Coffee shop at Crinan
Disabled access
The canal was constructed between 1793 and 1801 to carry ships from Loch Fyne to the Atlantic without rounding Kintyre. The towing path makes a very pleasant, easy walk and children really enjoy looking at the yachts passing through the 15 locks.

BALMEANACH NATURE WALK
Balmeanach, Fishnish, Isle of Mull
6 miles N of Craignure
Tel: (0680300) 342
Tea-room
Look for wild flowers, ducks, dragonflies, birds and rabbits by the stream. Also has a play area.

THE BOATHOUSE VISITOR CENTRE
Isle of Ulva, Aros, Isle of Mull
Tel: (06885) 264
Tea-room
There's lots of fun to be had when you combine a 2-minute ferry ride, an island and a walk. There are 6 signposted walks on the island as well as a visitor centre with displays of life on Ulva in the past.

AROS PARK

nr Tobermory, Isle of Mull
Half a mile S of Tobermory on A848
Tel: (06803) 346
P: Available
Picnic site
Toilets
Forest walks.

Watersports

BORROBOATS

Dungallen Park, Gallanach Road, Oban
Tel: (0631) 63292/66104
Various charges
Small boats (rowing and outboard), sailing dinghies and motor launch for hire by the hour, day or week.

NORTH SAIL SCHOOLS

Columba's Bay, Balcardine, Loch Creran
by Oban
Tel: (0631) 72591
Various charges
Sailing and windsurfing equipment for hire. Instruction available.

NERVOUS WRECK DIVING – WATERSPORTS

Ganavan Sands, Oban
Tel: (0631) 66000
Open: Daily 0900 – 1800
Various charges
Wet water rides, water-skiing, hydrosliding, sidewinder, bump-ride tubes.

ISLAY LEISURE

Cornabus Cottage, Port Ellen, Isle of Islay
Tel: (0496) 2042
Various charges
Canoe and windsurf hire. Instruction available. Boat trips, angling, guided walks and mountain bike hire.

QUARRY POINT VISITOR CENTRE

Crarae, Loch Fyne
A83
Tel: (0546) 86 258
Open: Daily, Apr – Oct 1000 – 1800
P: Available
Various charges
Restaurant and picnic areas
Boating and windsurfing, diving and fishing. Play area.

ARDBRECKNISH BOATING CENTRE

Ardbrecknish nr Inveraray
On B840, 2 miles from Cladich, between
Inveraray and Dalmally
Tel: (08663) 223
Open: All year
Various charges
Picnic beaches
Boats with oars, motors or sails for hire for safe family trips on Loch Awe. No experience required. Fishing tackle and tuition available for beginners.

LINNHE MARINE WATER SPORTS CENTRE

Lettershuna, Appin
25 miles SW of Fort William on A828
Tel: (0631 73) 227
Open: May – Oct 1000 – 1800
P: Available
Various charges
Picnic area, light refreshments
Learn to windsurf, sail or water-ski in a safe sheltered bay with a rescue boat on hand all the time. Small windsurf rigs and wet suits are available. Or you can hire a rowing, motor or sailing boat for a trip to the nearby seal colony and a picnic on one of the islands. The jetty can be used for launching your own boat if you prefer. There is a simulated clay pigeon shoot suitable for children.

PLACES TO EAT

Hotels and Restaurants

ARDENTINNY HOTEL
Loch Long by Dunoon PA23 8TR
Informal lunches and suppers in the Buttery or the patio garden which runs down to the sea. Bikes and boats for hire at the hotel. Recommended by Egon Ronay and the Taste of Scotland guide.

ARISAIG HOUSE
Beasdale, Arisaig PH39 4NR
Tel: (06875) 622
Modest bar lunches—such as soup and home-made bread—in de luxe surroundings.

THE GLASSARY
Sandaig, Isle of Tiree PA77 6XQ
Tel: (08792) 684
Very small restaurant recommended in the Taste of Scotland guide. A children's menu is available or they can choose off the main menu. A family room is available in the adjoining guest house.

INVERCRERAN COUNTRY HOUSE HOTEL
Glen Creran, Appin PA38 4BJ
Just off A828 at head of Loch Creran
Tel: (063 173) 414/456
Open: Mar – Nov
Children over 5 are welcome for Taste of Scotland lunches.

LOCH MELFORT HOTEL
Arduaine, nr Oban PA34 4XG
Tel: (08522) 233
Very flexible attitude to children. They can choose from the bar menu or have small portions off the main menu. High teas in the early evening. Recommended in the Taste of Scotland guide. Family rooms or adjoining rooms available. Baby listening service.

LOCHNELL ARMS HOTEL
North Connell, nr Oban PA37 1RF
Tel: (063171) 408
Children's menu, garden and a small selection of toys.

THE OLD LIBRARY LODGE AND RESTAURANT
Arisaig
Tel: (06875) 651
The proprietors like children. Simple country cooking.

Quick Meals and Snacks

COFFEE-BOOKSHOP
Dervaig, Isle of Mull
Tel: (06884) 234
Browse through the books (including some for children). Have a coffee or a glass of juice and a biscuit, and buy ingredients for your next meal from the specialist foods on offer.

CROFT KITCHEN
Port Charlotte, Isle of Islay
Good, inexpensive food available all day. Children's menu. Beach for children to play on. Primitive camping facilities are available (only WC).

DUART CASTLE TEA-ROOM
By Duart Castle, Isle of Mull
Open: May – early Oct
Excellent home-baking.

OLD BYRE HERITAGE CENTRE

(*see* ANIMALS AND BIRDS)
Dervaig, Isle of Mull
Tel: (06884) 229
Good tea shop with homely fare ranging from home-baking to thick vegetable soup.

Pubs

BARN BAR
Cologin, Lerags, by Oban
Tel: (0631) 64501
Home-cooked meals served all day. Children under 14 welcome till 2000. Children's portions available, pets' corner.

KINTRA OLD GRANARY
Kintra, Isle of Islay
A pub with a children's certificate serving good, moderately priced food. Very relaxed atmosphere and right by a beautiful beach – ideal for parents and children. Camping and bunkhouse facilities (*see* PLACES TO STAY).

Fast Food Chains

LITTLE CHEF
Spean Bridge
Tel: (039781) 297

THE PANCAKE PLACE
95 – 97 George Street, Oban

PLACES TO STAY

Hostels

Facilities at these hostels are Grade 1 and include hot showers, and heating during the winter. Book in advance to be sure of a family room.

SHYA – GLENCOE
Argyll PA39 4HX
Tel: (08552) 219
The hostel is within a few miles of good skiing areas.

SYHA – OBAN
Esplanade, Oban
Tel: (0631) 62025
Ferries leave from Oban for the Hebrides, Iona and Mull. Sandy beach a few miles away. Close to bus and train stations.

Caravan and Camping Sites

ARDGARTEN CARAVAN AND CAMPING SITE
2 miles W of Arrochar on A83
Open: Apr – Sep
££
One of the Forestry Commission's top-grade sites on the shores of Loch Long, with children's play area and boat launching facilities.

ARDUAINE CARAVAN AND CAMPING PARK
Arduaine, Argyll
20 miles S of Oban on A816
Tel: (08522) 288
Open: Mar – Oct
£
A grassy site by the water. Play area.

GLENCOE CARAVAN AND CAMPING SITE
On A82 Tyndrum – Fort William, 1 mile E of village
Tel: (08552) 397
Open: Apr – Oct
££
A top-grade Forestry Commission site.

GLEN NEVIS CARAVAN AND CAMPING PARK
Fort William PH33 6SX
nr Glen Nevis Centre
Tel: (0397) 2191
Open: mid Mar – Mid Oct
££
A large campsite, close to the Glen Nevis Centre where you can buy tea and coffee, or have some fun in the games room.

KINTRA FARM SITE
Port Ellen, Isle of Islay
tel: (0496) 2051
Open: Apr – Sep
£

KINTRA OLD GRANARY (see PLACES TO EAT)

SHEILING HOLIDAYS
Craignure, Isle of Mull PA65 6AY
Tel: (06802) 496
Open: Apr – Oct
££
Lots for children to do and close by the LITTLE RAILWAY (see RAILWAYS). Static tents on site or bring your own. Close to the beach and lochside, games room and good play area.

Hotels

BALLACHULISH HOTEL
Ballachulish PA39 4JY
Tel: (08552) 606
£££
Comfortable hotel on the shore of Loch Linnhe. Family rooms.

THE FALLS OF LORA HOTEL
Connel, by Oban PA37 1PB
Tel: (063171) 483

From ££
Comfortable hotel with pine bunks in the family rooms.

THE GLASSARY
See **PLACES TO EAT**
From ££

LOCH MELFORT HOTEL
See **PLACES TO EAT**
£££

241

THE NORTHERN HIGHLANDS AND ISLANDS

The Isle of Skye is the most popular destination for travellers in this area. Car ferries cross regularly from Mallaig and the Kyle of Lochalsh. But if your children don't travel well on narrow twisting roads, it might be more fun to go by steam train up the West Highland Line from Fort William to Mallaig.

Apart from the quiet pleasures of beachcombing, riding, walking and cycling, Skye has a reasonable range of things to do with children. There is an adventure playground at the Clan Donald Centre, a reptile zoo, and a number of museums depicting island life in bygone days.

The Outer Hebrides — Lewis, Harris, North and South Uist, Benbecula and Barra — are served by ferries leaving from Uig on Skye, or Ullapool which is further north on the mainland. The pace of life on the islands is slow and relaxing — there is not much to hurry for unless a rain squall threatens. The beaches on the western seaboard must be among the most magnificent in the country but they are not easy to get to — the journey to the islands takes at least 2 hours by ferry from Skye and between 5 and 8 hours from Ullapool.

Back on the mainland, the west coast scenery is quite spectacular — towering mountains, crofts huddled by the shore and pockets of golden sand. Palm trees grow well in the mild climate and the gardens at Poolewe are definitely worth a visit. Another fascinating garden has been developed at Achiltibuie where exotic fruit and vegetables are grown in a space-age dome.

The mountains give way to cliffs and sandy beaches on the north coast. John O'Groats is worth a visit just so you can say you have been to the most northerly point on the mainland. The ferry to Orkney leaves from Thurso, while a faster, passenger only, ferry crosses from John O'Groats.

Along the east coast, which is mainly moorland and peat bog, there are a number of excellent heritage centres and museums which tell the poignant story of the Highland clearances and the tough life led by the crofters.

Gaelic is still spoken in these grand corners of Scotland and even the signposts are printed in two languages.

PLACES TO VISIT

Animals and Birds

COUNTRYSIDE CENTRE (NTS)
Torridon
9 miles SW of Kinlochewe on A896
Tel: (044 587) 221
Open: End May – Sep, Mon – Sat 1000 –
1800, Sun 1400 – 1800
Disabled access

The museum has displays on local wildlife plus a video. The track leading from it to the nearby deer museum passes paddocks where orphaned deer are raised. Older children and adults can look for deer and eagles in the company of a ranger, but these walks are only for those who are fit and suitably dressed for the hills.

LLAMA WALKS
Dunbeath
tel: (05933) 217

Help to take 12 South American llamas for their walk round Dunbeath Strath. This takes 3 to 4 hours and includes time for a picnic lunch. Phone for details.

DUNCANSBY HEAD
John O'Groats

The main road ends at John O'Groats and from here there are interesting walks to Duncansby Head and the Stacks of Duncansby. Fulmars, auks, shags, guillemots and great skuas nest here, and seals may be seen close to the shore.

WATERFOWL AND COUNTRY PARK
The Croft, Drumsmittal nr North Kessock
3 miles N of Inverness

Open: All year, 0930 – 1830
££
Picnic area

Come and feed the ducks. There are 40 different species of ornamental pheasant, duck and geese and lots of ducklings, chicks and goslings.

KYLERHEA OTTER HAVEN
Kylerhea, Isle of Skye
Open: All year
Free
Picnic area

One of Britain's most thriving otter populations lives here. You might be lucky and see otters, eagles and falcons from the observation hide.

SKYE ENVIRONMENTAL CENTRE
Harrapool, Broadford, Isle of Skye
Tel: (0471 822) 487
Open: Mon – Sat 1000 – 1700
Free

The museum has wildlife and geological displays. There is a seashore study trail, and wildlife safaris can be arranged for all age groups.

SKYE SERPENTARIUM
The Old Mill, Harrapool, nr Broadford,
Isle of Skye IV49 9AQ
Tel: (0471) 822209
Open: Daily during summer seasons
1000 – dusk
£
P: Free

A reptile zoo with snakes, lizards, frogs and tortoises. If you are brave enough, you may be able to handle a snake under supervision – none of them are poisonous. It's a surprise to find that they are warm and dry to touch, not cold and slimy.

243

Beaches

Little gems of beaches are strung out along the rocky coast with longer stretches of sand at the Kyle of Tongue, Kyle of Durness, Dunnet near Thurso and Reiss near Wick. There are good shells on the beach at John o' Groats. This is such a remote area that you can be sure that the beaches are all clean and unpolluted.

TALMINE
nr Tongue
Turn off A838 at Achuvoldrach
Sandy beach with rocky outcrops, a burn and a harbour.

CORAL BEACHES
nr Dunvegan, Isle of Skye
On unclassified road 3 miles N of Dunvegan
A 20-minute walk takes you to white coral beaches. There is not much sand, just masses of tiny shells. Look along the high tide line for big clusters of coral.

Bike Hire and Cycle Routes

MOUNTAIN RESTAURANT BIKE HIRE
Strath Square, Gairloch
Tel: (0445) 2316
Open: All year, daily
Mountain and leisure bikes for adults and children. Daily, half-day or weekly rates. Evening hire in summer. Maps, locks, guides and trail snacks.

BICYCLE BOTHY
Ar Dachaidh, Badnellan, Brora
Tel: (0408) 621658
Open: All year
£ per half-day

Adult mountain bikes and children's bikes for hire. Also spares and accessories.

LEISURE ACTIVITIES
11A Princes Street, Thurso
Tel: (0847) 65385
Cycle hire, including children's bikes, spare parts and accessories.

THE BIKE AND CAMPING SHOP
The Arcade, 35 High Street, Thurso
Tel: (0847) 66124
Bike sales, hire including children's bikes, repair service.

ISLAND CYCLES
Struan Road, Portree, Isle of Skye
Behind new Arts Centre
Tel: (047 072) 284
From £ plus small charge for a helmet
Mountain bikes, tourers, 10-speeds and children's bikes for hire.

CYCLE CRAFT
Culmhor. Lairg Road, Bonar Bridge
Tel: (08632) 368
From £ per day
Adults and children's bikes for hire.

KYLE CYCLES
Old Plock Road, Kyle of Lochalsh
Tel: (0599) 4842
Open: Daily
Mountain bikes, tourers, children's bikes to suit all ages, child seats, panniers, maps and car bike racks for hire.

Boats and Boat Trips

DOLPHIN ECOSSE
Bank House, High Street, Cromarty IV11 8UZ
Tel: (03817) 323
££££
Family and school trips to see the

only known group of bottlenose dolphins living in the North Sea.

ULLAPOOL BOAT TRIPS
MacKenzie Marine, Green Pastures, Ullapool
Tel: (0854) 612008
Open: Easter – Oct
£££
Refreshments
Nature cruises to Isle Martin bird sanctuary and seal islands take 2 or 4 hours. Look for red deer, red-breasted mersanger ducks, arctic terns and peregrine falcons. Send yourself a postcard with a unique Summer Isles stamp from Tanera Mhor.

SUMMER ISLES
Mr I. MacLeod, Post Office, Achiltibuie
Tel: (085 482) 200
Open: Easter – Oct daily except Sun
£££
Morning and afternoon cruises daily from Badentarbet Pier, Achiltibuie. Go to the Summer Isles and see a seal colony basking on the rocks.

ISLANDER CRUISES
Ullapool
Tel: (0854) 612200/612264
Open: Easter – Oct
£££
Light refreshments
No disabled access
Half an hour on shore on a 3-hour pleasure cruise to the Summer Isles. See seals, dolphins, porpoises and whales if you are lucky. Dress warmly so you can stay on deck all the time.

MV PENTLAND VENTURE
Ferry Office, John o'Groats
Tel: (095 581) 353/342
£££

Day trips to Orkney take 45 minutes in a motor-boat.

LAXFORD CRUISES
5 Moffat Square, Scourie
Tel: (0971) 2409
Trips: Mon – Sat at 1000, 1200, 1400
£££
Look out for up to 50 different species of bird, and see if you can spot a seal colony basking on the rocks.

STATESMAN CRUISES
Heatherbrae, Inver, Lochinver
Tel: (05714) 446
£££
Trip up Loch Glen Coull to see seals and Britain's highest waterfall. The trip takes about 2 hours and leaves from Kylesku Old Ferry Pier.

ST DONAN
Kincraig, Lilles Hall Street, Helmsdale
Tel: (04312) 386
From ££
Trips to see the bird colonies on the cliffs.

Castles and Stately Homes

DUNROBIN CASTLE AND GARDENS
Golspie
On the A9, half a mile N of village of Golspie, 65 miles N of Inverness
Tel: (0408) 633177
Open: May, Mon – Thu 1030 – 1230; Jun – Sep, Mon – Sat 1030 – 1230, Sun 1300 – 1730
££
Tea-room
This is the ancient seat of the Earls and Dukes of Sutherland. The bed-

rooms, nurseries, study and other rooms give a glimpse of the lifestyle enjoyed by the Victorian dukes – who also owned four other stately homes in Britain. The museum has a working 19th-century fire-engine. The formal gardens are open all year, and you can walk in the castle policies free of charge when the castle is closed.

BROCHEL CASTLE
Raasay by Isle of Skye
At the far end of the longest unmarked road leading N on Raasay
The ruined stronghold of Clan MacLeod of Raasay gives a good idea of fortified living 400 to 500 years ago.

CLAN DONALD CENTRE
Armadale Castle, Isle of Skye IV45 8RS
On A851 close to Armadale Pier
Tel: (04714) 305
Open: Mid Mar – early Nov 0930 – 1730, gardens open all year
££
P: Free
Restaurant
Disabled access, wheelchairs available
An award-winning centre with a museum. Walks along the shoreline and through some of the oldest woodland on Skye. Find out more about the countryside on a ranger-led walk, visit the ruins of Armadale Castle and play in the adventure playground. The Skylark scheme organises daily walks and events for children, and there is an environmental playscheme called the Sleat Slaters on Wed/Fri afternoons in Jul/Aug. Children are also welcome to ceilidhs – check for dates and times.

DUNVEGAN CASTLE AND GARDENS
Dunvegan, Isle of Skye
Tel: (047 022) 206
Open: Mar – Oct 1000 – 1730; Castle only closed Sun
£££; free entry for Blue Peter Badge wearers
P: Free
Restaurant
No disabled access
Historic stronghold of the Clan MacLeod, looking out across the sea loch of Dunvegan. Children love 'firing' the cannons on the battlements at passing boats. Look down into the dungeon where realistic figures groan (not for those who are easily spooked). Distract the faint-hearted with the Highland cattle and walks through the water gardens and the woods. From May – Sep there are boat trips from the castle jetty to a seal colony (an expensive extra).

Caves

SAND OF UDRIGLE
Laide
Off A832, on the shore half a mile N of Laide
Free
There are 2 caves to explore as well as the strange rock formations nearby.

COVE
nr Poolewe
B8057 NW of Poolewe, on the shore near Cove
Free
The two caves are reached by a rather boggy route to the shore. Further along the cliff is a natural

stone arch which you can walk through at low tide.

SMOO CAVE
nr Durness
A838, 1.5 miles E of Durness
Tel: (097 181) 259
Open: All reasonable times; boat trips Apr – Oct, weather permitting
££ for boat trips
No disabled access

Three vast caves and a waterfall at the end of a deep cleft in the limestone cliffs. The entrance to the first cave looks like a Gothic arch. You can see the second cavern from a platform but it is more fun to go by boat to the second and third caves. The boat takes you right into the waterfall chamber where you land and walk 150ft further into the caves. Contact Durness Tourist Office for times of trips.

THE BRIG O' TRAMS
Wick
Free

A natural arch formed over hundreds of years by the action of weather and sea wearing away the rock.

Farms

DALMORE FARM
nr Alness
Signposted from A9 off Alness bypass
Tel: (0349) 883978
Open: Mon – Sat 1030 – 1700, Sun 1300 – 1700
Free
Tea-room, picnic area

A working farm with a special area for children which includes many rare breeds. Visit the farm museum, have a pony-and-trap ride and let off steam in the small playground.

HIGHLAND AND RARE BREEDS FARM
Avalon, Elphin by Lairg IV27 4HH
On A835 between Ullapool and Lochinver
Tel: (085486) 204
Open: May – Sep, daily 1000 – 1700
££
Refreshments available

A working croft with many native and traditional breeds of farm animals. There are farm-working demonstrations which include sheep-shearing and bottle-feeding of lambs. Watch the feed round at 1000 or go on a guided tour at 1400. There is a farm walk, pets' corner and shop.

CORVOST RARE ANIMAL CROFT
Ardgay nr Tain IV24 3BP
Tel: (08633) 317
Open: Daily from 1100
£

Red deer, goats, sheep, duck pond etc.

CORRAIDH CROFT RARE BREEDS
94 Laid, Loch Eribolleside, by Altnahara
Tel: (0971 511) 234
£
Tea-room

Rare breeds, live shellfish, pets' corner and exhibitions.

BORRERAIG PARK EXHIBITION CROFT
Glendale, nr Dunvegan, Isle of Skye
Off B884
Open: Mon – Sat 1000
£
P: Available

A good collection of antiquarian farm implements and livestock.

HILL CROFT OPEN FARM
6 Tortarder, Struan, Isle of Skye
Tel: (047 072) 242
Free
Rare breeds of animals.

CRAIG HIGHLAND FARM
Plockton
Unclassified road N of Kyle of Lochalsh
Open: 1000 – dusk
£
Come and feed the animals at a rare breeds conservation centre.

Fish

TORRACHILTY DAM
Marybank, nr Dingwall
Off A834 between Dingwall and Strathpeffer
Open: Jun – Oct
The Borland Fish Lift is named after a Scottish hydraulic engineer. Migrating fish swim into a chamber at the foot of a sloping shaft at the bottom of the dam. Water from the loch fills the shaft and the fish rise up with it until they spill out over the sluice.

Gardens

INVEREWE GARDENS (NTS)
nr Gairloch
On A832, 6 miles NE of Gairloch
Tel: (044 586) 200
Open: All year, daily 0930 – sunset
££
P: Available
Licensed restaurant
Disabled facilities – wheelchairs available
Palm trees, Himalayan lilies and giant forget-me-nots from the South Pacific all flourish here even though the gardens are further north than Moscow. Miles of quiet path to explore and a rocky beach to play on.

THE HYDROPONICUM – *see*
SCOTLAND AT WORK

Graveyards and Gruesome Places

CLOOTIE WELL
Munlochy
Free
The trees and fence around the wishing well are draped with thousands of rags. To have your wish granted you must spill a small amount of water before tying a rag on a nearby tree and drinking from the well. If you take away one of the rags you will succumb to the misfortunes of the original owner.

BADBEA
nr Ousdale
A signposted path leads from the lay-by to Badbea
The lonely settlement of Badbea was founded by tenants evicted from inland straths during the infamous clearances. The site is very exposed and tradition has it that children and livestock had to be tethered to prevent them being blown over the cliffs. Many of the inhabitants eventually emigrated to America or New Zealand around the turn of the century.

SPLIT STONE
nr Melvich
1 mile E of Melvich on A836
It is said that an old woman was returning from a shopping trip when she was chased by the devil. She ran round and round the stone and

the devil, in his temper, split it but the woman escaped.

WITCH'S STONE
Littleton, Dornoch
An upright slab with the date 1722 marks the place where the last witch in Scotland was burned.

WOLF STONE
nr Helmsdale
10 miles SW of Helmsdale on A9
A stone marks the spot where, in 1700, the last wolf in Scotland was killed.

Heritage Centres

WATER SAMPLING PAVILION
The Square, Strathpeffer
Open: Daily Easter – Oct
Sample the sulphur waters which made the spa renowned in Victorian times when people flocked here to 'take the water' for the good of their health.

TIMESPAN HERITAGE CENTRE
Helmsdale
Tel: (04312) 327
Open: Easter – mid Oct, Mon – Sat 1000 – 1700, Sun 1400 – 1700
£
An award-winning centre which retells the dramatic story of the Highlands – witches and warriors, maidens and murderers, prosperity and poverty, triumph and tragedy – using a mixture of life-size displays, sound effects and videos.

BAILLE AN OR AND SUISGILL
nr Helmsdale
A short distance up A897, the Strath of Kildonan
Baille an Or and Suisgill were the

site of the Great Sutherland Gold Rush of 1869. Many men from all over Britain came in search of gold and there is still some to be found today. Details about panning and permits may be obtained from the Tourist Information Centre in Helmsdale. Pans are available from the craftshop.

Museums

GAIRLOCH HERITAGE MUSEUM
Gairloch
Tel: (044 583) 243
Open: Easter – Sep, Mon – Sat 1000 – 1700
£
P: Available
Restaurant
Disabled access and facilities
See what life used to be like in this part of Scotland. There is a reconstructed croft house room where an old lady sings as she spins, a schoolroom and other displays on domestic work. Children can test their knowledge with the quiz.

DINGWALL MUSEUM
Town House, High Street, Dingwall
Tel: (0349) 62116
Open: May – Sep, Mon – Sat
£
Look in on a traditional Highland kitchen and see the dark interior of a smithy. Admire the workings of the old town clock.

GROAM HOUSE MUSEUM
Rosemarkie
Open: May – Sep, Mon – Sat 1100 – 1700, Sun 1430 – 1630; winter weekends
£
An award-winning Pictish Centre, with a fine collection of early Chris-

tian stones. There is a playable harp based on the design on the Nigg Stone. Videos on the Picts and the Brahan Seer are fascinating— especially one in cartoon form for children.

CROMARTY COURTHOUSE
Cromarty
Tel: (038 17) 418
Open: Apr—Sep, 1000—1800; reduced hours in winter
£

Go back 200 years—look into the prison cells and sit in the courtroom where the judge (an animated figure) passes sentence on a woman found guilty of stealing from a local hemp factory. Put on a Walkman and go on a Time Machine Tape Tour as you walk through the streets of the town.

HIGHLAND MUSEUM OF CHILDHOOD
Old Railway Station, Strathpeffer
Tel: (0997) 421031
Open: Daily
£

Tells the story of childhood in the Highlands through displays and recordings.

LHAIDHAY CAITHNESS CROFT MUSEUM
nr Dunbeath
On A9, 1 mile N of Dunbeath
Tel: (05933) 244
Open: Easter—Sep, daily 0900—1700
£
P: Available
Picnic area
Disabled facilities
An early 18th-century croft house with the stable and byre under the same roof. It is completely furnished

in the fashion of its time. Blind people are encouraged to touch things.

DUNBEATH HERITAGE CENTRE
Old School, Dunbeath KW6 6EY
Follow signs from A9 Dunbeath bypass
Tel: (059 33) 233
Open: Apr, Mon—Fri 1000—1700; May— Sep, Mon—Sat 1000—1700, Sun 1100— 1800
£
Picnic area by the harbour
Listen to seabirds and smell soup cooking as you look at the displays of life-size figures going about their business in a Highland community. There are many excellent walks round Dunbeath including the strath, seashore and the harbour area which are all part of the heritage trail. Look out for puffins and seals.

WICK HERITAGE CENTRE
Bank Row, Wick
Tel: (0955) 3385
Open: Jun—Sep, Mon—Sat 1000—1700
£

An award-winning museum. The 20 display areas include a harbour with real boats, a radio station, a cooperage, a kiln, a printing works, a smiddy and domestic rooms with period furniture.

COLBOST FOLK MUSEUM
nr Dunvegan, Isle of Skye
3 miles W of Dunvegan
Tel: (047022) 296
Open: Daily 1000—1800
£
P: Available
See what it would have been like to live on Skye 100 years ago. A pungent peat fire burns all day in the thatched 'black house' and there's an illicit whisky-still round the back of the building.

GIANT ANGUS MacASKILL MUSEUM

Dunvegan, Isle of Skye
Near public car park
Tel: (047022) 296
Open: Mon – Sat 0930 – 1800, Sun 1230 – 1700
£
P: Available

The museum contains a life-size model of Angus MacAskill, in the Guinness Book of Records as the tallest Scotsman and highest 'true' giant at 7'9'. He was born on Berneray in the Outer Hebrides in 1825, but was brought up in Cape Breton, Nova Scotia, where he died of fever aged 38.

THE OLD SKYE CROFTER'S HOUSE

Luib, Isle of Skye
On main Broadford – Sligachan road, 15 miles from Kyleakin
Tel: (04712) 427
Open: Daily 1000 – 1800
£
P: Available

A folk museum showing how crofters lived in the early 20th century without electricity, running water, TV or cars.

HOLMISDALE HOUSE TOY MUSEUM

Glendale, Isle of Skye
B884 W of Dunvegan
Tel: (047081) 240
Open: Mon – Sat 1000 – 1800
£

A collection of toys including dolls, books, games and meccano. Visitors are encouraged to touch the toys and can operate some of the games.

SKYE MUSEUM OF ISLAND LIFE

Duntulm, nr Uig, Isle of Skye
On A855 N of Uig
Tel: (047 052) 279
Open: Mid May – Oct, Mon – Sat 0900 – 1800
£
Disabled facilities

A group of 7 thatched cottages complete with wall beds, farming implements, a handloom and old photographs all dating from last century.

Novelties

WHALIGOE STEPS

Wick
Free
No disabled access

365 steps lead down the cliff to a small harbour where boats used to land their catches. Take care on the steps especially in wet or windy weather.

KILT ROCK

Isle of Skye
Off A855, 17 miles N of Portree
Open: All year
Free
P: Available
Disabled access

Even the rocks look like kilts in this part of the island! The 'pleats' are actually complex rock formations. These can be seen from the road but you can walk to the cliffs (take care at the edge) and to a nearby waterfall.

Picnic Sites

LAEL FOREST GARDENS

Inverlael
A835 Garve – Ullapool – Inverlael, sign-

posted, third carpark
P: Available
Forestry Commission picnic site with
waterfall, playfort and gardens.
Toilets.

LEDMORE
Dornoch
1 mile N of junction of A835 and A83
P: Available
Forestry Commission picnic site.
Toilets.

LOCH LINNHE
nr Fort William
6 miles S of Fort William on lochside at
Corrychurrachan
P: Available
Forestry Commission picnic site.
Toilets

CAMAS TORSA
Strontian

A861 from Strontian-Salen, then B8007,
1 mile W of Salen
P: Available
Forestry Commission picnic site overlooking Loch Sunart. Toilets.

KYLERHEA
Isle of Skye
A850 (Kyleakin–Broadford), then follow
signs through Glen Arroch
P: Available
Toilets
Forestry Commission picnic site.
Watch out for otters as this area is
famous for them.

Railways

THE WEST HIGHLAND LINE
Station, Fort William
Tel: (0397) 703791

Open: May–Oct, phone for details of timetable
£££
Refreshments on board
Take a trip back in time on a steam-hauled train. Steam and smuts stream out behind the *Lochaber* which travels from Fort William to Mallaig and back. On Sundays there is the option of joining a sea cruise to the Isle of Skye or into Loch Nevis before returning to the train.

Riding

EAST SUTHERLAND RIDING CENTRE
Culmailie Farm,
Golspie
Tel: (0408) 633045
From ££
Lessons and pony-trekking for all ages and stages. Beach rides and quiet woodland rides on reliable horses and ponies.

DUNNET TREKKING CENTRE
Drummuie, Westside, Dunnet
Tel: (084 785) 689/311
From £
Trek over the countryside or along miles of golden sand on Dunnet Beach.

SANDFORD RIDING AND TREKKING CENTRE
5 Ose, Struan, Isle of Skye
On A863 nr Bracadale
Tel: (047 072) 225
From £
Hourly trekking and hacking. Beginners welcome. Children are accompanied.

Scotland at Work – Past and Present

CNOC AND LOCHAN WILDLIFE
Burnside, Murkle, Caithness KW14 8YT
Off A836
Tel: (0847) 66382
Open: Daily 0900–2000 by appointment
P: Available
Free
Coffee shop
Have you ever wondered how animals and birds in museums look so life-like? During the tour you will see a skilled taxidermist at work.

DUNLIN DESIGNS
Burnside, Murkle, Caithness KY14 8YT
Off A836
Tel: (0847) 64460
Open: Daily in summer 1000–1700; Thu–Sun in winter 1000–1700
Free
See how to make soft toys, patchwork, quilting and embroidery in the same craft complex as CNOC AND LOCHAN WILDLIFE.

HIGHLAND FINE CHEESES FACTORY
Shore Road, Tain
Tel: (0862) 2034
Open: Mon–Fri 0930–1700
Free
Go on a conducted tour and find out how cheese is made – then taste the finished product.

CAITHNESS GLASS
Airport Industrial Estate, Wick
Tel: (0955) 2286
Open: Mon–Fri 0900–1630
Free
P: Available
Restaurant

Disabled access and facilities
Mother and baby room
See craftsmen making beautiful glassware and paperweights from the safety of a viewing gallery. There are also glass engravers and jewellers at work.

DOUNREAY EXHIBITION
Thurso KW14 7TZ
10 miles W of Thurso
Tel: (0847) 62121 x 656
Open: Apr – Sep Tue – Sun 1000 – 1600
Free
Picnic area, refreshments
Toilets
An interesting exhibition of nuclear power and the work taking place at Dounreay. There are 2 floors of videos, models and hands-on exhibits. Anyone aged 12 or more can also look round the Prototype Fast Reactor.

KYLEBURN CONFECTIONERY
Lybster
Off A9
Tel: (04932) 353
Free
Tea-room
Have you ever wondered how the writing gets into the middle of a stick of rock? Find out on a tour of the factory where you can see lettered rock and traditional boiled sweets being made.

CRAFT WORKSHOPS
John o' Groats
Free
See Santas, Xmas puddings, apples, cherries and multi-coloured, carved candles being made. There is also a potter and various other craftspeople at work.

LOVAT MINERAL WATER
Fanellan, nr Beauly
On A831 S of Beauly
Open: Mon – Fri 0930 – 1630
Free
Coffee shop
Have a look at one of the most modern bottling plants in Europe from the viewing gallery. Visitor centre.

ORCADIAN STONE COMPANY
Main Street, Golspie KW10 6RH
Tel: (040 83) 3483
Open: By appointment, daily 0900 – 1730 (not Sun in winter)
P: Available
Free
Go on a 30-minute tour of the workshops where dull-looking stones are cut and polished and transformed into sparkling jewellery. There is a large exhibition of local geology and fine mineral specimens.

THE HYDROPONICUM
Achiltibuie nr Ullapool
Off A835 N of Ullapool
Tel: (085 482) 202
Open: Apr – Oct, daily; tours at 1000, 1200, 1400, 1700
£££
P: Available
Restaurant close by
Disabled facilities
A space-age dome where plants are not grown in soil, but in water like the Hanging Gardens of Babylon. Ripe strawberries hang down from the roof, while alongside lettuces and cabbages there are bananas, figs, vines, lemons and flowers. Special arrangements can be made for school groups.

GREAT GLEN FOODS
Old Ferry Road, North Ballachulish PH33 6RZ
Tel: (08553) 277
Open: Factory visits all year, Mon – Fri 0900 – 1700
Free
Sample one of the 22 flavours of tablet in the shop and perhaps get some tips on how to make a perfect batch yourself.

Sport and Leisure Centres

LOCHABER LEISURE CENTRE
Belford Road, Fort William
Tel: (0397) 704359/703886
Open: All year
Various charges
Light refreshments
Swimming pool with chute, inflatables and rafts. Table-tennis, crazy golf, putting.

GREAT GLEN SCHOOL OF ADVENTURE
Great Glen Water Park, South Laggan by Spean Bridge PH34 4EA
A86 NE of Fort William
Tel: (0809) 3381
Open: Daily; watersports Apr – Oct
Various charges
Restaurant
Lots of sports and activities to try. Motor-boats, rowing boats, pedaloes and fishing tackle for hire. Also Australian half tennis, giant chess, swimming pool and games room with table-tennis. Tuition available for sailing, windsurfing, canoeing, water-skiing and cross-country skiing. Three-bedroom lodges to let on the site.

INVERHOUSE SPORTS
Culrain, Ardgay
On A9 between Dornoch and Tain
Tel: (054982) 213
Various charges
Bicycles, mountain bikes, grass track go-carts, radio-controlled racing, off-road motor-cycle tuition.

RAASAY OUTDOOR CENTRE
by Isle of Skye IV40 8PB
Ferry from Sconser on A850, Isle of Skye
Tel: (047862) 266
Various charges
Sailing, sea and loch canoeing, wind-surfing with specialised 'kiddy-rigs', archery, orienteering, rock-climbing and abseiling. Expert tuition for beginners on day/half-day basis or residential Activity Weeks. Minimum age 9.

Swimming

A fun session in an indoor heated pool is an appealing alternative to a dip in the sea if it is cold and wet outside. There are pools at ALNESS ACADEMY, POOLEWE, TAIN, THURSO, GOLSPIE, PORTREE and KYLE OF LOCHALSH.

Walks

NEPTUNE'S STAIRCASE
Banavie nr Fort William
3 miles NW of Fort William off A830 at Banavie
P: Available
Disabled access
Watch boats being raised 64ft along a series of 8 locks which were built almost 200 years ago.

Watersports

DRASCOMBE SAILING SCHOOL
Avoch, Black Isle
Tel: (046373) 493
Open: Apr – Oct
Various charges

Sailing on the Beauly and Moray Firths. Group or individual lessons. Families welcome.

GAIRLOCH WATERSPORT CENTRE

Gairloch
Tel: (0445) 2131/2333
Open: All year
Various charges
Learn how to windsurf, water-ski, canoe or parakite. Fishing rods for hire – bait supplied.

ARDMAIR POINT CARAVAN SITE AND BOAT CENTRE

Ardmair nr Ullapool
Tel: (0854) 2054
Various charges
Windsurfing, sailboarding and canoeing. Rowing and motor-boats for hire. Good campsite.

WEST HIGHLAND MARINE LTD

Badachro nr Gairloch
Tel: (0445 83) 291
Open: All year
Various charges
Hire Canadian canoes, sea kayaks, rowing boats with outboard engines and sailing dinghies. Lifejackets for very small children are available. Explore the tiny beaches around the bay.

WHITEWAVE CANOEING

Idrigill, Uig, Isle of Skye
Tel: (047 042) 414
Various charges
Learn sea kayaking and windsurfing on half or full-day courses. All equipment provided.

LEISURE MARINE

Shore Front, Plockton
Tel: (059 984) 306
Various charges

Canoes, rowing boats, sailing dinghies and motor-boats for hire. Seal trips at 1500. Fishing. Bike hire from Off the Rails (tel: 059 948 423).

Waterfalls

CORRIESHALLOCH GORGE (NTS)

Braemore nr Ullapool
A835 at Braemore, 12 miles SSE of Ullapool
Tel: (0463) 232084
Open: All times
Free
P: Available
No disabled access
The Falls of Measach plunge 150ft into a spectacular gorge which you can cross via a suspension bridge. Viewpoint.

FALLS OF ROGIE

2 miles W of Strathpeffer
Open at all times
Free
P: Available
No disabled access
The word 'rogie' comes from the Norse language and means 'splashing, foaming river'. From the suspension bridge which spans the falls you may be lucky enough to see salmon leap.

FALLS OF SHIN

nr Bonar Bridge
A836, 5 miles N of Bonar Bridge
P: Available
No disabled access
Spectacular falls through a rocky gorge famous for the salmon leaping. Display board about the life-cycle of salmon near the carpark.

EAS COUL AULIN FALLS
Old Ferry Pier by Kylestrome
At the head of Loch Glencoul, 3 miles
W of A894
Tel: (097 183) 239/(05714) 446
Open: Cruises daily in summer at 1100, 1400, 1600
Take a boat trip (*see* STATESMAN CRUISE—**BOATS AND BOAT TRIPS**) to the tallest waterfall in Britain which drops 658ft. Look for seals and herons.

CASSLEY FALLS
Off A839 about 10 miles W of Lairg
Very attractive falls and walkway alongside. Salmon can be seen leaping during the summer months.

PLACES TO EAT

Hotels and Restaurants

CAPE WRATH HOTEL
Durness IV27 4QF
Tel: (097181) 274
Open: Mar–Jan
Just by ferry to Capeside. Lots of grass outside to play on. A quiet fishing hotel. Soup and sandwiches in the lounge bar are good value.

THE CEILIDH PLACE
West Argyle Street, Ullapool IV26 2TY
Tel: (0854) 612103
Open: All year
Families welcome.

FLODIGARRY COUNTRY HOUSE HOTEL
Flodigarry, Staffin, Isle of Skye
Tel: (047 052) 203
Delicious and generous afternoon teas served in a quiet conservatory.

KINLOCHBERVIE HOTEL
Kinlochbervie IV27 4RP
On B801 off A838
Tel: (097182) 275
Open: Jan–Dec
Very cosy small restaurant with good food and fast service. High-chairs available.

INCHBAE LODGE HOTEL
Inchbae by Garve IV23 2PH
On A835, 6 miles W of Garve
Tel: (09975) 269
Good food in an informal atmosphere. Bar lunches from 1200, suppers from 1700. Featured in Taste of Scotland guide. *See* PLACES TO STAY.

KESSOCK HOTEL
North Kessock, by Inverness IV1 1XN
Tel: (046373) 208
Tasty bar lunches and very good with children.

OLD HOUSE HOTEL
Muir of Ord IV6 7UH
On A832, half a mile W of village
Tel: (0463) 870492
Open: May–mid Oct
Bar lunches feature in Taste of Scotland guide and children are made very welcome. Fluent French spoken.

PRIORY HOTEL
The Square, Beauly IV4 7BX
Tel: (0463) 782309
Families with children welcome for bar lunches or suppers (starting at 1730). Recommended in Taste of Scotland guide.

ROYAL GOLF HOTEL
Dornoch
Tel: (0862) 810283
Open: Mar–Oct

THE SEAGULL
Breaknish, nr Broadford, Isle of Skye
Good lunches – prawns, salads, soups and vegetarian lasagne.

THE STEADING RESTAURANT
Gairloch IV21 2BP
Tel: (0445) 2449
Open: Easter–mid Oct, Mon–Sat 0830–2100 (1700 Apr/May)
Coffee shop/restaurant in converted 19th-century farm building right by GAIRLOCH MUSEUM (*see* MUSEUMS). There are special dishes for children. Dogs must be tied in the shady courtyard but they may be given a

bowl of water. Recommended in Taste of Scotland guide.

THE THREE CHIMNEYS
Colbost, Dunvegan, Isle of Skye
On B884, 4 miles W of Dunvegan
Tel: (047 081) 258
Snack lunches from £2.50 (though you could spend much more), available between 1230 and 1400.

WHOLEFOOD CAFÉ AND RESTAURANT
Highland Design Works, Plockton Road, Kyle of Lochalsh
Tel: (0599) 4388
All the food is cooked on the premises, with specialities being seafood and vegetarian dishes. Recommended by Egon Ronay's *Just a Bite*, 1992.

Quick Meals and Snacks

BIADH MATH
Railway Station, Kyle of Lochalsh
Tel: (0599) 4813
Open: Easter – Oct, Mon – Sat 1000 – 1700, Sun 1100 – 1600, 1830 – 2100
Home-made seafood and vegetarian dishes, children's meals, light lunches, coffees and home-baking.

BUNILLIDH RESTAURANT AND TEA-SHOP
Helmsdale
Tel: (04312) 457
Open: Mon – Sat 1000 – 2100, Sun 1100 – 2100
Local seafood, baked potatoes, home-made cakes and pastries. Recommended in the Good Food Guide and Les Routiers.

DUNNET HEAD TEA-ROOM
Brough, Dunnet

On B855
Tel: (084 785) 774
Open: Apr – Sep
Snacks, 3-course meals, vegetarian choices, additive-free meals, high teas and a children's menu.

LOCHBAY TEA-ROOMS
1/2 MacLeod's Terrace, Waternish, Isle of Skye
Tel: (047 083) 235
A very small restaurant which, according to one family, serves the best winkles outside Brittany.

Pubs

BADACHRO INN
nr Gairloch
Tel: (044 583) 255
A casual, friendly pub with bar meals available anytime during opening hours. Children can play in the garden which overlooks the sheltered bay or sit in the TV room in the evening.

THE OLD INN
Gairloch
Tel: (0445) 2006
Bar lunches with a riverside room for families with children. Featured in the Good Beer Guide and on TV's *Wish You Were Here*.

Ice-Creams

CATHEDRAL CAFÉ
Dornoch
Good ice-creams.

PLACES TO STAY

Hostels

SYHA—CARBISDALE CASTLE
Culrain, Ardgay IV24 3DP
Tel: (054 982) 232
Book in advance to be sure of a
family room. A good area for cycling
and pony-trekking.

SYHA—GARRAMORE
Morar PH40 4PD
Tel: (06875) 268
Family rooms can be booked outwith July/August and Whitsun holidays. Lovely silver sand beach near
the hostel.

SYHA HOSTEL—KYLEAKIN
Isle of Skye IV41 8PL
Tel: (0599) 4585
Book in advance for family rooms.
Bikes may be hired locally.

SYHA—TORRIDON
nr Kinlochewe IV22 2EZ
Tel: (044587) 284
Book in advance to be sure of getting
a family room.

SYHA—UIG
Isle of Skye IV51 9YD
Tel: (047 042) 211
Book in advance to be sure of a
family room. Pony-trekking, cycle
hire, canoeing and fishing are available in the area. Ferries bound for
the Outer Hebrides leave from Uig.

Caravan and Camping Sites

APPLECROSS CAMP SITE
Applecross, Strathcarron IV54 8LS
*On minor road off A896 W of Loch-
carron*
Tel: (05204) 284
Open: Apr—Oct
From £
Grassy sheltered site.

ARDMAIR POINT CARAVAN SITE AND BOAT CENTRE
nr Ullapool
3.5 miles N of Ullapool on A835
Open: Easter—Oct
From ££
Equipment for watersports is available on the site. *See* **WATERSPORTS**.

BALMACARA CARAVAN AND CAMPING SITE
*From the E, on A87 take 2nd road on R
after Reraig village*
Open: mid Apr—Sep
£
Forestry Commission site set in open
woodland, by a river.

GLENBRITTLE CAMPING AND CARAVAN PARK
Isle of Skye
Tel: (047 842) 232
£
Wonderful views of the Cuillins.
Toddlers and young children would
be happy pottering on the wide
shallow beach but it may be a bit
dull for older children as the Cuillins
are too rugged for youngsters.

GRANNIE'S HEILAN' HAME
Embo, Sutherland
Tel: (0862) 810260
Open: All year
From ££

Large site with access to the sea. Play area.

PITGRUNDY CARAVAN PARK
Dornoch
Tel: (0862) 810001
Open: Easter – mid Oct
From ££
Close to the sea. No tents.

SEAVIEW FARM CARAVAN PARK
Dornoch
Tel: (0862) 810294
Open: May – Sep
From £
A path from the site passes through farmland on the way to the beach which is only 10 minutes away.

SCOURIE CARAVAN AND CAMPING PARK
Harbour Road, Scourie, Sutherland
Tel: (0971) 2217/2060
Open: Easter – Oct
From ££
An attractive site near the sea.

Hotels

INCHBAE LODGE HOTEL
by Garve IV23 2PH
On A835, 6m W of Garve
Tel: (09975) 269
£££
Children are free, and there is free trout fishing at the bottom of the garden.

OUTER HEBRIDES

PLACES TO VISIT

Aeroplanes

BARRA AIRPORT
Traigh Mhor (Cockle Strand), Barra
Famous sands where the planes from Glasgow, Stornoway and Benbecula land on the beach. The timetable is governed by the tides, so check for arrival and departure times.

Ancient Monuments

DUN CARLOWAY (HS)
Isle of Lewis
Off A858, 16 miles from Stornoway
Free
A 2000-year-old Iron Age dry-stone defensive tower or broch. It is so well preserved that one wall still rises to over 30ft.

CALLANISH STANDING STONES (HS)
Isle of Lewis
Close to A858
Free
Tea-room nearby
As you walk along the avenue of 19 huge megaliths or standing stones towards the circle of 13 more stones, try to imagine why anyone should

want to go to the effort of dragging them here and then erecting them. Whatever the reason, this mammoth task was carried out between 3500 and 5000 years ago and the stones now rank second to Stonehenge in importance.

Beaches

The beaches on the Outer Hebrides are amongst the most remote, the most peaceful and the cleanest in Scotland.

BACK AND NORTH TOLSTA
nr Stornoway, Isle of Lewis
N of Stornoway on the B895
One of the areas on the east coast of Lewis with lovely beaches.

TRAIGH NA BERIE AND UIG
Isle of Lewis
On the W coast of Lewis
Traigh na Berie (*see* **PLACE TO STAY**) has a very basic campsite (not hot water or showers) but this is more than compensated for by the beautiful scenery. Uig Sands is a huge beach where the historic Norse-carved

Lewis Chessmen were found. They are now in the British Museum.

TRAIGH MHOR AND PORT GEIRAHA
Isle of Lewis
At the end of the B895, N of Stornoway
Lovely beaches. You can also see the 'bridge to nowhere' built by Lord Leverhulme for a road he intended to run to Ness but which was never built.

LUSKENTYRE
Isle of Harris
W of Tarbert
The west coast of Harris has many long beaches with Luskentyre being one of the biggest and most famous.

Other good beaches on Harris include SEILABOST, HORSABOST, NISABOST, SCARISTA and BORVE.

AISGERNIS
South End, South Uist
Off A865
The beach can be reached from the village. It runs the length of South Uist's western seaboard.

TANGUSDALE
nr Castlebay, Isle of Barra
Hotel nearby
Sandy beach with rocky outcrops.

VATERSAY, ISLE OF BARRA
Causeway to the island from Castlebay
The island has two beautiful beaches separated by machair, a stretch of sandy pasture dotted with tiny wild flowers. One faces east, the other faces the Atlantic.

Bikes

ALEX DAN CYCLE CENTRE
67 Kenneth Street, Stornoway, Isle of Lewis
Tel: (0851) 704025
Cycle hire, including children's bikes and child seats, repairs.

BARRA CYCLE HIRE
29 St Brendan Road, Castlebay, Barra
Tel: (08714) 284
Cycle hire with special rates for firm bookings.

HEBRIDES HOLIDAYS
11A Tabost, Isle of Lewis
SE of Stornoway, off the A859 to Tarbert
Tel: (0851) 88288/88408
£ per day
Mountain bike hire for over-10s.

Castles

KISIMUL CASTLE
Castlebay, Isle of Barra
On a tiny island in the bay
Tel: (08714) 336
Open: May – Sep, Wed, Fri and Sat afternoons only
£ including the ferry
Partial disabled access
Kisimul has been the home and stronghold of the MacNeils of Barra for about 800 years. Clansmen like Ruari the Turbulent were notorious for their lawlessness and piracy in the past.

Museums

SHAWBOST SCHOOL MUSEUM
Isle of Lewis

263

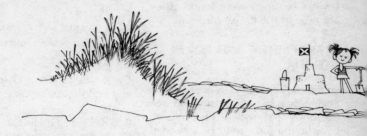

A858, 19 miles NW of Stornoway
Tel: (0851) 71 213
Open: Apr–Nov 1000–1800
Free (donation)
No disabled access
Created for the Highland Village Competition in 1970, the museum illustrates the old way of life on Lewis.

LEWIS BLACK HOUSE (HS)
Arnol, Isle of Lewis
15 miles NW of Stornoway on A858
Tel: (0851) 71501
Open: Mon–Sat
£
P: Available
Disabled access
A good example of a traditional thatched Hebridean dwelling. There is a central peat fire in the kitchen but no chimney, so the smoke has to find its own way out through cracks and gaps. The animals lived under the same roof, in the byre.

KILDONAN SCHOOL MUSEUM
Kildonan, South Uist
Café next door
Historical and archaeological items of interest to children over 8 are on display.

Novelties

BUTT OF LEWIS
Ness, Isle of Lewis
No disabled access to the lighthouse
The lighthouse is built on the edge of the cliffs at the most northerly point of Lewis. Take care, especially on windy days.

WHALEBONE ARCH
Bragar,
Isle of Lewis
On W coast of Lewis
Free
This arch is made from the huge jawbone of a blue whale that came ashore in 1920. The harpoon which killed it was still attached to the body and forms the centrepiece of the arch.

Parks and Playgrounds

LADY LEVER PARK
Stornoway,
Isle of Lewis
In the town centre
The park surrounds Lewis Castle (not open to the public) and the wooded

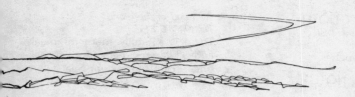

grounds overlook Stornoway harbour. There is a playground nearby.

There are also small play areas at TARBERT and SEILABOST, Harris.

Sport and Leisure Centres

LIONACLEIT COMMUNITY SCHOOL (*Sgiol Lionacleit*)
Lionacleit, Benbecula
On B892
Tel: (0870) 2211
Restaurant
Disabled facilities
A community school with a swimming pool and other sports facilities as well as a children's library, a theatre and a museum. Visitors are welcome to come to the ceilidhs and other events during the summer.

NICHOLSON/LEWIS SPORTS CENTRE – *see* SWIMMING

Swimming

CASTLEBAY COMMUNITY SCHOOL
Castlebay, Isle of Barra
Tel: (08714) 471
A swimming pool, games hall and library.

NICHOLSON/LEWIS SPORTS CENTRE
Sandwick Road, Stornoway, Isle of Lewis
Tel: (0851) 702603
Open: Public sessions outside school hours
Swimming and canoeing, table-tennis, squash and racquet ball, 5-a-side football, badminton, tennis and unihoc.

LIONACLEIT COMMUNITY SCHOOL – *see* SPORT AND LEISURE CENTRES

PLACES TO EAT

BORRODALE HOTEL
Daliburgh, South Uist
Tel: (08784) 444
Good pub lunches.

CASTLEBAY HOTEL
Castlebay, Barra
Tel: (08714) 223
Good lunches in the Puffin Grill.

CRAIGARD HOTEL
Castlebay, Barra
Tel: (08714) 200

ORASAY INN
Loch Carnan, South Uist
Tel: (087 04) 298
A small, friendly, family-run inn serving traditional and oriental food which you can eat out-of-doors in the summer. Meals to take away are also available.

POLLOCHAR INN
Pollochar, South Uist PA81 5TT

At S end of the island
Tel: (08784) 215
There is a family room for meals, and children's helpings are half-price. Beach at the door. Seal colony nearby.

ROSEVILLA TEA-ROOM
Tarbert, Harris
Good snacks and main meals, coffee and baking. A bit pricey . . . but there's not much competition in the Outer Hebrides.

STONEYBRIDGE COMMUNITY HALL
Stoneybridge, South Uist
Lovely fresh home-baking and a friendly, relaxed atmosphere. Children can use the games hall for 30p – it has limited facilities but is handy for using up some energy on rainy days.

PLACES TO STAY

Campsites

TRAIGH NA BERIE – *see* BEACHES
On the W coast of Lewis
Token charge £

No facilities apart from toilets and a cold water tap. Beautiful setting looking out to the Atlantic but be prepared for a long, slow drive there on the narrow roads.

ORKNEY AND SHETLAND

The 163 islands that make up Orkney and Shetland are a wonderful place to go for a quiet, 'away-from-it-all' holiday. The main attraction of the islands are the many archaeological sites which include relics of the Viking occupation, and the beautiful beaches which are at their best in the driest, sunniest months of April, May and June.

You are never more than 3 miles from the sea—ideal for beach-loving youngsters who can build castles in the sand or make their own rings of standing stones on the rockier beaches. For older children, there are great opportunities for birdwatching and canoeing or sailing. There are few cars and fewer hills, so the islands are good for cycling. You could visit a different island every day on the scheduled ferry services, or go by plane to the more remote ones where the landing strips are bumpy fields.

Although at its nearest point, Orkney is only 6 miles from the Scottish mainland, things are done a little differently on the islands: a wall runs right round the island of North Ronaldsay to keep the sheep on the beach where they eat seaweed instead of the precious grass which grows inland; near Kirkwall you'll see road signs warning drivers to look out for otters crossing the road, and at the Boys Ploughing Match at St Margaret's Hope, the miniature ploughs are pulled by children, not horses!

The sparsely populated Shetland Islands are 60 miles north of Orkney. They are almost as close to Norway as they are to Scotland, and the Scandinavian influences are clear in the dialect and place names. In fact, the islands were given to Scotland in 1469, as dowry for Margaret, daughter of King Christian I of Norway, who married James III, King of the Scots.

The traditional burning of a Viking longship marks the end of the long dark winter at Up Helly Aa. But January is not the best time to visit Shetland for the first time—come instead in the summer when the sun barely sets at night and you can take a trip round Lerwick harbour in another longship, the *Dim Riv*. Go trekking on native Shetland ponies, swim in the small but excellent leisure pools and explore some of the beaches and ancient monuments.

ORKNEY

PLACES TO VISIT

Ancient Monuments

GRAIN EARTH HOUSES (HS)
Haston, Kirkwall
Tel: (031) 244 3101 (HS, Edinburgh)
Open: On application to key keeper
Free
Disabled access
An iron-age souterrain with an entrance stair leading to an underground passage and chamber.

GURNESS BROCH (HS)
Aikerness nr Kirkwall
Off A966 at Aikerness, about 4 miles NW of Rendall
Tel: (031) 244 3101 (HS, Edinburgh)
Open: Check for opening hours
£
P: Available
No disabled access
A broch is a fortress tower with a spiral staircase built into the cavity between its massive double walls. Gurness Broch once was over 40ft high but the ruins now stand about 10ft high and are surrounded by stone huts and a deep ditch. It was built over a well so the Iron Age inhabitants could withstand a long siege. The broch was also inhabited in the Dark Ages and Viking times.

MAES HOWE (HS)
nr Kirkwall
Off A965, 9 miles W of Kirkwall
Tel: (0856) 76217
Open: Apr – Sep, Mon – Sat 0930 – 1900, Sun 1400 – 1900; Oct – Mar, until 1600
£
P: Available
Partial disabled access
Tea-room close by
An enormous burial mound, 115ft in diameter, dating back to c.2500 BC, and containing a burial chamber which is unsurpassed in Western Europe. It was already 4000 years old when Norsemen broke into it to shelter from a storm, and according to the Orkney-inga Saga, two of them went mad. Some time later, Viking crusaders left runic inscriptions on the walls which say things like 'Ingaborg is the most beautiful of women' – Viking graffiti! To get into the chamber you have to creep through a 40ft stone-lined passage.

MIDHOWE BROCH AND CAIRNS
Rousay
On the W coast of the island of Rousay
Open: All reasonable times
Free

No disabled access

Rousay has about 200 chambered cairns and other reminders of ancient man—but this is the best on the island. It is built on a promontory cut off by a deep rock-cut ditch. Midhowe Stalled Cairn, 'an elongated ship of death', is nearby.

SKARA BRAE (HS)

19 miles NW of Kirkwall on B9056
Tel: (0856) 84815
Open: Daily, Mon—Sat 0930—1900
(1600 Ot—Mar); Sun 1400—1900 (1600
Oct—Mar)
£
P: Available
Partial disabled access

This Neolithic village was occupied about 5000 years ago by farmers and herdsmen. The main settlement is made up of 8 houses joined by covered passages. Walk along the tops of the walls and look down into rooms equipped with stone beds, fireplaces, cupboards and dressers. The village was covered by drifting sand for 4500 years but was revealed again by a storm in 1850. There is also a beautiful sandy beach.

Animals and Birds

MARWICK HEAD NATURE RESERVE (RSPB)

Marwick Bay
Off B9056, N of Stromness; access along path N from Marwick Bay
Tel: (0856) 850176
Open: All year
Free
P: Available

These 300ft high cliffs have huge and spectacular colonies of seabirds, including puffins. Go there in April—July when the birds are nesting but don't be surprised by the noise and the smell.

Bike Hire and Cycle Routes

STROMNESS CYCLE HIRE

54 Dundas Street, Stromness
Tel: (0856) 850255
£ per day

Mountain bike hire, some with child seats.

Boats and Boat Trips

Mainland is surrounded by lots of interesting islands which are serviced by scheduled inter-island ferries. Explore a different island each day and have fun walking, beachcombing, seal spotting and so on.

SCHOONER ENTERPRISE

Snowberry Villa, East Road, Kirkwall
Tel: (0856) 3441

Trips by boat to visit wildlife areas and sites of nautical and archaeological interest.

NORTH ISLES BOAT CHARTERS

Rowandale, Finstown
Tel: (0856) 76 551
Operating: mid Jun—Aug

Bird and sealife trips on Mon and Sat. During the rest of the week the ferry goes from Kirkwall to Sanday, Stronsay, Egilsay and Rousay.

Farms

ORKNEY FARM PARK

Finstown KW17 2JT
Take A986 from Finstown and follow the signs
Tel: (0856) 76 243

Open: Mid May – Sep, daily 1000 – 1800
£
P: Available
Picnic area under cover in the informa-tion booth
Partial disabled access

Visitors are able to wander between the breeding pens of rare and endangered species of cattle, pigs and sheep. Ducks and geese live on the landscaped ponds which have walkways to let you go near without getting wet feet. Children can touch the baby animals in the pets' corner.

DOEHOUSE FIBRE FARM
Tenston, Sandwick, South Ronaldsay
Tel: (0856) 84 546
£

Learn about cashmere goats, angora rabbits, weaving and spinning. The entry cost includes a pony ride and a go on the spinning-wheel.

Graveyard and Gruesome Places

TOMB OF THE EAGLES
Liddle Farm, South Ronaldsay
Tel: (0856) 83 339
Open: Apr – Sep, 1000 – 2000; Nov – Feb 1000 – 1300
£

The tomb was discovered a few years ago by a farmer. He was looking for fencing material and in the process uncovered a 5000-year-old burial place containing the remains of 340 people and the talons of many sea-eagles.

Museums

SCAPA FLOW VISITOR CENTRE
Lyness, Hoy

Open: All year, Mon – Fri 0900 – 1600 (Sat – Sun, May – Sep 1030 – 1530)
Café
Take the ferry from Houton to Hoy (tel: 0856 81 397 for times and prices). The centre is a few minutes walk from the pier.
£

Scapa Flow was a major naval base during both World Wars. There are many sunken warships including HMS *Vanguard*, HMS *Hampshire* and HMS *Royal Oak*. The German Imperial High Seas Fleet was scuttled here as well. You can pretend to operate a deck gun from the HMS *Hampshire* or a 6.5-inch gun reco-vered from one of the German ships. A favourite with children tired of looking at ancient monuments.

CORRIGALL FARM MUSEUM
Harray
Tel: (0856) 77 411
Open: Mar – Oct
£

Old Orkney farm implements and buildings.

KIRBUSTER FARM MUSEUM
Birsay
Tel: (0856) 77 268
Open: Mar – Oct
£

A fire burns in the middle of the room all year round, so be prepared to get smoke in your eyes as there is no chimney.

STROMNESS MUSEUM
Stromness
Tel: (0856) 850025
Open: Mon – Sat 1030 – 1230, 1330 – 1700
£

A small museum with stuffed birds, eggs, model ships and a feature on

the scuttling of the German Fleet at Scapa Flow in WWI.

Riding

HROSSLAND TREKKING CENTRE
Hilltoft, Burray
Tel: (0856) 73 307
£ – ££
Riding and pony-trekking around Burray. Lessons, riding holidays. Children welcome.

Scotland at Work – Past and Present

LINDOR SHEEPSKINS
Braevilla, Rendall KW17 2NZ

On A966, 4 miles from Finstown
Tel: (0856) 76 356
Open: All year 1000 – 1700
Free
P: Available
See how soft fluffy sheepskin rugs are produced in a 30-minute tour of the tannery.

Swimming

SWIMMING POOL AND
SPORTS CENTRE
Kirkwall

Watersports

DALE KITCHEN – *see* PLACES TO EAT

271

PLACES TO EAT

Quick Meals and Snacks

DALE KITCHEN
Evie
Tel: (0856) 75 318
Good wholesome food, lovely baking and snacks available all day. Evening meal at 1830. Books and magazines by the fireside (no fireguard so watch babies and toddlers). There is a good beach and broch nearby. Canoes and windsurfers for hire.

POMONA CAFÉ
Albert Street, Kirkwall
Tel: (0856) 87 2325
Good fast food with small portions available. Bottles can be warmed for babies.

TORMISTON MILL
opposite MAES HOWE (see ANCIENT MONUMENTS)
On A965 W of Kirkwall
Lovely home-baking. Ducks to feed and grass to play on.

TRENABIE'S
Main Street, Kirkwall
A good place for people-watching. Favourite elevenses-stop with local children because of the ice-cream sodas.

WYLIE'S TEA-ROOM
Dounby
On A986
Great family eating on a Sunday when you can have as much as you like for a fixed 'high tea' price. Highchairs available. It is near CORRIGALL FARM MUSEUM (*see* MUSEUMS) which is very popular with children.

Pubs

Stromness pubs are at their best during the folk festival (3rd weekend in May) when fiddlers and fiddle music abound.

FERRY INN
Stromness
A lively pub with a large eating area. Although small portions are available, it is best suited to older children. Cosy atmosphere especially on winter evenings.

SCORRABRAE INN
Orphir
On a minor road off A964
Good views and lovely hill walk directly behind the pub. Good pool room off main bar.

PLACES TO STAY

Hostels

SYHA—KIRKWALL
Old Scapa Road, Kirkwall KW15 1BB
Tel: (0856) 872 243
Advance booking required for family rooms. Bikes may be hired locally. Close to sandy beaches and, for the less hardy, the indoor swimming pool.

Camping and Caravan Sites

EVIEDALE CAMPSITE
Dale, Evie, Orkney KW17 2PJ
By A966, N of village
Tel: (0856) 72 254/270
£
There are cottages to rent and a very small campsite. *See* DALE KITCHEN (**PLACES TO EAT**).

NESS POINT CARAVAN AND CAMPING PARK
Stromness, Orkney KW15 1JG
On S side of town
Tel: (0856) 3535
Open: Mid May—mid Sept
£
Beautiful location for both tents and caravans but rather exposed if the weather is poor.

PICKAQUOY CARAVAN AND CAMPING SITE
Pickaquoy Road, Kirkwall, Orkney KW15 1RR
On W outskirts of town, off A965
Tel: (0856) 3535
Open: Mid May—mid Sept
£
Play area with swings, climbing frame, etc. Only 10 minutes walk from St Magnus Cathedral and town centre.

SHETLAND

PLACES TO VISIT

Ancient Monuments

MOUSA BROCH (HS)
Island of Mousa
Accessible by boat from Sandwick, Shetland
Tel: (031) 244 3101 (HS, Edinburgh)
Open: Boat hire May – Sep afternoons, also Sat and Sun mornings, some evenings
Free, ferry ££
No disabled access
The best preserved example of an Iron Age broch tower. These have only been found in Scotland and were built about 2000 years ago as fortress towers over the top of a fresh-water well. The tower stands over 40ft high and you can climb the rough staircase which goes up between the inner and outer walls. Winner of the Castle of the Year award in 1989.

JARLSHOF (HS)
Sumburgh Head
22 miles S of Lerwick
Tel: (0950) 60112
Open: Apr – Sep, Mon – St 0930 – 1900, Sun 1400 – 1900; Oct – Mar closed from 1600 and Tue/Wed afternoons
£
One of the best sites of its kind in Europe. The settlement was occupied in the Neolithic, Bronze and Iron Ages as well as by the Vikings, and some parts date back 3000 years. It was covered and preserved by sand about 1000 years ago and only revealed after great gales at the turn of the century. Historians think that the first people to live here ate a lot of limpets because there are large 'middens' of empty shells left from Neolithic feasts. Visitor centre and museum.

Bike Hire and Cycle Routes

PUFFIN PEDALS
Mounthooly Street, Lerwick, Shetland ZE1 0BJ
Tel: (0595) 5065
Open: Mon – Sat, all year, 0915 – 1645
Bikes for over-5s (no charge for safety helmets), and child carriers available at nominal charge.

Boats and Boat Trips

DIM RIV
Sailings from Lerwick from Jun – mid Aug
£

Pretend to be a Viking and take a trip round the harbour on a 40ft replica of a traditional Norse longship complete with painted dragon figurehead. The tourist office takes bookings and has details of sailing times.

Farms

CROFTING AND WILDLIFE TRAIL
Burland, Tondra nr Scalloway
Between Scalloway and Burra
Free (donations)
A marked route round a working croft. Amongst the many unusual farm animals are Tamworth pigs — the rarest and oldest breed of pig in Britain — and Shetland hens which lay green eggs. The ducks, hens and geese are housed in a traditional duck house made from an old up-turned boat.

Museums

SHETLAND CROFT HOUSE MUSEUM
Voe, Dunrossness
On unclassified road E of A970, 25 miles
S of Lerwick
Tel: (0595) 5057
Open: May — Sep, Tue — Sun 1000 — 1300,
1400 — 1700
£
P: Available
No disabled access
A mid 19th-century thatched Shetland croft house with 100-year-old furniture. There are also outbuildings and a working water-mill.

LERWICK TOY SOLDIER MUSEUM
Toll Clock Shopping Centre, North Road,
Lerwick
Open: Mon — Fri 1000 — 1700, Sat 0930 —
1730
Free
Thousands of old and antique toy soldiers, some dating from the 1870s. The shop sells modern model soldiers.

Parks and Playgrounds

There are small play areas in virtually every village around Shetland. SANDWICK play area has a skateboarding track with ramps and humps which is fun for those with bikes and trikes too. KING HARALD ST PLAY PARK has tennis and putting.

Riding

BROOTHOM PONIES
Dunrossness
Tel: (0950) 60556
££ per hour
Riding and trekking on Shetland ponies; 4 to 5-year-olds can have walks on a lead rein. See mares and foals.

MILLCROFT FARM AND RIDING CENTRE
Brindister, West Burrafirth, Bridge of Walls
Tel: (059 571) 427
Open: Mon — Sat 0800 — 2200
A working croft with a children's play area and a child-minder who looks after babies and toddlers while parents and older children ride or have lessons. Novices can go for walks on safe, friendly ponies.

CLICKIMIN LEISURE CENTRE—*see*
SPORT AND LEISURE CENTRES

Sport and Leisure Centres

The Shetland leisure centres and swimming pools all provide excellent modern facilities.

UNST LEISURE CENTRE
Baltasound, Unst
Tel: (095 781) 577
£
Badminton, squash and swimming pool with a children's lagoon complete with toys, armbands, rings and inflatable seats.

CLICKIMIN LEISURE CENTRE
Lerwick
Tel: (0595) 4555
£
Cafeteria
Variety of indoor sports in the large games hall, football pitches, pony-riding and activities for children. Creche.

YELL LEISURE CENTRE
Mid Yell
Tel: (0957) 2222
£
A small leisure pool, snooker and indoor sports.

WHALSAY LEISURE CENTRE
Whalsay
Tel: (08066) 678
£
Badminton, 15m swimming pool, squash courts.

ISLEBURGH COMMUNITY CENTRE
King Harald St, Lerwick
Tel: (0595) 2114
£
Café
Snooker, pool and badminton. The junior youth club (8 to 12-year-olds) has a programme of activities, competitions, trips and a Christmas show.

Swimming

NORTH MAINLAND POOL
Junior High School, Brae
25 miles N of Lerwick
Tel: (080 622) 321
£
Leisure pool with lagoon area for very young children. Mother and toddler sessions, pool games, monster sessions.

LERWICK POOL
Hillhead, Lerwick
Tel: (0595) 3535
£

UNST LEISURE CENTRE, YELL LEISURE CENTRE, WHALSAY LEISURE CENTRE—*see* **SPORT AND LEISURE CENTRES.**

Walks

SHETLAND FIELD STUDIES GROUP organise guided nature walks around the islands during the summer. Contact the tourist office for details.

PLACES TO EAT

Hotels and Restaurants

BURRASTOW HOUSE
Walls ZE2 9PB
3 miles W of Walls
Open: All week, Mar – Oct
Booking required for lunch which is served between 1230 – 1430. Children's helpings, also afternoon teas. Recommended in the Good Food Guide.

CANDLESTICK MAKER
33 Commercial Road, Lerwick
Tel: (0595) 6066
Open: 1000 – 2300
Good value food and reductions for children.

'DA PEERIE FISK' RESTAURANT
Busta, Brae ZE2 9QN
Tel: (080622) 679
On W side of Busta Voe. L off A970 on to Muckle Roe road then L again after 600 yds.
Open: Daily in summer from 1200
Disabled facilities
Restaurant specialising in local seafoods and features in the Taste of Scotland guide. Relatively expensive but children get reduced prices.

ST MAGNUS BAY HOTEL
Hillswick ZE2 8RW
Tel: (080623) 372
36 miles N of Lerwick
Open: Daily
Children welcome for inexpensive bar lunches. Featured in the Taste of Scotland guide.

WEST SANDWICK RESTAURANT
Yell
Tel: (095 786) 204
Tasty, inexpensive food. Children can have small portions and there are toys to play with. Preparing the 'bill' can take longer than anticipated so ask for it in good time if you are rushing for a ferry.

Quick Meals and Snacks

COMMUNITY HALLS
Open: Sunday afternoons in summer
The community halls round the islands open for tea and home bakes – well worth a visit if you are passing.

HOLMSGARTH SNACK BAR
P&O Terminal, Holmsgarth, Lerwick
Open: Daily from 0800 (0900 on Sundays)
Good cheap food and lots of space for toddlers to run around. This is an important consideration if they have been strapped into their car seats for several hours!

PUFFINS
Mounthooly Street, Lerwick
Tel: (0595) 5065
Open: Mon – Sat from 0900
Mother and baby room
A 'coffee shop' serving excellent light lunches and snacks – home-made soup, filled rolls and home-baking. Real coffee with refills at no extra charge. High-chairs and toddler's beakers are available and children can amuse themselves with the toys that are provided.

SKIBHOUL STORES
Haroldswick, Unst
Tel: (095 781) 371
The shop has a café where you can make your own tea or coffee. Potted versions of local history and photographs are displayed under glass on the table-tops and there are uninterrupted views of the North Sea.

VIKING CAFÉ
Commercial Road, Lerwick

At the bus station
Mother and baby room
A good place to grab a bite of inexpensive 'fast food'.

Ice-Creams

LESLIE'S DELICATESSEN
Market Cross, Lerwick
Open: Mon – Sat 0830 – 1800
All sorts of ice-creams.

PLACES TO STAY

Hostels

SYHA—LERWICK
Isleburgh House,
King Harald Street,
Lerwick ZE1 0EQ
Tel: (0595) 2114
Book in advance to be sure of getting a family room. Bikes may be hired locally. Ferry boats to Iceland and the Faroes leave from Lerwick.

UNST YOUTH CENTRE
Gardiesfauld,
Uyeasound,
Unst
Tel: (095 785) 237
There are no campsites on Unst but the youth centre provides the cheapest accommodation and is proving very popular.

Four old bothies at ESCHANESS, VOE, WHITENESS and WHALSAY have been renovated recently to provide accommodation in historically interesting buildings.

Camping and Caravan Sites

CLICKIMIN
Lochside, Lerwick
Tel: (0595) 4555
£
A very good campsite beside the CLICKIMIN LEISURE CENTRE (*see* SPORT AND LEISURE CENTRES).

FETLAR CAMPSITE
The Garths Campsite, Leagarth, Island of Fetlar
Near village of Hubie on B9088
Tel: (095783) 226
Open: May—Sep
£
A grassy, level site to the south-east of the island.

LEVENWICK CAMPSITE
Levenwick Campsite, Levenwick
By A970 18 miles S of Lerwick
Tel: (09502) 207
Open: Apr—Sep
£
Level grassy site with birdwatching and cliff scenery nearby.

INDEX

Notes: (W) indicates that the place is open in the Winter; (S) that it is open on Sundays; and (F) that entry is free.

PLACES TO VISIT

PLACES TO EAT